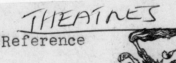

PILLARS OF DRURY LANE

A Julian Wylie Pantomime at Drury Lane. Christmas 1934–5

It is *Cinderella* and in the cast are Phyllis Neilson-Terry, June, Revnell and West, Billy Danvers, Dan Leno Junior, and Clarice Hardwicke

PILLARS OF DRURY LANE

W. MACQUEEN-POPE

WITH 65 ILLUSTRATIONS

LONDON
HUTCHINSON

Hutchinson & Co. (Publishers) Ltd.
178–202 Great Portland Street, London, W.1

London   Melbourne   Sydney   Auckland
Bombay   Johannesburg   New York   Toronto

First published 1955

Printed in Great Britain
by The Anchor Press, Ltd.,
Tiptree Essex

To

PRINCE LITTLER

under whose expert guidance
Theatre Royal, Drury Lane,
enjoys an era of Prosperity
and who upholds the traditions and glories
of that wonderful place.
A great man of the Theatre, a tireless
worker in the cause of Theatrical Charity,
he is himself an enduring
Pillar of Drury Lane.

CONTENTS

LIST OF ILLUSTRATIONS

9

The Author wishes to acknowledge with gratitude the documentation and the memories sent to him by his old and valued friend, Dick Milton, concerning the pantomimes and dramas of Sir Augustus Harris and Arthur Collins.

Before the Curtain Rises

ONCE upon a time—all fairy tales start like that—that place of recreation called a Theatre was the Aristocrat of the Entertainment World. It remains so today—but these are not the days when aristocracy has any power. A long pedigree, purity of breeding—these things do not matter any more—save to those who have them and feel pride in it. Today a bank balance is supreme, and men and women find greater satisfaction in the possession of the latest form of luxury car—or in the glory of a mink coat—than in a storied ancestry.

In the Machine Age, it is machinery which matters—science is slowly but surely strangling romance—and employing its victim to bring about its own doom. Where people once read about gallants in cloaks and wigs, with flashing swords and galloping steeds, now they prefer Space Ships. Boys are more interested in stories concerning the presumed beings of another world than this—beings who are practically machines themselves—than pirates, highwaymen, crooks, or even cowboys. The Theatre aristocrat always had rivalry of some sort—but rivals of a much lesser degree. The first London theatres had bull and bear baiting to compete for custom—but the Theatre won. Pleasure gardens, routs, ridottos, masquerades—all had their vogue but the Theatre rose steadily in stature. The Music Hall claimed many devotees and swept the country from its lowly start in Lambeth. But the Theatre had now developed its own aristocracy in the shape of the Actor-Managers.

Then came the first challenge of the Machine—the cinema, the moving pictures.

That challenge crept in, as it were. These animated pictures, as people called them, became last turn at a Music Hall, an additional attraction at the Egyptian Hall, to mix with the magic of Maskelyne and Cooke, and were not regarded seriously. Yet a great man of the Theatre had seen their possibilities, none other than Sir Augustus Harris himself, the fabulous Druriolanus. But even he never dreamed . . .

The Theatre paid little or no attention to this new thing for some time. These upstart machines—these advanced magic lanterns —mostly operated in shops which were otherwise empty, with the projector in full sight, a man to rewind the film, and someone playing ceaselessly more or less appropriate music on a piano of indifferent tone. The figures on the screen were all in a tremendous

hurry—and well they might have been for it always appeared
to be pouring with rain. Then—effects were introduced. Coconuts
reproduced the sound of horses' hoofs—a theatre trick of course, and
a good one—real bells were rung, real revolvers fired.

But the Theatre went on, its head in the air. By degrees, this
new form of entertainment, these animated pictures, took on a real
name—they became The Cinema—and theatres of a kind were
built, for their proper exhibition. The Theatre itself regarded them
as booths. Then certain of those theatres, which surrounded London
like a belt of amusement, began to go over to the cinema—the
Parkhurst in Islington surrendered, so did others. Still the Theatre
paid little attention. But the rot had set in.

A new menace arose—easy and quicker transport to the West
End. The motor-bus and the Tube. Business at the local theatres
began to fall off. The public could get into the West End easily and
comfortably. They went to see the big names instead of the touring
companies.

The Theatres felt the pinch before their rivals the Music Halls.
Those Halls still had star attractions on their bills—whereas the
Theatres mostly had the No. 1 or No. 2 Companies sent out by
George Edwardes, Frank Curzon, Robert Courtneidge and George
Dance—and there were others. Those great people who wisely
never surrendered to the lure of the West End—and would play
there for seasons only—packed those suburban theatres when they
visited them, as they did in the provincial playhouses—Fred Terry
and Julia Neilson, Martin Harvey—later to be knighted—the
Gilbert and Sullivan Operas, and, later, Matheson Lang. Again,
there were others. But the mechanical transport and the mechanical
film were undermining the Theatre and also, but more gradually,
sapping the Music Halls.

There were so many suburban playhouses—just think of some:
the Lyric, Hammersmith; and the King's; the Grand, Fulham; the
Coronet, Notting Hill Gate; the Richmond Theatre; the Ealing
Theatre; the Britannia, Hoxton; the Grand, Islington; the Parkhurst, Islington (mentioned above—and the demise of which was
made certain when a great theatre, the Marlborough, was built
next door to it); the Alexandra, Stoke Newington; the Opera
House, Crouch End; the Dalston; the Camden; the Surrey; the
Borough Theatre, Stratford; the Deptford; the Broadway, New
Cross; the Elephant and Castle; the Metropole, Camberwell; the
Brixton; the Kennington; the Royal, Kilburn; the Crown, Peck-
ham; the Shakespeare, Clapham; the Artillery Theatre, Woolwich;
the Terris, Rotherhithe; the Standard; the Duchess, Balham;

Mortons at Greenwich; the Pavilion, Mile End—and that is not a complete or exhaustive list. Gradually they began to fall out—some closed, some tried to turn themselves into Music Halls, some became what were then called 'Picture Palaces'. . . . The power and glory of the Theatre was departing.

In 1912 there were no less than forty-eight Music Halls in the London area alone—with a total accommodation for 70,000 people per performance—and many of them did it twice nightly too. Between them they took over £8,000 every evening. How many are left now—and what would the gross takings be? One by one they too vanished. Some turned themselves into theatres—and failed as did the theatres who tried to turn themselves into Music Halls— some went over to the pictures—some just faded away, like the old warriors they were.

The First World War revivified the Theatre but hit the Music Hall—strange as it may seem. For the men home on leave wanted to go to a show—and parents went with them, many of whom had never visited a theatre before. They found it far less sinful than they had anticipated—they liked it. They went again. But the Music Halls had adopted Revue—and lost their great attraction, the Individuality of the single turn which made them unique. Individuality is one of the playhouse's—variety or straight—greatest assets. Some of the London Music Halls became revue houses purely and simply— the Empire and Alhambra and the Palace as cases in point. And a lot of the smaller houses followed suit—the London Pavilion and the Oxford being examples. So it was a moot point as to whether they were Theatres or Music Halls.

Then, when the aftermath of war had scarcely cleared away, came the great industrial slump. That hit all places of entertainment, but the cinema weathered it best—for films had now grown great and important—and the cinema could send the stars into the most remote villages—which the Theatre could not. And picturegoing was cheap and had become a habit.

On top of that came the greatest blow the Theatre had ever suffered since Cromwell closed it down entirely in the 17th century. That was the advent of the 'Talkie'. This new mechanized entertainment which could meet the Theatre on level terms of speech and far outdo it in variety of scene and speedy change—swept the country. The Theatre did little to hit back, indeed, it made no effort. It relied on its prestige. It had not realized—or it would not do so—the changed conditions of life, the public outlook, the alteration in taste—the difference in monetary value. The cinema gave far more for the money—it made no restrictive rules—you could drop in . . . it was easy. Still, most theatres resisted any alteration in their usual procedure—what had been, must be—and a great number did not allow smoking. The public had become more free and easy.

It was the Provincial Theatre which suffered most. It was still offering touring companies, excellent in themselves—but the cinemas were presenting names which had captured the imagination of the public by intensive publicity. Also, these stars came from Hollywood, and although they were only shadows, they had the romance of distance—you could see the actors of the Theatre any time in the flesh.

In 1889 there were 370 theatres listed in the British Isles—quite apart from the numberless halls, Corn Exchanges, Assembly Rooms, etc., which 'fit-up' companies constantly visited, and also quite apart from the 'portable' theatres, of which many still existed. How many are left today? There were 175 accredited Music Halls, taking no account of the vast quantity of small halls which also gave Variety shows. Again, how many are left today?

This vanishing of theatres, which received a new fillip whilst this book was being written from the threatened destruction of the St. James's and the Stoll, is no new thing. It has been going on for years and replacements have been few and not in any way commensurate with the gaps—even in London's West End.

In London alone in the last fifty years or so a very large number of theatres have vanished—some from natural causes, change of taste and competition, some from inability to meet the alterations demanded by the London County Council and other public bodies —and some from enemy action. Those gone for good include the old Globe, the Olympic, the Gaiety, Toole's, the Opera Comique, the Aquarium Theatre (which became the Imperial), the Princess's in Oxford Street, the Royalty, the Lyceum, the Shaftesbury, the Grafton, the Playhouse, the Little, and Daly's. The Queen's still awaits rebuilding, and the Kingsway talks of re-opening. The replacements have been the Strand—originally the Waldorf—the Aldwych, the Duchess, the Phoenix, the Whitehall, the Saville, the Piccadilly, and the Fortune—whilst the Prince Edward, the Carlton, and the Leicester Square, although intended as theatres, very soon succumbed to the films and other forms of entertainment. All those theatres mentioned above were visited by the author of this book. So sixteen have gone and two are still out of action. In their place stand six newer ones. Nothing is likely to be done to fill that gap. In all probability it will grow. Indeed, that seems a certainty.

So it will be seen that the Theatre has been losing its power and

EARLY PILLARS

Upper left: Thomas Killigrew, founder of Theatre Royal, Drury Lane
Upper right: Mrs. Powell *Lower left:* James Quin *Lower right:* J. S. Munden

Upper left: Alfred Bunn *Upper right:* Madame Malabran *Lower left:* Alexander Pope *Lower right:* Samuel Whitbread

its appeal to the great mass of the public for a long time. It is nothing new. That statement concerning the loss of appeal will be hotly contested, but the figures speak for themselves.

Those now vanishing suburban theatres, by the way, were not shabby, second-rate places by any means. Not all of them were first class, but the majority were splendid playhouses, comfortable, with good accoustics, excellent lines of sight, spacious and well appointed. They were run by responsible firms and had responsible and efficient managers. Prices were cheap but the fare offered was the best obtainable. And the stages were real stages, capable of taking any attraction. They were designed by men who were practical. They could and did accommodate the biggest shows which Drury Lane could send them. They had plenty of 'side' room, plenty of scene docks, room to move and proper equipment. They were superior to many of the stages in far more recent West End theatres. And, every Christmas, they staged their own pantomimes, magnificently dressed and produced and magnificently cast. The pantomimes at the old Grand Theatre, Islington, were famous, so were those at the Britannia, Hoxton. But they were all first class. You would find stars like Marie Loftus, Marie Lloyd, Julie Mackey, Winifred Hare, Simeta Marsden, Alexandra Dagmar, Harry Randall, Harry Tate—in suburban pantomimes, and it was the same in the Provinces. They all had star casts and those pantomimes were strongly supported—the local inhabitants took pride in them. And yet they did not detract from the crowds which went to Drury Lane and the other big West End pantomimes.

Prices were popular, graded to suit the neighbourhoods. An average might be Stalls at 4s.; Dress Circle 3s.; Balcony 2s.; Pit 1s.; Gallery 6d. Boxes ranged from £2 2s. to £1 1s., and were popular with pantomime parties. Of course, they made a little extra on the 'early doors'. Total receipts could be from £150–£175 per performance—and in the biggest, rather more. There was a good margin of profit.

But they have gone, the Provincial Theatres have dwindled almost to vanishing point—not counting the Repertory Companies —and now it is the turn of the West End to wilt as well.

How has all this come about? By seniority the Theatre is still the Aristocrat of the Entertainment World. But like human aristocrats, it finds itself in parlous times. Of course, every Theatrical Management always insists it is doing splendid business—even when just about to withdraw a failure. Theatre managers are the supreme optimists. They have to be or they could not exist in that mad world of the Theatre. For nobody who is really sane can live therein.

B

Nobody who can take a level view and calculate the ordinary business risk has any place in that extraordinary realm which is not a business at all, which is not even a good gamble. It is, at best, a gamble with a gamble. If you go on a racecourse and back a horse, at least you get a run for your money. If you back a play, you stand a good chance of not getting a run at all. Yet, somehow, it goes on. There are no rules—no goodwill. You stand or fall by what you offer on each occasion. You send up the curtain on a new production. Two to two and a half hours later, down it comes and you have either made a fortune—or lost one. The odds are that if you make a fortune, you will lose it the next time you ring up on a new play. Business men have no place in the Theatre. It is the realm of the idealists who have the glorious insanity of the Theatre in their blood. No ordinary commercial man can stand the strain or the hazard. Many men have made fortunes from business and gone into the Theatre to run it on business lines. They have all crashed. Yet those without an ounce of business in their constitution but who have the Theatre in their topsy-turvy brain have risen to fame and— sometimes—to fortune. The Theatre is a place for Theatre People, not for business tycoons. That was why the Theatre reached its highest point in this land under the Actor-Managers. Those men were the craftsmen of their profession, living on their job, lavishing their care and technical knowledge on their productions as did Sheraton on his furniture, Gainsborough on his pictures, Cellini on his precious metal work. They were commercial managers, of course —they made certain calculations of their risks—but it did not worry them unduly. They knew that figures did not really matter until after they had completed their work and placed it before the public. How could it be valued before then? A play has no value except that which the public gives it. A tremendous, costly production may be a dead flop, a little drawing-room comedy a smash-hit and money-spinner. The old Actor-Managers brought their actual experience to bear upon their public. They created their following, they created their atmosphere, they gained their clients and kept them. Also, they achieved continuity of policy. They sold branded goods—the public knew what they were buying. Of course they were commercial—but they ran a professionally commercial Theatre which is an entirely different thing from just a commercial one.

But the First World War, the rising costs, the entry of specu-lators into what they thought was a Tom Tiddler's Ground where money was easy, ousted the Actor-Managers. These speculators did not know what they did—that the Theatre between 1914–18 was being buoyed up by an artificial boom. There are only a limited number of theatres and the speculators, by constant demand, forced up rents and terms in general. The actors, seeing the trend, wanted more money—and who shall blame them, except from the long point of view—and the Actor-Manager could not stay the course. He had been content with not very vast profits. He had kept prices down. He had not been saddled with an Entertainment Tax put on as a war-time measure but lasting through a peace and another war —and rising, too, as time went on. He had taken personal interest in his following and had tried to make theatre-going pleasant and easy by means of courtesy, dignity and the finest quality, given in generous measure. A short play always had a 'curtain raiser' in front of it, for the convenience of those who had stood waiting for a long time outside—but available to the smart people in the more expensive seats, if they chose to come. They made no charge for cloakrooms or programmes—their refreshment tariff was reasonable—and they did their best to please. A complaint was instantly dealt with. The customer was always right. The world of 'I couldn't Care Less' had not arrived. And the Theatre prospered.

The acting was of the highest standard. It had to be or the players were out of work. No actor or actress then expected to play in the West End without some years of training and experience in the Provinces. And when, thus matured, they sought jobs, their names were known. They were given parts which the managements knew they could play—or they would not have got them. They were 'produced', it is true, but they were not told how to speak every line, given every inflexion or movement; they did not start their education afresh with every new play. They were trained people. They knew they had to do their best. They had no side-lines—no films, recordings, television or broadcasts to earn extra money. They could just act and if they did not act well enough, out they went.

In place of the Actor-Manager came the management by remote control—the managers who conducted their business from their offices—engaged other people to do what the Actor-Managers did themselves and decided that all was fish that came into their net— people who do not say they are in the Theatrical Profession but in Show Business. So up went the prices, on went the charge for programmes and cloakrooms—as many extras as possible were crowded in. Seating capacity was the first consideration and it led to the banishment of pits and galleries and increased prices—which again helped the vicious circle of rising expenses. The margin got less and less. Seating capacity is not of first importance in a theatre.

What matters—and the only thing which matters—is what takes place on the stage—that is what fills the seats.

Accountants rose to power in the Theatre. But somehow or another, their figures seldom came right—you cannot work very accurately on estimates in the Theatre gamble and they found that they could only make their figures add up after the shows were produced. Then, all too often, it was too late. One theatre accountant proudly boasted that he knew exactly how many tins of polish it took to keep the brass-work clean, how many yards of carpet there were in the theatre, how much soap was required for cleaning and all that sort of thing. But he never solved the problem of how to make that brass-work, those carpets, dirty by means of the public crowding in to do so. There were men at the other extreme, too. More than once a play has been put on which had not an earthly chance of being a financial success—however good it might be artistically—because the expenses were greater, every week, than the money it was possible to get into the theatre. Yet that mad optimism prevailed—and does so still. . . .

Four things matter in the Entertainment Industry—the aristocratic theatrical portion of it—a theatre, a play, the actors (in the collective sense, including actresses) and—the audience. In a sense, the latter is the most important of the lot. Without it—there is no Theatre. It must be enticed in.

The Theatre itself is vastly important but it is interdependent upon the play. A play without a theatre is a document on a manager's desk, without life, waiting to be born. A theatre without a play is one of the most depressing things in the world. By day a closed, almost derelict unemployed building, with a hang-dog, ashamed air, the 'blue-blanking' which covers its display boards being the symbol of it and its owner's real feelings. By night, it is a dark gap in the glittering cavalcade of street lighting, a thing which cowers in the shadows, more obviously unemployed than by daylight. But when that Theatre finds its soul, which is a play, the play finds its body, which is the Theatre, and that combination finds its heart and sets it beating—and the heart is the players who are to perform, a very different state of things obtains. The Theatre comes alive, animate, vibrant, glowing with electric signs and activity. Then, and then only, is the whole thing endowed with life. And then and then only can the fourth part of the combination, the Audience, be expected to create the entity. Then that Theatre, in its collective sense, begins the job for which it was intended—and its job is to create Illusion.

Sir Herbert Tree, who was the incarnation of Theatre, said, "I take it that the whole business of the Stage is . . . Illusion." And how right he was—and how he understood that Art. A theatre is a factory like any other workshop which manufactures goods, but what it makes is magical—it makes Illusion.

A theatre has a story to tell, just as thrilling and interesting as any of those who played there—or visited it. Yet tens of thousands of the people who go there know nothing about them at all, except their names. There was a time when theatres shared the limelight with their players—when playhouses like Daly's, the Gaiety, the Haymarket, the Criterion, the Savoy, the St. James's, His Majesty's and Drury Lane meant a good deal. That was because great people worked there, and sold branded lines of Illusion . . . created something of that illusive thing called Goodwill, which is so hard to obtain in the Land of Illusion.

Those men who controlled those theatres were either Actor-Managers or creative geniuses—George Edwardes, Cyril Maude, Sir Charles Wyndham, Gilbert and Sullivan with D'Oyly Carte, Sir George Alexander, Sir Herbert Tree, Sir Augustus Harris and Arthur Collins. Those men created Illusion and their productions formed that indefinable something so valuable in a theatre, called 'Atmosphere'. And everything which happened, or had happened, in a theatre added to it—made that atmosphere more apparent, more bracing to the imaginative mind. Every play produced, every man and woman who acted, added something to that atmosphere.

Theatres are not only places of entertainment, places where Illusion is sold, but they are battlefields as well, arenas of desperate engagements, great victories, humiliating defeats, triumphs and disasters. All that adds to the feeling which a theatre can convey to those who love it. Battles between player and player for glory and precedence, battles between management and players, and most bitter of all, battles between theatre, play and players—and the audience which does not see things their way.

Something of what happens always remains for those who have the right senses. Old mummers, dead and gone, yet leave something behind in the places where they played—and to them play was their life.

That is why the older a theatre is, the more potent is its atmosphere. The new theatres are more impersonal, not enough has happened therein to fill them with memories—with those strange ghostly influences of effort made and strength expended, which haunt so pleasantly the older playhouses. If you really love the Theatre, either as your profession or as a playgoer, you will be conscious of it. Those old players are still there, whispering of their successes and failures, their victories and defeats, the plays which were acclaimed, and those which failed, all down the years, still seeking your applause, it would seem. It is not merely the age of a building which gives it atmosphere, it is what has happened there. It is the impalpable something left behind by all those who have striven so hard to please, worked so unceasingly to give the public whom they serve just an hour or two of Illusion. The greater the people, the greater the atmosphere—but everything adds some trifle to the strange ether of effort expended which can be felt and appreciated by those in tune with it.

No cinema can supply that feeling, nor will one ever succeed in doing so. There you have no personal effort at all, just shadows on a screen, tinned voices, operated by machinery—no personality to make its invisible yet enduring mark at all. In centuries to come no cinema-goer will thrill to think that he or she sits in the place where Valentino flickered on the screen, where the other members of that vast horde of 'stars' of celluloid filled the place with their shadows. It cannot happen. They were not there—those people, clever and talented as they were. They appeared in countless thousands of places—and ubiquity kills the personal memory and the power it can give to atmosphere. Perhaps such a thing might be found in a studio—but the public cannot go there.

But with a theatre it is different. Here is the actual place where the great ones worked in the flesh, where it all happened. There, at Daly's, was *The Geisha, The Merry Widow*—so much more magic— there at the Gaiety were Gertie Millar, Edmund Payne, George Grossmith and Connie Ediss, supported in their turn by the mighty ones of the older Gaiety—by matchless Nellie Farren and Fred Leslie, Royce, Edward Terry, J. L. Toole, Florence St. John, Kate Vaughan and delightful dainty Sylvia Grey, who still lights the world as a nonagenarian. At the Haymarket shone Benjamin Webster, Elliston, Henderson, J. B. Buckstone, whose ghost still lingers in the place he loved, Fielding, old Samuel Foote who first made it famous —and Cyril Maude, whose polish and perfection gave it the shining radiance it still contains—for the Haymarket is very rich in atmosphere indeed. The Criterion's atmosphere was first made—and made very enduringly—by Sir Charles Wyndham and Mary Moore, afterwards Lady Wyndham—and what they wrought remains today. The Savoy was built for a specific reason—the Savoy Operas, and the creators of those, Gilbert, Sullivan and D'Oyly Carte, who built it, made its name immortal. One cannot go there without sensing them—and that is atmosphere, too. The St. James's, for so many years the unluckiest theatre in London, found its real master in 1891, when George Alexander took it over—and turned ill fortune into glittering success. He conferred on that most gracious theatre his own personality, his distinction of manner, taste and talent—his dignity, his elegance and his immense sense of Quality. You can feel it all still—it is the 'atmosphere' of the St. James's. Alexander was knighted in 1911 and it seems as if the accolade was laid upon his theatre too.

Her Majesty's—now again bearing its original name—was built by Tree—and is his monument. He was the only Actor-Manager ever to build his own theatre—and he created the atmosphere by his compelling personality and his towering theatre genius directly it was built. It is perhaps right to say he did more than that—his heaven-sent gift of Illusion was laid with the very bricks, mixed with the mortar, buttressed the very foundations—for Her Majesty's was full of atmosphere on its very opening night—and that never happened to any other theatre anywhere.

And so to Drury Lane—Theatre Royal—the oldest of them all, the oldest theatre in the world still used as such. Fire has ravished it, reconstruction has been busy on it, bombs have hit it from enemies who came by night—but nothing has ever destroyed it— nothing has ever diminished that atmosphere which it contains— and, short of complete destruction, nothing ever will.

Great things have been happening there for 283 years—there age and events have built up the layers of memories, the lingering echoes of events and effort, into something which everyone who enters it must feel—of which even the most callous and uninterested are aware. There is a magic in the very name—and Drury Lane is known and famous all the world over. Old in years, it is young in spirit, for that rich atmosphere is the blood in its veins, fine, red blood which courses strongly and keeps it vigorous and active despite its burden of nearly three centuries—or perhaps because of it.

Think of the plays performed there—think of the great ones who have trodden its stage—think of the famous people who have visited it or had their hand in the running of it.

For the greatness of a theatre and its own particular atmosphere is supplied by those who have controlled its destiny—turned its wheels, kept it alive and open—and who have contributed to its gifts of Illusion. Those people are the pillars of a theatre. Drury Lane may and indeed does stand on those arches which Sir Christopher Wren built so strongly and securely between 1672 and 1674. But those are merely the support for the platform on which stand the human pillars who have made the mighty playhouse so great and famous—the men and women who have wrought there, either as players, as managers, as dramatists or producers—who have created its shows, guided its destinies and left their share of the atmosphere of achievement which fills it today. Some have succeeded, some tried and failed—some retired before their powers left them, some died in harness, their great ambitions still unfulfilled . . . but all of them were creators—creators of that duty of the Theatre, creators of Illusion. They had their own ways of doing it, their own methods and their own secrets. But all of them helped to build Drury Lane—that storehouse of memories, that theatre of majesty.

Men and women, they shall be called up and asked once more to strut their little hour upon the stage—to live again in the world of imagination, if they can indeed be evoked and re-created by the written word. Many books could be written about many theatres—some have their chronicled histories, some have not. Theatre Royal, Drury Lane, already has its story outlined by the same hand which now attempts, not to tell the story over again, for this book is in no sense a history, but to throw the sunshine of the Theatre—that thing beloved of theatrical folk which is still called Limelight although it is by no means so today—on those odd, and often fantastic folk, unlike ordinary human beings in so many ways, filled with that divine madness which the Theatre induces in its workers. For it is not possible to be sane in the everyday sense if one is to be of the Theatre. In that topsy-turvy world, where everything is done the other way round, the beings who inhabit it must be see-ers of visions, living lives apart from the workaday world, speaking often a jargon of their own, obsessed by their own personalities, vain, self-confident yet fearful, frightened yet brave, working for themselves yet as members of a team—all to one end—that success may come and failure be unknown. Sometimes they win, sometimes they lose—but something remains of their great gambles in the greatest gamble on earth—the Theatrical Profession. They, in their turn, kept that vast playhouse alive and vigorous and its continuity down the years until today it is their monument. Only a selection can be made in the small space of this volume—but those singled out for display herein all had one thing in common—a knowledge of their job, a deep and abiding love for the place for which they laboured, and that courage which made them pit their wits and their imaginations against the great hosts of the General Public, at once their supporters and their enemies. They had to forget their own likes and dislikes and strive to find out what that constantly changing thing, Public Taste, would find acceptable. There are no rules in the Theatre, save one—the rule of giving the best in the best manner. You cannot learn what to do, but you can learn what not to do. And acting, the life's blood of it all, cannot be taught, but it can be learnt. And it is best learnt there upon the stage of a theatre in front of those who are at once the friends and foes of the learner, according to whether he learns his lesson or not.

But, in every instance, they all believed in the same thing—that Acting is the great Art of the Theatre—the means by which it lives or dies. An auditorium of some sort you must have, a play you must have, but Acting has the last word. A theatre without actors is useless, a play is just so many words on paper—until the art of the actor brings the touch of life. Strangely enough, acting is often at its best in periods when there are no outstanding plays or dramatists. It is, primarily, the actors whom the public go to see. It is they who create the Illusion. It is they, by their art, who can interest and excite. Bad acting can kill a play, good acting can often get a bad play near to success—sometimes to complete achievement thereof. Not always, but sometimes. The Actor came first in the Theatre. As soon as Thespis had stepped forward—and acted—then the dramatists followed. And when acting is exciting, then the Theatre blossoms like the rose. For the great actor or actress can hypnotize an audience into forgetfulness of their surroundings—and that is Illusion, that is what the Theatre is for. The greatest periods of Theatre History were those when Acting was strong and virile. Today, the grey age of understatement, we have quiet, subdued acting. Very, very seldom is one carried away. The Theatre therefore loses its great asset of excitement—it becomes a sedative whereas it should be a tonic. An actor or actress must project their personality and art into the most distant recesses of the playhouse—they must compel their audience. They must be larger than life. One of the secrets of the success of the films is that they are always larger than life.

To do the Theatre job properly, it is necessary always to be larger than life, to remember that one's force has to conquer mentalities of all kinds. A theatre audience is never a complete entity, it is a conglomeration of different tastes, different intellects, varying intelligence. The men and women who have to bring that mass of humanity under their spell, must realize that and call magic to their aid. It is not enough to let them sit back in their seats and come towards you of their own accord—if, indeed, they will. They must be conquered, they must be entranced, they must be made to think that what they are watching is Reality—whereas it is mere Illusion. That can seldom be attained by undertones, inaudibility and dim lighting. The great theatrical magic of Illusion must be injected into those who watch, so that they lean forward—and are carried away themselves into the Land of Illusion.

Those who will be called upon to cross these pages all knew that. They were the Creators of Illusion—and they were the Pillars of that greatest Temple of Illusion the world has ever known—Theatre Royal, Drury Lane.

CHAPTER ONE

The First Pillar

THE first Pillar of Theatre Royal, Drury Lane, might also be called its foundation stone as well, for he was its creator, its builder and its first manager. His name was Thomas Killigrew. Without him, that famous theatre, the Temple of the English Drama, might never have existed. It is not to be supposed that when he built his playhouse, he gave one thought to the idea that it would become a landmark in the world history of the Theatre, a place revered, a monument to our Stage and one of the sights of London. He loved the Theatre, he wanted to build one—and he did.

What manner of man was he? Whence came this desire to run a playhouse? It was apparently inherent. Yet he was of gentle blood and not one of the despised and persecuted sections of the public who earned a precarious living by acting, for ever at war with authority and the Church, often in the stocks and the lock-up, frequently in the pillory and always in danger of having their ears cropped or their noses slit. It was, indeed, Thomas Killigrew, Gent, who stopped all those things, as will be shown. He wrought better than he knew, he built for posterity and he struck such a blow for the Profession he loved—and entered—that he completely revolutionized its social standing.

The tens of thousands who visit Drury Lane, to see its plays, never waste a thought on Thomas Killigrew, yet they owe much to him. How many members of his profession, suddenly confronted with his name, would know much—or indeed anything—about him? Yet they are indebted to him for far more than they realize—even when told.

Thomas Killigrew was the son of Sir Robert Killigrew, Kt., of Falmouth in Cornwall. He was the fourth son of his father, so there was no question of inheriting the title—that went to his eldest brother William in due course—nor did Thomas, despite his immense popularity with his King, his loyal service and his work in creating the first Theatre Royal the world ever knew, receive a knighthood or a title at any time. He died Thomas Killigrew, Gentleman, as he was born. There were twelve Killigrews in that family, and seven of them, three of the boys and four of the girls, gained considerable fame and eminence.

Thomas Killigrew was born in London, on 7th February, 1612, at his father's house in Lothbury in the City of London. Some authorities attribute his birthplace to Hanworth, in Middlesex, where his father had a manor, but Master Thomas, for all his Cornish blood, was a Cockney, born well within the hearing of Bow Bells. And he loved his London as a true Cockney should.

He was educated well but he did not go to a University, as did his brothers. William, the eldest, went to St. John's College, Oxford, and Dr. Henry Killigrew, the youngest, to Christ Church at the same University. All these three brothers, William, Thomas and Henry, had something in common. They were all dramatists—and dramatists of some distinction, which might be thought curious in sons of an ancient County Family in those days. But at that time, starting from the Tudor Renaissance, literary merit was esteemed a virtue and a desirable accomplishment. Some wrote books and learned treatises, very many wrote poetry, but the Killigrews wrote plays. Somewhere or other there seemed the taint of the Theatre in the blood and it came out in that generation. Although the plays of William (afterwards Sir William) were of considerable merit—he wrote four plays for certain and one which is attributed to him—he also wrote many essays and views on life—he does not bulk in Theatre history as does his younger brother Thomas—the complete man of the Theatre. Henry Killigrew, the youngest, became a B.A. at Christ Church and was one of the quadragesimal collectors. He became an M.A. in 1638 and when the Civil War broke out he joined the Royalist Cause and became Chaplain to the King's Army and a Doctor of Divinity. He was then appointed Chaplain to the Duke of York and was given the twelfth stall in Westminster Abbey. He suffered, as did the entire Killigrew family, for its loyalty to the Crown. But on the Restoration he became almoner to the Duke of York, superintendent to the affairs of his Chapel, Rector of Wheathampstead, in Hertfordshire, and finally Master of the Chapel Royal, Savoy. Not a very likely background for a dramatist, but such he was. He got it out of his system quite early on. He wrote his play to be performed in celebration of the wedding of Lord Charles Herbert to Mary Villiers when he was seventeen years old. It is not clear as to whether it was actually performed on the occasion for which it was written, or later, but it was produced at the Blackfriars Theatre and certain of the critics of the day cavilled at it. They said it was monstrous and impossible that a boy of seventeen should conceive such sentiments as he put into the mouth of one of his characters. The character thus complained of was Colanthes. However, Lord Falkland took up cudgels on behalf of the author and said he did not see how it was either monstrous or impossible, since the author was exactly that age when he wrote those words and sentiments. And Ben Jonson praised it too. Dr. Henry wrote no more plays but he revised *The Conspiracy* before it was published in 1653 and renamed it *Pallantus and Eudora*.

The Theatre virus ran most strongly, however, in the veins of young Thomas. He was destined for the Court and it seemed that a University education was not considered to be of benefit to him there. At any rate, he did not go. He received a pretty good education, either at some school as day boy or from a private tutor, and although he absorbed a good deal of general knowledge—especially of literature and the classics—he did not concern himself with gaining erudition. He was about the streets a good deal—perhaps as good a form of education as any—and he was always haunting the playhouses. That was his idea of heaven. Just as small boys today spend their Saturday morning in the cinema, Master Thomas would betake himself, whenever occasion offered—and it is pretty certain that he made the occasions suitable—to the Theatre, especially the Red Bull, which was in St. John's, Clerkenwell, and therefore not far from the Killigrew home in Lothbury. There he not only watched the plays but actually played in them when he got a chance. One can picture this small boy, quite entranced by the illusion of the Theatre—primitive as it then was—carried away by the art of the actors—there were no actresses—standing in that open-air theatre, formed out of an inn yard, as its name suggests, which was the 'Blood Tub', the home of melodrama of the time. But it was a theatre, where there was acting, and that was enough for young Thomas. He was there as often as he could manage. And there were red-letter days at the Red Bull, for at times the manager, or stage manager (called the Prompter then), would come out before the show started and shout to the crowd outside—and for the most part those crowds were made up of boys, hoping to see the show for nothing, as their descendants crawled under the canvas of the circus tents. "Who will go and be a devil and he shall see the play for nothing?" Doubtless young Thomas headed the rush. He would see the play—he would actually get on the stage as a little devil in the grand finale—and what bliss that was, to act as well—and go home excited and starry-eyed, with his mind fully made up as to what he was going to be when he was a man. Well, that youthful ambition was fulfilled, though much lay between the conception of the idea and its fulfilment. In case present-day readers wonder where the devils came into the play, it was quite usual to have a lot of them, to represent the forces of evil in the amazing heroic stories which the

dramas of the time presented. Good must prevail, even though the
hero died heroically—and the villain would be seized by the Powers
of Evil and carried off to Hell, with general rejoicings, by the
audience in general and the boys and players representing devils in
particular. There would be fireworks and any quantity of red fire
to make the whole thing impressive to the working folk—mostly
illiterate—who frequented the Red Bull—and to drive home to
them the age-old message of Melodrama—that Virtue wins and Vice
loses. And there is no doubt that Master Killigrew thought the
whole thing very fine indeed. The theatre-tainted blood coursed
through his veins.

There is no actual record of when he first went to Court, to serve
his King, Charles I. He became a Page of Honour. Probably
somewhere about 1626—when he was fourteen. He became very
popular there. He used to joke about his lack of education—or at
any rate of the lack of University polish—but he could hold his own
with anyone by means of his own wit and smartness. Also he knew a
great deal about the romantic works of the day—and Romance was
in fashion. He had read what the great ones had written, and
remembered it and could quote fluently. There are certain reports
about his travels, though when he found time to undertake them is
certainly not clear. His duties as page did not give him leisure to be
away from Court. It is more likely that his travels were confined to
London, of which his knowledge, like that of Sam Weller, was
extensive and peculiar—and Sam Weller was educated in the
streets of London too, as were Charles Morton (destined to create
Music Hall) and John Hollingshead—destined to create the Gaiety
Theatre. It is a pretty good University for those who serve the
Theatre. That Killigrew kept his eyes open and saw all that was
going on, is proved by the fact that he wrote a very detailed account
of what he saw when an impostor claimed to have exorcised devils
out of the minds and bodies of certain nuns in a London convent.
His account of this, very vivid and well observed, was in the Pepysian
Library at Magdalene, Cambridge.

He did well at Court, he was in favour with the King—and in
high favour with the Queen, Henrietta Maria, who doted on the
Theatre and plays. His salary was £100 a year. He had to imple-
ment that and there were ways of doing it. He was doubtless mixed
up in intrigues and backstairs ventures—taking favours for whispered
words in the ears of the great, conniving at illicit romances—it was
all part of the job and the times.

But he stood very well with the Queen—and to stand well with
her was to do the same with the King. She loved poets and players

as much as George II said he detested them. Plays and masques were in constant request, for the private Court Theatre at Whitehall—the Queen and the Royal children appeared in them—on Sunday nights, too! And it is to be believed that even Charles I would act upon occasion. Killigrew took the chance this offered. He had the family gift for playwriting—it was most strongly developed in him—and before the Civil War broke out he had had three of his works produced there and had appeared many times as actor. There is not much on record of his acting powers. Probably he got by for he had plenty of confidence. But his plays were good and too good just to see the light at private performances—Royal though they might be. These Royal performances were in the nature of 'try-outs' too, for other plays besides those of Killigrew afterwards got transferred to public playhouses. In his case, the theatre was the Phoenix —originally called 'The Cockpit'—in Drury Lane, so Thomas Killigrew began his professional theatrical career in the very street whose name he was to make world famous by reason of his own theatre. These plays were *The Prisoner*; *Claracilla*; and *The Princess, or Love at First Sight*. They were produced almost consecutively— during 1637 or 1638. They were presented by Beeston, who was almost the first owner of a Theatre Royal, inasmuch as he was allowed to call his company 'His Majesty's Servants'. But he never got written permission to do so and eventually he lost favour.

If Killigrew had not travelled in his youth, as did most young men then, he certainly went abroad when attached to the Court, but on a diplomatic mission and attached to the suite of Walter Montagu. They went to France and Italy, and visited Rome and Naples. That was in 1636 and there is good cause to believe that Killigrew wrote his plays whilst he was away, or at least two of them. And if not actually whilst he was away, then almost immediately on his return. He gathered background and colour from that brief foreign trip of four months—and the plays are very much alike in character and texture. *The Prisoner* was written before he went away and is slightly different in form. When he came back, in 1636, he got married to his first wife, Cecilia Crofts, at Oatlands in Surrey. And he got those plays produced. So it is almost certain that he wrote *Claracilla* and *The Princess* whilst abroad—the folio suggests it—the first in Rome, the second in Naples.

Pepys, commenting on a subsequent performance of *Claracilla*— after the Restoration—says it was 'acted before the troubles'— meaning the Civil War. They were all just the sort of plays the Queen would like—Tragi-Comedies of a romantic nature, with fine senti-ments and well-turned lines—of little depth but pleasant on the ear.

Killigrew knew his classics and myths well enough to get what he wanted from them—and he had a good wit of his own to add some sparkle. The plots were pretty complicated—comedy scenes were interlarded, but the themes were full of simple and pure sentiment. This was in Pre-Restoration days. *Claracilla* was the best of them, for it had plenty of action and movement and carried its 'auditors' away with its clever construction and force. It held the boards for a long time. It was a very actable play. Pepys did not like it much— but he really liked very little which did not have a favourite of his in the cast—but admits 'there are some good things in it'. But Killigrew was not to become a complete man of the Theatre yet; his plays were not to make him a distinguished figure in the world of the Drama. A greater one than he could devise broke out in 1642, when King Charles I went to war with a great section of his own subjects and the Civil War broke out.

Killigrew was, of course, on the side of the King. There is no actual record of what he did, nor whether he actually fought in battle for the King, but there is no doubt at all that he worked for the Royal Cause with activity and probably success, because in September 1642 he was arrested and locked up—placed in the custody of Sir John Lenthall, 'on suspicion of raising arms against Parliament'. Now Killigrew was the ideal Cavalier. He was brave, careless, largely improvident, but he had address and a witty tongue. He had also great energy and was popular with all classes, because he was a good mixer and always in the playhouses. London was a small city—and celebrities were well known. Handsome Tom Killigrew with his persuasive tongue, his knowledge of men and women gained from his own experience and that of the Court, could be a thorn in the sober sides of the Parliamentarians—so into prison he went. The Royalists thought him of sufficient importance to exchange him for a prominent Roundhead who had been captured at Edgehill. That was in July 1643, so he had been in durance for about ten months. Then he joined the King's forces and doubtless fought in the field. Things went against the Crown, and with disaster in sight, Queen Henrietta Maria sailed for France with the Royal children, escorted by a small body of loyal Cavaliers, and Thomas Killigrew was one of them. If he had travelled little on the Continent before, he was to repair that gap in his education now. The Queen sailed from Falmouth—the home town of the Killigrews.

The refugees went to Paris, and what happened to them there— and what happened to poor Charles I, foolish, misguided, gallant man—is a matter for ordinary history. But Killigrew remained with the vestige of the Court and worked for the man he now regarded as

ABD-EL-KADER—FROM AN AUTHENTIC FRENCH PORTRAIT.

Left: Gustavus Vaughan Brooke, the tragic tragedian, in the character of Othello. He owed his first London success in this character to the admiration of the public for a Moorish chieftain Abd-el-Kader—who had performed deeds of heroism and who is seen above

Upper left: Samuel Foote *Upper right:* Balfe, the composer *Centre:* A scene from the famous melodrama *The Whip*. *Below:* The Rotunda at Drury Lane showing statues of Edmund Kean and Shakespeare

his King, afterwards to be Charles II. And dark-haired, dark-skinned, cynical and clever Charles Stuart made Killigrew his friend. They had the same tastes, they were both wits, they both loved the Theatre. But Charles lacked that energy and sometimes astonishingly clear sight of Killigrew, who although he treated his exiled King with deference on public occasions, would give him sharp and good advice in private. Killigrew was rather unscrupulous and would always take a chance—he would have been no good in the Theatre had he not done so. He had a way with him and was an accomplished diplomat—again a theatrical gift of value. Charles refers to him in a document, in 1647, as 'our diligent and faithful servant'—of course, in Latin. Charles held him in great esteem, because Killigrew could make him laugh; and often the wily man wrapped up his good advice in a joke, which the King assimilated. Charles sent him on important business to Italy in 1647 and he did it well. He was made Groom of the Bedchamber to the Duke of York, then at The Hague. Thus he had the ear of Royalty always at his command. But when Charles I was executed and his son became King in exile, Killigrew was at once recalled to Paris and joined the personal entourage. Charles then made him an Ambassador and sent him to Italy again, to Savoy, to Florence, places of the utmost importance to the Royal Cause—and then as Resident Ambassador in Venice, one of the greatest cities in the world, of immense power and political significance.

There are some stories about this appointment. It is said that the King, who was absolutely penniless, did not see his way to support his Ambassador. Killigrew had a remedy for this. He would borrow money from the English merchants there, he said, in the King's name and for the King's business—and they would be pleased to lend it to him. It is said that the King demurred at this idea; it does not sound likely because Charles would go to any shifts, at all times of his life, to lay his hand on cash. But there again Killigrew showed that keen theatrical strain—never do business with your own money but always with somebody else's. Anyway, Thomas Killigrew went to Venice as Ambassador. It has been said that he had to be removed therefrom because of his dissolute and vicious behaviour. But that is not true. Clever, astute Killigrew outwitted the Cromwellian representatives in Venice—he made rings round them to the extent that the Protector became annoyed and frightened for his power in Venice and made representations to the Court there that this wicked Malignant should be sent packing—or else. . . . Cromwell and his Army were a world power, a fact which is often forgotten. The Venetians knew his military skill. They had heard what he and

C

his Ironsides had done to the French at Dunkirk and they wanted no bother with this grim, iron master of arms. So representations were made and Charles had no option but to recall Killigrew. But Killigrew had made good use of his time there, besides his diligence in conducting the King's business. He had studied the Italian Theatre—he had done the same in France and wherever he went. That was the mainspring of his life. He had an idea of his own—to put into force when he got home. He never doubted that his King would reign again.

He stood high in favour with his Royal Master and friend. When Charles left Paris for The Hague, in 1654, Killigrew went too. And there he married his second wife, a Dutch lady named Charlotte de Hesse, who brought him a fortune of £10,000, the same dowry as his first spouse. He served his King, he had a house of his own in Maastricht—and he often worked for the States-General as well on delicate politicial missions—and probably secret service, too. Also, he went on writing plays. He wrote *The Parson's Wedding*—part of it only, for he finished it when he got home; *Cicilia and Clorinda*—or *Love in Arms* (which was in two parts); *Thomaso* or *The Wanderer*, also in two parts; *Bellamira*, *The Dream*, or *The Love of Shadows* and *The Pilgrim*. Only one of them ever saw the lights of an English stage and that was *The Parson's Wedding*. But it kept him busy and he scribbled much poetry too. Sir John Denham wrote a little poem which touched off Tom Killigrew round about this time, when, his Venetian Embassy over, he was with the Court and Groom of the Bedchamber to Charles—a constant companion and a confidant, too. . . .

> Our Resident Tom
> From Venice is come
> And left all the Statesmen behind him
> Talks at the same pitch
> Is as wise, is as rich
> And just where you left him, you find him.
>
> But who says he's not
> A Man of much Plot
> May repent of this false accusation
> Having plotted and penn'd
> Six plays to attend
> On the farce of his Negotiation.

Killigrew wrote seven, not six, plays, but the last was probably written after Denham's playful satire.

King Charles came into his own again in May 1660, and when *The Royal Charles* sailed into Dover, Samuel Pepys of course went aboard and met the Quality, as he loved to do. He records, 'amongst others, Thomas Killigrew (a merry droll, but a gentleman of great esteem with the King).'

Once home, Killigrew set about his ambition, his theatrical enterprise—which had as its object the building of his own theatre. He joined hands with Sir William Davenant and together they persuaded the King, who needed little persuasion, to make them joint controllers of London's theatres. Davenant had kept the flag of the Theatre flying nobly during Cromwell's closure of the play-houses. He and Killigrew were friends. And the King had already made Killigrew his Master of the Revels, which caused legal trouble later. Of the adventures of Davenant and Killigrew together and separately, their establishment of themselves as dictators of the Theatre, their battles with Sir Henry Herbert, who claimed, with some justice, to be the actual Master of the Revels, and their parting company with each other with a gentleman's agreement, strictly kept, never to interfere with each other's affairs—there is a full report in *Theatre Royal* and it need not be repeated here. Of the two men who might be said to have founded the modern theatre—or the actual theatre upon which ours of today is founded—for their methods and playhouses differed much from those in vogue up to the Restoration—Davenant was by far the abler business man and manager—also the better producer. But Killigrew had the vision, the ideas, and the Romance. He was the popular man and he was the founder of the first Theatre Royal, to which he gave some of his own personality—seeming to weld it into the bricks and mortar and into the atmosphere—which still retains it. He is summed up in Pepys' small phrase, 'a merry droll'. Davenant was much more stern and serious, a lover of discipline—Killigrew was easy-going, he persuaded rather than led, he suggested rather than ordered. But he got his own way.

And first, from the King, he got that Order to 'erect a Company of Players, such company to be our Own Company of Comedians'— a title which all companies appearing at Theatre Royal, Drury Lane, still bear, no matter what their nationality or composition; and secondly he got the Patent or Royal Charter which made his play-house Theatre Royal.

That Charter is all important. Up to its granting the Theatre and its players had been persecuted for years—for many, many centuries. Every man's hand was against them—especially that of the Church and the Civic Authorities. They were outcasts, they were masterless men, and even when wearing the livery of some great nobleman, they were not safe. The stocks and the pillories gaped for them and often held them—their ears were cropped and their noses slit. But when Tom Killigrew got that Royal Charter from Charles II, that was the end of persecution. Now the Theatre was Royal—it was free—it was stabilized. It was part of the ordinary life of the country—not a doubtful and semi-criminal pursuit. The Theatre was established and free. That was what Thomas Killigrew did—or persuaded his King to do—for the Theatre, and Drury Lane still stands foursquare as a memorial to it. That Charter which the King granted had another very important clause:

"Whereas the women's parts in plays have hitherto been acted by men in habits of women, at which some have taken offence, we do permit and give leave from this time to come that all women's parts be acted by women."

And so, by virtue of Killigrew's Drury Lane, women came upon the stage, and the Theatrical Profession was the first in which men and women met on terms of equality. Now, there had been actresses on the French and Continental stage for years before that. Killigrew had seen them. So had Charles II. He had taken an interest in them, and did not see why on his return home he should not go on seeing them—nor did Tom Killigrew. So into the Charter went that paragraph—it adds also that this change is introduced in the interest of the morals of the King's beloved subjects (and we know what a stickler he was for morals). There are those who say the King allowed women on the stage because, prior to their admission, he had gone to see a representation of *Hamlet* and had been kept waiting for some time whilst the actor who was to play the Queen was closely shaved. But one thinks that the interest the King took in actresses had far more to do with it. For he continued to take the liveliest interest in the English actresses new come to their calling—there is the instance of Mistress Nell Gwynne . . . and others.

How Killigrew raised his money and built his theatre has all been told. He made a success of it from the word 'Go'. He had the favour of the King and the Court, the nobility and gentry and was popular with the general public. He was an easy-going manager but he knew his way about. He had always done that. When he married his first wife, Cecilia Crofts, a Maid of Honour to the Queen, he had nothing but what he might get by his Court service. She had £10,000—as did his second wife. He managed later, as Master of the

Revels, to get a fee out of The Wardrobe—for this appointment was the modified form of King's Jester and allowed its holder great latitude of speech, and he could say what he liked without fear of reprisal. Tom Killigrew was too good-natured to speak much ill of anyone. He never lacked for anything by reason of not asking for it. His idea was that if you asked for a lot you might get something, if you asked for a little you probably got nothing. So he always asked for as much as possible. He was able to run a lottery for some years, doubtless at a good profit. And he certainly asked for a lot when he requested the King to give him that Charter for his proposed theatre in Drury Lane—and he got it.

The King, as easy-going as Killigrew, could refuse this laughing Cavalier—this man of charm and wit and considerable brain— nothing. And Killigrew knew it. He was always asking, with a smile on his face and an assurance that he would never be rebuffed. He asked for—and got—things to which he was never entitled. He asked to be made Keeper of the Greenwich Armoury, to wipe off his personal expenses [sic] in attending the King in exile. He got it. There was a parcel of silver plate knocking about which was said to be the property of Oliver Cromwell and appeared not to have an owner. Killigrew made an application—and got it. Some woodlands in Northamptonshire appeared to belong to nobody; Killigrew put in a claim and they became his. He got a share in granting licences to pedlars and petty chapmen, and also on butts for long-bow practice. Once he gave a bond of security for £500—the bond fell in. Killigrew asked to be relieved of it. He was relieved all right. No good sinecure fell vacant but his application went in—and he got quite a few of them—one as Water Bailiff in particular he secured for his two sons on his death. And that £100 a year which he had earned at the Court of Charles I had, of course, not been paid since the Civil War. He claimed the arrears and compounded for an annual pension of £100. A man of enterprise who was never averse to a gamble or taking a risk—the ideal theatre manager, as he turned out to be.

But he could speak straight on occasion even to his friend and benefactor Charles II. He loved the King but he was not afraid of him. They were familiar friends. It so fell out that King Charles, in dalliance with his numerous lady friends, had for a very long time neglected to attend the meetings of the Privy Council and had flouted those who had dared to suggest that this was a dangerous thing to do. A nice storm was brewing. Killigrew took a hand. As Groom of the Bedchamber, he had immediate access to the King and he startled that monarch by appearing before him dressed as a pilgrim equipped for a long journey. There was the pack, the staff, the shell, all the 'props' properly worn and in order. The King was astonished. He asked Killigrew where he was going. "On a long journey," replied that man. "Oh, and where to?" asked the interested monarch. "To hell," bluntly replied Killigrew. The astonished King asked him why he was bound for that unpleasant destination. "Well," said Killigrew, "I am going to fetch back Oliver Cromwell that he may take care of the affairs of England, of which it stands so sadly in need and which his successor seems to ignore. And yet I know one man who might do it instead of Oliver, if he would." "And who is he, pray?" queried the King. "A certain Charles Stuart," answered Killigrew, "who could be a noble and wise king, if he would take the trouble and leave the women alone." The King roared with laughter, and was for a long time constant in his attendance at Privy Councils. But after a while he grew lax again and his councillors were greatly incensed, especially the Duke of Lauderdale, a man of violent temper and impetuous manner. He stormed out of the council chamber shouting with rage and uttering words in respect of the King which were, if well justified, nevertheless very dangerous to utter had an enemy overheard them. But instead of a foe he met Tom Killigrew, who smiled sweetly upon him and asked what was the matter. The Duke told him in no modified terms. Killigrew warned him good-naturedly to be careful of what he said about His Majesty—and then offered to lay a wager. He said, if the Duke would return to the Council, he, Killigrew, would see to it that His Majesty was there too in less than half an hour. Lauderdale, who could not believe it, laid a level bet of £100 —and went back to the Council. Killigrew hastened to the King. Without mincing matters, he told Charles exactly what had happened. Then he added, with a twinkle in that rather wicked eye of his: "I know that Your Majesty hates Lauderdale, though the necessity of your affairs compels you to carry an outward show of civility. Now, if you choose to be rid of a man who is thus disagreeable to you, you need only go this once to Council; for I know his covetous disposition so perfectly that I am well persuaded, rather than pay this Hundred Pounds, he will hang himself out of the way, and never plague you more." The King was so amused that he went straight away to the Council—to the discomfiture of Lauderdale and to the delight—and enrichment—of Killigrew.

Killigrew got his money to build his theatre—that was easy for him. The terms and conditions of the sharing amongst the original venturers and company have all been set out, as have all particulars of the theatre. Up it went, and it opened—the first Theatre Royal the world had ever seen, a precedent for all time and an influence on foreign courts. For if there had never been a Theatre Royal, Drury Lane, there might never have been a Comédie Française—and a landmark in the International World of the Theatre for ever. The work of Thomas Killigrew, Gent—a merry droll.

What was he like to look at? There are not many pictures of him extant. As a younger man he was slight and quite good-looking, with a longish nose, a sensitive mouth and rather dreamy eyes; but with the suggestion of a smile around both mouth and eyes. He wears his hair long, of course, and he is fondling a dog—and he loved dogs and they loved him. A later picture shows him as far more robust and square-looking; it is the work of a Dutch artist who may have seen him that way. But it shows him as he was when he founded Drury Lane, a man of fifty-one years of age, experienced in the ways of the world, twice married, used to the hardships of exile, the ups and downs of the world, the intrigues of courts and embassies, equal to any emergency from friend or foe, the adviser and confidant of his King, the master of the first Company of King's Comedians— and more than that, the manager of the first actresses who ever trod the stage. He coped with the tantrums and temperaments of those ladies; and it was under his management that the first one appeared, at the little theatre in Vere Street, Clare Market, which he was running whilst Drury Lane was being built.

He was easy-going but he was never a fool. He was perhaps a bit lazy but he did his work. He saw to it that his theatre, when built, was well run and gave the public the best possible value. He was very proud that he was able to light it, after a while, with real wax candles instead of tallow and make other improvements. He was also given to looking ahead and he founded one of the first academies of dramatic art—to train the young idea—and set it up in Moorfields, although nothing much came of it, or of the other in The Barbican.

He had his troubles to face all along the line, but he did yeoman service in his theatre. He gave the public what they wanted—he staged spectacular shows as well and he had real horses on the stage—a tremendous sensation, as early as 1665, in a play called *Hyde Park*. He made Charles Hart his joint leading man, with Major Mohun and Shakespeare's great-nephew, his general manager, to break the first flow of troubles, but he had to meet them in the end; he met plenty. As always in the Theatre, finance is a knotty and arguable point. Killigrew had his shareholders with whom to cope and his company, many of whom were on a sharing basis. There wa nothing but smiles when things went right—but when bad t me came, as they always do in Theatreland—then it was all Killig fault. But somehow he managed to ride the storm. He had to be the diplomat and keep the peace between the numerous lady favourites of his King, when they came to the Theatre. And he had to cope with the King himself, when he visited it—but that he could manage easily. Incidentally King Charles II was the first monarch ever to go to the Theatre: prior to that the Theatre had gone to the monarch.

He had two tremendous blows. The first fell when the Great Plague shut his theatre down completely—indeed, all playhouses—from 5th June, 1665, until 29th November, 1666. That was a sad blow. He lost his most popular leading lady—Nell Gwynne—when the King carried her off in 1670; she had reigned for only five years but she remains for ever Sweet Nell of Old Drury. He had serious opposition to face when the widow and sons of his old friend Sir William Davenant opened the Duke's Theatre, in Dorset Gardens, in 1672—but he weathered that. Then his worst blow fell, in 1672—when fire destroyed Theatre Royal. This might have crushed a lesser man and even a man with more capital than Killigrew possessed—and he had very little. But like the man of the Theatre he was, he refused to accept defeat. He took refuge at the old theatre in Lincoln's Inn which Davenant had run. He had no money, no costumes, no scenery or properties, all had been consumed in the fire. But he made the best of it; he met disaster with a joke and called himself and his company 'The Shipwrecked Mariners'. He determined to rebuild. He canvassed the rich and influential—he got the money together and those who supported him were called 'Adventurers'—an apt name. And he rebuilt Drury Lane Theatre. He was determined to do so and he did. Nothing stopped this easy-going, seemingly lazy, jest-loving Cavalier, for he adored the Theatre. It was in his blood. He built again—and he built well. His second Theatre Royal stood on the same site and was the same size as that of today. He had the best architect possible—no less a person that Sir Christopher Wren. But it was very expensive. His first theatre had cost, to build and equip, the sum of £2,400. This second and much larger playhouse, with the finest architect in the land—cost £4,000. Think of that in terms of today! It seemed vast then, it is cheap and staggering now. But the theatre was very plain and workmanlike; there was no money for artistic embellishment. That did not worry Killigrew. He knew that what happened on the stage was what mattered—and saw to it that the best was provided. He got it opened in 1674.

So he was, actually, twice the Father of Drury Lane—the creator of the first and second Theatres.

He was ageing and he left things to his sons, Henry and Charles, and neither of those sons was any good. There were battles with the company, disaffection and desertions, accusations of sharp practices and, naturally, family rows. The sons claimed that their father did not keep his word to them—and Charles especially was a thorn in his side. Neither of them inherited any of their father's qualities.

Worn out with battles and worries, but cheerful and joking to the last, Thomas Killigrew died at Whitehall, on the 19th March, 1682. He was seventy years of age and had lived every one of them.

He should always be remembered by all those interested in the British Theatre. For it was by his work that the Theatre became free. Davenant, it is true, kept it alive during the enforced closure of the Commonwealth, whilst Killigrew was in exile with his King. But it was Killigrew who was the King's friend, who persuaded Charles to make him and Davenant the masters of Theatreland. It was Killigrew who got the document which entitled him to 'erect' a Royal Company of Players and thereby stop the centuries of persecution. It was Killigrew who got the Charter for Drury Lane from Charles II; for although Davenant had secured one from Charles I in 1639, he had never been able to make it operate. It was Killigrew's players who were the Royal Servants, wearing the Royal Livery— still worn at Drury Lane—and twelve of whose actors became Court officials. He it was who created and built the first Theatre Royal the world had ever known—a theatre which goes on today with prosperity and power. Thomas Killigrew—as much as Burbage—was the Father of the English Theatre, and the man to give it freedom.

He was just the right type. He had supreme confidence and never admitted defeat. He always believed that, if disaster came tonight, success was just around the corner. Nothing dismayed him, nothing checked his enthusiasm. He loved the Theatre, he wrought for it and he wrought lasting good. He was the supreme optimist. He was a gambler always ready for a throw with Fortune, never downcast if he lost, never unduly triumphant if he won—taking it all in the day's work. When crippling blows fell, he shook them off and was ready to start again. Not a business man in the real sense of the word, but a man of understanding, knowing that the Theatre is not a business but a gamble with a gamble and always ready to take it on. And win or lose, he never complained. In other words, he was the ideal theatrical manager. Today, nearly three centuries after he built it, Theatre Royal stands as his monument. Most of the millions who go there never give him a thought—do not even know his name. Yet he made it all. And something of him remains in that unique atmosphere of that unique house. For despite its majesty, Drury Lane is never overpowering. It is magnificent, it is regal, but it is always friendly and welcoming—it always has a smile. It inherits that, woven into its atmosphere, from the 'merry droll' who created it. Something of the two theatres he knew and in which he worked still remains in that splendid building—one tiny portion of the first theatre—and quite a lot of Wren's work. And the original Charter of course still exists. But there is another trace of Killigrew at Drury Lane, for all to see—visible there at every performance. For the footmen there wear the Royal Livery—the only building outside the Royal Palaces where it can be seen. They wear it by virtue of that Charter given to the first and most enduring Pillar of Drury Lane—that double pillar and double foundation stone—Thomas Killigrew, Gentleman; the merry droll who made Old Drury.

CHAPTER TWO

Pillars of the Early Structure

THIS book or record is not intended to feature once again all those mighty names which throng the story of the world's most famous Theatre but to give credit to those of whom not so much is generally known, but who in their turn supported that playhouse and by their efforts added something to its atmosphere and, by their service, welded something into its story.

Those who look for the sagas of Betterton, Garrick, Macklin, Cibber, Siddons, Kean and other giants will not get much result. But the lesser people have stories just as strange and exciting, just as full of endeavour and achievement, disaster and failure as their better-known brothers and sisters. There were many men who were pillars of the first Drury Lane Theatre who have too little in the way of remembrance. And amongst them towers the handsome face and form of Edward Kynaston. All that most people who remember him at all recall of him is that he played women's parts. So he did, but he played men's parts too and he bulked largely in the making of Old Drury.

He was born of a decent county family—the Kynastons of Otely in Salop. He was apprenticed to old Rhodes, once a famous 'prompter' in pre-Restoration days, who turned bookseller at Charing Cross and kept many actors from starving during the forced closing of the Commonwealth. This was, of course, a most respectable calling and Kynaston got his head full of the Stage from his surroundings. No wonder he took to it; and with his extreme good looks, of course, he was made to play girls' parts in the days before actresses were allowed on the Stage. There is no actual record of his birth nor of when he actually first appeared on the Stage, but he lived to a good age—well past sixty—and he died in 1712, being buried in the churchyard of the Church of St. Paul, Covent Garden, the Actors' Church. He was on the Stage for forty years, from 1659 until 1699, and he may well have played before that, for he was a member of Killigrew's first company. Only, if he played during the Commonwealth it would be at the surreptitious performances arranged by Davenant. It is most probable that he got stage-struck during his apprenticeship by being thrown amongst so many people of the Theatre.

Of all the actors who played women's parts he is easily the most famous. There were, of course, plenty of others and most of them played at Drury Lane in their day, after, however, they had given up the petticoats. Hart himself, Killigrew's star and general manager, graduated that way, so did Burt and Clun—both members of the first company of His Majesty's Comedians. The first-named, after he shed the petticoats, proved a fine actor and had no superior as Cicero in *Cataline*. He had to surrender Othello, in which he excelled, to Hart, who had played Cassio, at the direct command of Charles II. But Hart was said to be as great as Othello as Betterton was as Hamlet. Clun was said to be better than the famous Major Mohun as Iago and only Lacy excelled him in *The Humerous Lieutenant*. His big hit was as Subtle in *The Alchemist*, of which the public never wearied. He met a tragic end, being stabbed in Kentish Town, then well in the country, on his way home to his lodgings with, we are told, 'a lady on his arm and some liquor under his belt'. One of his assassins was captured and hanged for the night's work. All play-goers mourned poor Clun. It must not be imagined that these men—most of whom had graduated in the parts since boyhood—who played women's roles were in any way effeminate. Quite the reverse. Clun had a girl with him when killed. Burt was a married man with a family, and Hart an early lover of Nell Gwynne's—and many other ladies.

But although all those men were pillars of Old Drury none of them save perhaps Hart excelled Kynaston as a performer, and not Hart in all ways, either. There are statements that Kynaston was born in 1619, which would have made him ninety-three when he died—which is impossible. He was certainly playing in 1659 and perhaps before. Say he was seventeen then; that makes him seventy, which would be about right.

There is no doubt as to his looks—or his acting ability; it is amply attested by contemporaries of standing—by men of no less knowledge and ability than Pepys and Colley Cibber himself. Pepys was a man whose judgment was not always sound—he was one of those people who 'knew what he liked'—but he recognized the art and the looks of Kynaston. He speaks of him first in 1660 when he saw him play Olympia in *The Loyal Subject*, and says he made the loveliest lady he ever saw. He went drinking with Kynaston and a friend afterwards, too.

He saw him play a poor woman, a gallant and a pretty woman all in the same play—*The Silent Woman*—and he says he was the prettiest woman and handsomest man in the house. Colley Cibber, who never saw him play as a woman, gives him unstinted praise. Ladies of fashion made much of Kynaston and took him riding in their coaches, competing for the honour of his company. It does not appear to have turned Kynaston's head at all.

When women entered the Profession and Kynaston played according to his sex, he was splendid. It is then that Cibber praises him. He says the actor had something of a formal gravity in his mien, and a stately step which was probably due to his having to be careful of petticoats (when he was wearing them). However, even that proved an asset. Cibber says: "it misbecame him not in the art of Leon, in Fletcher's *Rule a Wife*, etc., which he executed with a determined manliness and honest authority well worth the best actor's imitation. He had a piercing eye and in characters of heroic life a quick imperious vivacity in his tone of voice that painted the tyrant truly terrible." Cibber lays down that Kynaston's two outstanding parts were Morat in *Aurenge-Zebe* and Muley Moloch in *Don Sebastian*. In those parts he showed a fierce lion-like majesty which made the spectators tremble with admiration. And that acute observer says that Kynaston was better than Barton Booth himself as Morat, which is saying something, and pays Kynaston the greatest tribute one actor can pay another when he says that when he himself was Syphax in Addison's *Cato* he tried to play it as he imagined Kynaston would have done. Kynaston was a fine King in Shakespeare's *Henry IV*, endowing it with real majesty and manliness combined.

Kynaston had a long and distinguished career. He was much respected, and when the Duke's Theatre, Drury Lane's rival, surrendered to its senior brother, as it were, and the union of the two companies took place to play at Drury Lane, it was Kynaston who dealt with the matter for Old Drury. He created only about a score of original characters, but they were good ones.

He was a popular man and a popular player but he had his enemies. He admired the style of dress affected by Sir John Sedley when he was a young man and imitated it. This displeased Sedley who had him beaten up by hired ruffians. They pretended they thought he was Sir Charles, when walking in Hyde Park. The actor then imitated Sedley on the stage and was beaten up again—so badly that the play had to be abandoned for the night and he could not appear for a week. Sedley did not deal with Kynaston himself, maybe it was beneath him to thrash a mere actor, let alone fight him.

Powel, a brother actor of a dissolute nature, did not like Kynaston either. Powel, suffering very much from the 'morning after' feeling, was being very sick when Kynaston came across him and asked him what was the matter. "Who wouldn't be sick," demanded the disgruntled Powel, "after listening to your voice?" It is said that at times Kynaston had a rather didactic and stilted utterance. But Powel had personal spite for there were no other complaints—quite the reverse, indeed. Downes, the celebrated prompter at Drury Lane, whose record *Roscius Anglicanus* is of such tremendous value, said of Kynaston that it was a matter of dispute amongst the critics as to whether any woman—when women came to play the female parts—ever did it as well or touched the heart more deeply than he did. And we have Cibber's record that when he gave up the female roles and played male parts "every sentiment came from him as if it had been his own, as if he had himself that instant conceived it, as if he had lost the player and were the real king he personated". He is speaking of Shakespeare's *King Henry IV*. That sounds like pretty good acting—and it cannot be said of many actors today. Some held him the equal of Betterton, but it is not conceivable that he was so. It is however very likely that he had played Juliet to Betterton's Romeo before women came on the Stage—and of course therefore before Mary Sanderson, who became Betterton's beloved wife and who was the first woman to play Juliet.

Cibber thought that Kynaston remained on the Stage too long— he would have liked him to retire before he was well past his prime. But Kynaston did not think so. When he was past sixty his teeth were still as white and regular as when he had played Juliet.

He was a happily married man and a householder, with a well-furnished and handsome home, in which he took pride. He probably understood women pretty well; maybe wearing the skirts for so long taught him about them. His memory failed towards the end and his vivacity and spirit began to leave him. Then he too left the Stage. He died quite well-to-do, which is more than many of them did in those days—or after—and certainly more than Betterton succeeded in doing, although his misfortunes were no fault of his own. Kynaston made a lot of money; for although his titular salary was £3 a week, he had a share and extras. He kept that money and he left it to his son, whom he had educated very well. That son, very wisely, did not go on the Stage. His father had given him a good education and he became a mercer in Covent Garden. He too did well, and he gave his son a good education—perhaps he always remembered that gentle blood ran in his veins. That son—Edward Kynaston's grandson—entered the Church and obtained the ministry of Aldgate. And then, despite the fact that his father had been in trade and his grandfather an actor—his genteel relations in Shropshire acknowledged him as one of their kin. One thinks old Edward Kynaston would have laughed at that.

Kynaston's dust is somewhere in the churchyard of St. Paul's, Covent Garden, near where he played as one of the first company at Drury Lane, one of the original members of His Majesty's Own Company of Comedians, near where his son carried on a lawful and successful business. He, who had been a leading lady himself, lived to play heroes to leading ladies. He was more than just a handsome man playing female parts—he was a very good actor indeed, almost a great one, and a just and faithful servant of Drury Lane Theatre, for whose benefit he did much. He is indeed a Pillar of Drury Lane.

The name of Kynaston still graces the Stage, too.

John Lacy was a considerable pillar of 'The Lane', and also one of the original company. One of his claims to fame is that he instructed Nell Gwynne in the art of acting, and probably had an easy job. But he is worthy of far more remembrance than that. He had started life as a dancing-master, and had then been a lieutenant in the Army before he took to the Stage. He was a handsome man, both of face and figure, and having taught dancing, he moved with grace. The public worshipped him and he was one of the especial stage favourites. He is classed, with Mohun, as Charles II's favourite actor, but that volatile king seems to have had as many favourite actors as he had favourite ladies, for so many claim that title. That Charles took a personal interest in his company of comedians is made clear by the fact that he directed that Hart should play Othello instead of Clun—he took upon himself the job of casting director. One presumes that Clun's loyalty suffered something of a strain as regards this switch-over. But still, King Charles loved the Theatre—and all theatrefolk and good playgoers should be eternally grateful to him for what he did for it. He was not without criticism. He expressed his annoyance that all the villains should always be dark-visaged men in long black periwigs—for that description fitted himself. He was sure there were as many fair villains as dark ones—and wanted to see them so depicted.

There is, however, no doubt of Lacy's great talent. He could play nearly anything—Evelyn the diarist confers on him the title of 'Roscius'. He held his popularity for over twenty years. His stage wardrobe was really remarkable—and many gentlemen went to inspect it and wonder at it. In those days actors supplied all their own clothes. He was one of the very great Falstaffs—sharing that distinction with Quin, Betterton and, much later, Sir Herbert Tree. He took great enjoyment in playing parts which enabled him to make 'cracks', as they would now be called, at courtiers and men and women in high positions. These gentry despised the actors and the actors liked to get their own back—especially Lacy. There is no doubt that many of the 'gags' were his own and never in the script. He enjoyed it—and so did the audience. But one day he went a bit too far, or so thought the King, when the words were reported to him. Notwithstanding that this was one of his favourite actors—he had Lacy locked up in The Porter's Lodge, in Covent Garden. The play in which he uttered his unpleasing words was *The Silent Woman* written by Howard. He was kept in durance for a few days, to cool him down, and then released. On his return to the theatre, Howard complimented him on being out of prison. Lacy was probably not in a good temper. He turned on Howard—who was an Honourable and cousin to an Earl—and told him he had written such a lot of nonsense in the part of Captain Otter that he had had to try and improve it, and that had caused the trouble. And he further informed the honourable sprig of the nobility that he was far more of a fool than a poet. That annoyed the Hon. Howard, as might be expected. A mere actor to speak to him—a man of noble blood—in such terms! It was not to be stood. So he smacked Lacy across the face with his glove. Lacy, caring nothing for blue blood, saw red. He raised his cane and gave Howard a good hard crack over the head with it. The bystanders expected to see the outraged cousin of the Earl draw his sword and run Lacy through the body. But Howard did no such thing. He rushed straight to the King and told him of the outrage. Charles, who may have been of the same opinion as Lacy, nevertheless had to take some action. He ordered Drury Lane to be closed—and closed it was—so that the whole company suffered for Lacy's bad temper.

The nobility and gentry were delighted that the actors should receive so sharp a lesson, for they considered these common people were getting far too insolent and should be kept in their place. But the ordinary folk were on the side of the actors and murmured against being deprived of their playgoing. Nobody knows what his fellow players said or did to Lacy. He fell very ill shortly after and was likely to die. It is said that a Bishop visited him to impart spiritual consolation and that Lacy refused either to see My Lord Bishop or to listen to his words. It is rumoured that the Bishop was an old friend of his, but it is puzzling to know what Bishop then would have consorted with mere play-actors. However, the King effected a cure. He sent word to Lacy that all was forgiven and forgotten and Lacy recovered pretty quickly. And once more he became Charles's favourite comedian—until he died in 1681. One of his great characters was that of Teague in *The Committee*—a farce afterwards cut down a good deal and sometimes called *The Honest Thieves*—and also *Killing No Murder*. As a stage Irishman he had no equal; he was also

Above: Sir Augustus Harris *Below:* Arthur Collins;
both great Pillars of Drury Lane

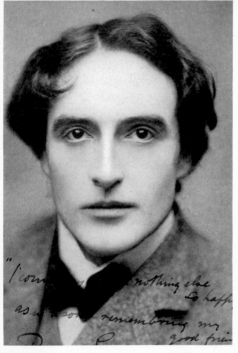

PILLARS OF MELODRAMA
Upper left: Lyn Harding
Upper right: Constance
Collier *Left:* Basil Gill

first-rate as Frenchman or Scotsman, an excellent Tartuffe, and very good as comic old women. He could play fine gentlemen, stupid fops or rogues with equal facility.

Next to his Falstaff probably his greatest stage achievement was the character of Bayes (he created it) in that satire of the Duke of Buckingham's entitled *The Rehearsal*. In that, egged on by Buckingham, he gave a most lifelike imitation of Dryden, the poet-dramatist, who had to go and see it and pretend he liked it. For Lacy was not only a fine actor but a magnificent mimic. *The Rehearsal* was a very famous play and held the stage for generations; always the part of Bayes was played by a great star—Garrick liked it very much—and some leading personality of the day was held up to ridicule. Women played it too, and the last great exponent of it was Old William Farren, who called himself the 'Cock Salmon of them all' in his day —who played it in 1819.

And Lacy was the first. When he died he left a play which was produced posthumously. It was called *Sir Hercules Buffoon*, and Tom Durfey, a man with a very long and crooked nose but a very shrewd and biting wit, wrote the prologue for it. He described Lacy as the standard by which true comedy might be measured, and he said, in the prologue, that if the play did not succeed:

> All that we can say on't
> We've his fiddle but not his hands to play on't.

Naturally Lacy, being a dancing-master, was expert on the fiddle. His portrait—a triple one at that—was painted by Wright and etched by Hopkins, is quite well known, and hangs at Hampton Court. John Lacy, comedian, man of many parts, wit, soldier, dancer and actor, was one of the early Pillars of Drury Lane.

The playwrights deserve remembrance, too, in the Theatre's colonnade. And one of the most remarkable was William Wycherly. He was born about the year 1640, and was eldest son of Daniel Wycherly, Esquire, of Cleve, in Shropshire, which seems to have had something theatrical in its soil, for the Kynastons came from there, too. When he was fifteen years old he was sent to France to have polish put on his education, and whilst there he embraced the Roman Catholic persuasion. But on his return to England, being entered as a gentleman-commoner at Queen's College, Oxford, he abjured the Roman Church and once more became a Protestant. On leaving Oxford, he entered the Middle Temple. But Charles II was on the throne, the town was gay, naughty and licentious. It had far more attractions to Wycherly, who was a wit himself, than the

D

dry study of the Law. So he became a wit amongst wits and had a
very good time indeed. He loved the Theatre; he went constantly to
the play; he was always in and out of Drury Lane Theatre. And he
decided to become a playwright himself. He succeeded, too. His
first one was produced at Old Drury and was *Love in a Wood; or St.
James's Park*. It was a success. Now the greatest wits sought him out
and he became acquainted with Her Grace the Duchess of Cleve-
land. That acquaintance grew very speedily and ripened fast—and
soon he was on the most intimate terms with her—in the full meaning
of the phrase in those loose-moralled days. George Villiers, Duke
of Buckingham, himself a dramatist, thought highly of him and
became his great friend. The Duke was Master of The King's Horse
and he made Wycherly one of his equerries. And Wycherly became
Colonel of a regiment, Captain-Lieutenant of his own Company.
Wycherly did very well, for there were perquisites in the Army then.
King Charles II also thought very highly of him and showed him
marks of great esteem. He showed him a very signal favour indeed.
For Wycherly fell ill of a fever, at his lodgings at Bow Street, and the
King himself did him the honour of paying a special visit to him, to
see how he was getting on. This was most unusual, even in Charles's
easy-going life. He found Wycherly ill and very low-spirited, so he
told the poet-playwright to take a trip to the South of France, saying
that he believed the air of Montpelier would cure him. Now it was
easy for a king to give a subject such advice as this, however well
intentioned, for there was little hope that Wycherly could afford
such a trip. But the King went further and said that he would defray
all expenses up to the sum of £500. It was easy for Charles to make
such promises, too; but on this occasion he kept his word and
Wycherly got the money. He went to France, spent the rest of the
winter at Montpelier and came back in the spring, completely
restored to health. He waited on his Sovereign to express his gratitude. The King was delighted at his recovery and showed him further
favour. He told Wycherly that he had a son—one of the many who
did not stand in succession to the Throne, of course—and that he
wanted this boy educated and brought up like a gentleman. He said
the boy could have no better tutor, no more efficient mentor, than
Wycherly, and Wycherly got the job of training the little Royal
illegitimate, and had £1,500 a year as salary.

But Royal favour was fickle in those days and Charles was not
the most constant of monarchs. Easy-going and democratic, he was
also quick to take offence and be enraged. Wycherly managed to
lose the Royal smile and favour. He had by this time written his
play, *The Plain Dealer*, which was held in great esteem. Before taking

over his duties as tutor, he paid a visit to Tunbridge Wells, then an exceedingly smart resort—Nell Gwynne lived there for some time under the 'protection' of my Lord Buckhurst—gravitating between there and Epsom. With Wycherly went his friend Mr. Fairbeard, of Gray's Inn. They were promenading along Wells Walk and stopped to look in the bookshop there. Wycherly, an author, had an author's anxiety to see if they stocked his works, for his plays were published— a custom of those days. Just as they gazed into the bookshop and entered it to make sure there were copies within, a very smart carriage drew up and out of it got a beautiful young lady of very obvious wealth. She went into the bookshop, too. To Wycherly's joy and pride she asked the bookseller if he had a copy of *The Plain Dealer*. Any author will know how Wycherly felt. Mr. Fairbeard took a hand. "Madame," he said, "since you ask for 'The Plain Dealer', there he is for you." And he pushed Wycherly towards the fair lady. She was the Countess of Drogheda, recently widowed. Wycherly gazed at her in admiration. "This lady can bear plain dealing; for she appears to be so accomplished that what would be a compliment to others, would be plain dealing to her." The Countess was pleased. But she replied: "No, truly. I am not without my faults, sir, any more than the rest of my sex—and yet, notwithstanding, I love plain dealing and am never more fond of it than when it tells me of them." One fears the pretty Countess was fishing for further compliments. "Then, Madame," said Mr. Fairbeard, "you and The Plain Dealer seem designed by heaven for each other." The upshot was that the Countess and Wycherly went for a stroll together. Next day he called upon her and visited her daily whilst at Tunbridge Wells. When she came back to Town—she lived in Hatton Garden—the daily visits continued. And very shortly Wycherly and his Countess were married.

But he had made a terrible mistake. He had not told the King. Gossip was rife in those days and no doubt Old Rowley knew all about this affair, but Wycherly, a favourite of his and his son's tutor, owed it to his Royal Master to tell him of the approaching wedding and beg his approval. He omitted to do so and Royal disfavour fell upon him. So this wedding, which looked so promising for both parties, brought social ruin to both. For his neglect of the King was regarded as a sign of contempt. Furthermore, Wycherly never went to Court, as he should have done, and this was regarded as ungrateful in him—ingratitude most rank and shameful. That was something the King could not bear. He had been accused of it himself, though never openly of course. So Wycherly lost his job as tutor and the Royal smile as well. He had his wife to balance it. But his absence from Court, it appeared, was not his own wish but his wife's command. She held the purse-strings and she was very jealous of this witty and much courted, celebrated husband of hers. She could not bear to let him out of her sight. They lodged in Bow Street, a fashionable thoroughfare then, opposite the Cock Tavern. If Wycherly ever visited the inn, with his friends, he had to have the window of the room in which he sat wide open with the curtains drawn back, so that his wife could see that there was no woman in the company.

It was far from being a happy marriage, but she died not long afterwards and she must have loved him, for she left him her whole and very considerable fortune. But he was not to enjoy that, for she had relatives who were disappointed at not being in the Will and were as jealous of Wycherly, for another cause, as his wife had been. The Will was hotly disputed and the whole affair cost him so much in litigation and other expenses that he fell into debt. His creditors pressed and he could not pay. So he was thrown into a debtors' prison and there he languished for several years. There seemed no hope of his ever getting out. And then, most dramatically, luck smiled again and Royal favour returned. The Merry Monarch was dead and his more serious but unpopular brother, James II, was on the throne. Whatever James's faults may have been—and they were many—he was a Stuart, and like all Stuarts he loved the Theatre. He went to see *The Plain Dealer*—the very play which was the root of Wycherly's trouble, the success of which had got him married to his Countess—a success for which he paid dearly. But this time it stood him in good stead. James II liked the play immensely. He enquired about Wycherly, found out his circumstances, gave immediate orders for his release and the payment of his debts and a pension of £200 per annum so long as the author remained in England. So Wycherly was free again.

But that curious trait in his nature—which made him anything but 'The Plain Dealer' of whom he had written so entertainingly and which had prevented him from braving his wife's anger and going to Court to make his peace with Charles—again stood in his way. He was ashamed to give the Earl of Mulgrave, whom James had sent to clear up his affairs, a full and true account of his liabilities. He suffered under the attempt to pay the undisclosed portions, with the fear of prison alive in him and the knowledge that if the King knew of his reticence he would be in trouble again. His life was a burden to him. Then his father died. He, as eldest son, inherited, but this was not much good to him, for he found that he was only tenant of the estate for life. The security was not good enough to enable him to borrow sufficient to pay off the again closely pressing creditors. But he found a way out, although after his first marriage it did not seem a choice he was likely to make. He married again and made a jointure. He always said that he was resolved to *die* married, although he did not like *living* in that state. His bride brought him £1,500. The greater portion of this he used to pay his debts.

Well, poor Wycherly did not have to live long in the state he disliked—and he did die a husband, for eleven days after the ceremony he passed away, on 1st January, 1715. He was buried in the Church of St. Paul, Covent Garden, and became one of the company of its illustrious theatrical dead. He wrote four plays: *Love in a Wood; or St. James's Park*, *The Gentleman Dancing Master*, *The Country Wife* and *The Plain Dealer*. All of them, save *The Gentleman Dancing Master*, were first produced at Drury Lane, the exception was at the Duke's Theatre. He had published a book of poems in 1704, and a lot more of his works, in prose and verse, were published posthumously in 1728.

Alexander Pope, the poet, when a very young man went to see Wycherly, who was then old. Wycherly heard his works and was very pleased with him; hailed him as a rising genius and wrote him many letters, which Pope cherished and eventually published.

Wycherly was a very considerable dramatist, one of the greatest of those who have been labelled 'Restoration'. His plays are well made, and his characterization splendidly observed, formed and handled. Although they reflect the morals of their time, loose enough in all conscience, there is a feeling that Wycherly himself, although of those times and living like the others, yet had something of a horror of it all and a leaning towards better things. He was a curious man in many ways, unstable and perhaps a moral coward. He never faced up to facts, he was always in a muddle—and he even seemed to have muddled his religion. He became a Catholic, he reverted to Protestantism, yet, when he died, it was a Catholic priest who gave him the Last Sacrament—and then he was promptly buried in a Church of England grave. Yet with it all, he was a great man of the English Theatre, his plays endure and are worth seeing if revived —and worth reading, too.

A contemporary of his wrote of him: "Mr. Wycherly is universally allowed the first place among the English Comick-Poets who have writ since Ben Jonson. His *Plain Dealer* is the best comedy that ever was composed in any language. The only fault that has been found in it, is its being too full of Wit; a fault which few authors can be guilty of. He has also writ three other plays, the best of which is *The Country Wife*."

Well, Wycherly was not the foremost of the dramatists, nor was *The Plain Dealer* the finest comedy in any language—it owed a good deal to Molière. But he had wit, skill, sparkle and the gift of humanity. And he is a very worthy pillar in Old Drury's colonnade.

There is one more in this period who deserves a place and remembrance, for although his stage career was short—only about six years in all—he made a great impression and was extremely popular. His name was Richard Estcourt. He seems to have had the delectable poison of the Theatre in his veins from early boyhood— how it got there cannot be known. He was of quite good family and born at Tewkesbury in 1688. He was well educated at what was called 'The Latin School' in that delightful town. In other words he studied the classics. But there was the gypsy in him somewhere and he left the dead languages and did a bolt to join a company of strolling players. He seems to have impressed them, or they had a very good eye for talent, for he persuaded them to let him play women's parts. He knew the hue and cry would be out after him and thought by playing leading ladies he would be the better disguised. He made his first appearance at Worcester, playing Roxana in *Alexander the Great*. But his people were on his track. However, still dressed as a girl, he evaded them and got as far as Chipping Norton before he was captured and taken home. His father decided to deal drastically with him, so he removed him from Tewkesbury, a quiet place, and took this stage-struck youth to London—the heart of Theatreland—and there bound him apprentice to an apothecary in Hatton Garden. Mr. Estcourt, senior, does not seem to have been a man of much common sense. Young Dick went to the theatres and found that he liked them, but that he did not like medicine either to take or to dispense. So he ran away again, and could not be found. Once again he joined the strollers and this time got clear of the country over to Ireland. There he made a success. He came back to London and was engaged at Drury Lane. By this time the family had given him up as a bad job. He made his first appearance at Drury Lane as Dominic in *The Spanish Friar* and scored a big success— because he gave a very close imitation of Leigh, the celebrated actor, whom he had seen play it. And thereby he disclosed his talent. Estcourt was no great actor but the best mimic of his time. Colley Cibber saw through him and said he owed his success simply to his ability to give exact reproductions of the greater actors he had seen play the parts he now essayed. But Sir Richard Steele begged to differ. He said: "It has surprised me as much as anything in nature, to have it frequently said that he was not a good player. When a man of his wit and smartness could put on such an utter absence of

common sense in his face as he did in Bullfinch in *The Northern Lass*
and an air of insipid cunning and vivacity in the character of
Pounce in *The Tender Husband* it is folly to dispute his capacity." Off-
stage, Estcourt was extremely good company and that was what
Steele liked, so he may have been prejudiced. He said, "The best
man I know for heightening the revelry of a company is Estcourt,
whose jovial humour diffuses itself from the highest person at any
entertainment to the meanest waiter." Estcourt was a prince of good
fellows and no snob.

Although Cibber slighted Estcourt's acting ability, he praised
him as a mimic. He said of him that "he was such an extraordinary
mimic that no man or woman, from the coquette to the Privy
Councillor, ever moved or spoke before him but he could carry their
voice, look, mien and motion instantly into another company". But
Estcourt created one or two famous parts as well, although mimicry
was his strongest line. One day he was taken by Mr. Secretary of
State Craggs to see Sir Godfrey Kneller, the great painter. There
he gave impersonations of celebrities they all knew: Godolphin,
Somers—many famous folk. Then Estcourt mimicked Craggs himself and Kneller was overcome with joy and roared with laughter. So
Craggs winked at Estcourt who immediately gave an impression of
Kneller. The painter stared and cried out: "Nay, nay, now you are
out, man. By heaven, that is not me"—thereby paying Estcourt a
great compliment. He would recite at festive gatherings and also do
his mimicry—and was not too proud to pocket gifts of money given
him.

The Duke of Marlborough thought highly of him, and treated
him as a friend—and even made him presents of money. To get money
out of the Duke proves that Estcourt must have been remarkable
indeed. Estcourt himself liked good company and revelry in the
tavern although he kept sober. It was maybe this social side of him
that made him forsake the Stage, on which he had been so set, and in
1711 he took over the Bumper Tavern, in Covent Garden. The
Spectator poked a bit of fun at him: "Estcourt had lain in, at the
Bumper, Covent Garden, neat, natural wines to be sold wholesale as
well as retail, by his old servant, trusty Antony Aston. As Estcourt is
a person altogether unknowing in the wine trade, it cannot but be
doubted that he will deliver the wine in the same natural purity
that he receives it from the merchants."

When the Beefsteak Club was founded Estcourt was made its
'Providore'—its caterer; and when acting in this capacity to the
chief wits and poets of the period he wore a small gold grid-iron
suspended round his neck by a green ribbon.

He was one of the most popular men of his day, always amusing and witty, never out of temper. He had polished manners. He wrote two plays: *The Fair Example* in 1706 and one called *Prunella* which is undated.

He died in 1713 and was amongst the actors once again, in St. Paul's, Covent Garden. His theatrical career belonged to Drury Lane and he is worthy of remembrance in its annals.

CHAPTER THREE

James Quin—Who Never Forgot

IT WAS the misfortune of James Quin, actor, to be a giant amongst giants, which attracts less attention than being a giant amongst pigmies. It is the reason why the name of this truly great actor is little known today. He lived greatly in great days, a colourful personality in colourful surroundings. He was not only the leader of the English Stage for twenty years, whose word was law in the Theatre and before whom mighty managers quailed, but he was also a great wit, a great duellist and a great gourmet. He could have been famous in any of those roles. He was also one of the best-hearted and most generous men in his Profession. If he never forgot a slight he never forgot a favour, and he repaid both in full. He was a great opportunist and if opportunity did not present itself, he created it. He knew fortune and misfortune but his courage and ingenuity often turned bad luck into good.

Quin was born in King Street, Covent Garden, on 24th February, 1693, scion of an old Irish family (his grandfather had been Lord Mayor of Dublin). Rumours were rife concerning him in his lifetime and some said that his father was an American, but he did not agree with that. He said his father was an English gentleman, who, some years after his son's birth, settled in Ireland and encumbered his small fortune by over-generosity and benevolence—traits which, if the story was true, he inherited. Anyway, he had received a good education—first at a grammar school and then at Dublin University. Whatever may be the facts, the first misfortune that young Quin encountered was to find that he was illegitimate by accident. His mother had unwittingly entered into a bigamous marriage with his father, believing her first husband dead. But he was not; he turned up again and he carried his tearful and protesting wife away with him—the other alternative was disgrace and prison. But Quin's father regarded his son James with deep affection and brought him up as his legitimate heir. He had every prospect of a modest but sufficient patrimony. His father brought him to London and apprenticed him to the Law—he had chambers in the Temple. But young Quin preferred the pleasures of the Town to those of the study and much preferred to read plays and the works of Shakespeare to the drier matter prepared by Coke and other jurists. He went in for a life of gaiety, not to say dissipation. Then his father died. The fortune was not large, but relatives did not see why the illegitimate James should have it. They went to Law, they upset the Will and Quin had not the means to contest it.

He saw that he could not make his living at the Bar—he did not know enough Law and it was a slow job anyway. But he knew a lot of Shakespeare, he had "an expressive countenance, a marking eye, a clear voice, full and melodious, an extensive memory, a happy and articulate pronunciation and a majestic figure". It all pointed to the Stage. There no questions were asked, no references required—and often no knowledge expected. He knew Booth and Wilks, two of the greatest actors, personally, and he had become very friendly with another, named Ryan. It was to Ryan that he broached the subject of going on the Stage. And Ryan agreed enthusiastically. Chetwood, Prompter at Drury Lane, who wrote a history of the Stage, claims that he discovered Quin when that man was playing a small part in *The Committee* at the Smock Alley Theatre, in Dublin. But when a man becomes famous he has many 'discoverers'. Ryan introduced him to the management at Drury Lane, got him an engagement for the ensuing season—and put him up to the tricks of the trade. And Quin never forgot the favour. He had several parts allotted to him and he studied them assiduously, but being of an amorous nature, he found relaxation in conducting an intrigue with the attractive wife of a linen draper in the Strand. Her husband being away, he took the lady to a bagnio nearby. The husband surprised them. Very naturally he flew at his wife to chastise her. Quin drew his sword in her protection, the husband, also armed, drew to protect himself. The swords clashed and the linen draper fell, wounded in the thigh. He issued two writs against Quin, one for *crim. con.* and the other for assault and battery. Quin fled to Ireland. There he acted at the Smock Alley Theatre and there Chetwood probably saw him. But he already had his Drury Lane engagement, which his absence prevented him from fulfilling. When the affair had blown over, Quin returned, and went to Ryan who got him back to Drury Lane.

He made his first appearance there in 1718. He found that advancement went by seniority and not by talent and that the Theatre of those days reeked with personal jealousies and intrigues. He played only small parts and he was not considered at all. He became one of the band of minor players who were called 'the faggots'. It did not suit James Quin—he waited upon opportunity. And opportunity came. One night, when *Tamerlane* was to be played—and played by special order of the Lord Chamberlain— Mills, who was to have played Bajazet, fell ill at the last moment.

There were no understudies. Quin saw his chance. He offered to undertake the very thankless job of reading the part. Nobody else wanted to do so—so he got the chance. He read it so well that he made quite a success. The next night he had to play again. And now that prodigious memory of his came into play—for he now knew every word of that long part by heart. He played it magnificently, not fluffing a word, and he was acclaimed by the audience. Now, he thought, a grateful management will give me decent roles. But no; he was pushed back amongst the faggots again. So he took a great risk. He left Drury Lane, who let him go, not knowing what they were losing. There was only one other theatre open to him, Lincoln's Inn, ruled by Rich. Quin applied for a job and got it. He was allowed to play some better parts—Banquo, and The Lieutenant of the Tower in *Richard III*, but nothing much. Then, in 1720, when he had been for two years on the Stage, Rich decided to revive *The Merry Wives of Windsor*. It was typical of him to take this decision when there was not, to his knowledge, an actor in his company who could play Falstaff. There was a good deal of confusion. Quin, the opportunist, asked to be allowed to attempt it. Rich was horrified. He looked at Quin, up and down, and took snuff. "Hem," he said. "You attempt Falstaff"—(sniff, hem)—"you might as well think of acting Cato after Barton Booth. The character of Falstaff, young man, is quite another character from what you think" (sniff, sniff, hem, hem). "It is not a snivelling part that—that—in short, anyone can do. There is not a man amongst you that has any idea of the part but myself. It is quite out of your walk. No, never think of Falstaff" (sniff, sniff), "never think of Falstaff—it is quite—quite—out of your walk, young man." Quin told his friend Ryan about this and Ryan heard him speak the part. Ryan then went to Rich and prevailed upon him to give Quin an audition. Quin did well. Rich, still very reluctant, but seeing nobody else in view, at last allowed him to take the chance. The night came with Rich in despondent mood. Quin entered and began to act. He surprised and astonished that audience; they had never seen such a Falstaff as this, who seemed to have stepped right out of Shakespeare's brain, exactly as his creator had conceived him. He was cheered, his performance was constantly interrupted by shouts of laughter and applause—and at the end he was acclaimed by an excited and delighted house. Ryan, who had come over to play Ford, was overjoyed. Quin had stepped into fame. He was now leading man at Lincoln's Inn and a force in the world of the Theatre. He never forgot the help given him by Ryan. When that fine actor fell on bad times, owing to being shot in the throat by footpads, so that his voice was impaired, Quin helped

him greatly, and played Falstaff at his benefit for many years. Even
when he had retired to Bath and was in failing health he would still
come to Town to do so. But at length he had to refuse. He had lost
some of his front teeth, so he sent a characteristic message to Ryan,
when the usual request came. "Dear Friend," he wrote, "there is no
person on earth that I would sooner serve than Ryan, but, by God,
I will *whistle* Falstaff for no man." He gave Ryan £1,000 instead,
saying he was leaving it to him in his Will anyway, and if he liked to
have it now, he was welcome, and would save legacy duty. Thus did
he repay his debt to his early helper. It was typical of the man.

Drury Lane had lost Quin to Rich at Lincoln's Inn. There Quin
became a great actor and a great attraction. He had differences of
opinion with Rich—who had told him he could not play Falstaff—
and when Drury Lane made Quin an offer, he went back there
again. All Rich had was an actor called Delaine, not in the same
street with Quin, but still very popular and with a following. And on
that subject of Falstaff it is interesting to recall what old Tate
Wilkinson, who knew the Theatre backwards, said of Quin's
performance: "Quin, with a bottle of claret and a full house, the
instant he was on the stage was Sir John Falstaff himself. His comely
countenance, his expressive eye, his happy swell of voice and
natural importance of deportment, all united to make up a most
characteristic piece of acting; and when detected in a lie, there was
such a glow of feature and expression as will never be equalled."
There is a testimony from an experienced man who became a Royal
Patentee himself in respect of York. And Samuel Foote, by no means
prone to praise but given to sarcasm and destructive mimicry, said of
him, "I can only recommend a man who wants to see a character
perfectly played, to see Mr. Quin in the part of Falstaff, and if he
does not express a desire of spending an evening with that merry
mortal, why I should not spend one with *him*, if he would pay my
reckoning." Even Davies, given to faint praise, allows that Quin was
the best Falstaff since Betterton.

Back at Drury Lane, Quin found himself faced with the difficulties of the amateur management of Fleetwood. But he did his
best. He became general manager and, on the death of Mills, the
star of the theatre where he had quite recently been 'a faggot'. Quin
had a way with him, he had dignity and importance—he made both
managers and actors fear and respect him. He was also pretty hot-
tempered and a fine swordsman, not averse to a duel. So he more
than held his own. But he had a tough team with which to deal, for it
included Charles Macklin, that remarkable man who revolutionized
the art of acting by his performance of Shylock—(playing it in direct

opposition to the manner of Quin), who was found guilty of manslaughter and got away with it and who lived to be 107 years of age.
Indeed, on that memorable night when Macklin threw over the
tradition that Shylock was the 'comic' of the show and played him
with such force and fierceness that King George II was frightened
out of his life, Quin played Antonio.

At Drury Lane Quin could show them what he could do. That
remark of Rich's, about the futility of his attempting to play Cato
after Barton Booth, rankled in his mind. He determined to risk it,
for Booth, considered matchless in this part, had retired. Everyone
tried to dissuade Quin, even Rich, when he heard about it. But
Quin had assumed the mantle of Booth and 'led the stage'. He knew
he was taking a gamble, for the greater part of his audience would
have seen Booth himself. He was risking his whole reputation, but he
had plenty of pluck. He was not one of those actors who feared to
follow another in a part and so risk comparison, he had confidence in
himself. In that he resembled the late Godfrey Tearle, who frequently
took up parts in the middle of the run of a play and always made his
own deep impression. Quin was to play Cato in the same theatre and
on the same boards as Booth. He was brave, but he was artful. He
caused the public announcements to be worded "The part of Cato
will be only *attempted* by Mr. Quin." Thus at the outset he dis-
armed the Boothites. So Quin 'attempted' Cato and his success was
never in doubt for one moment. He swept all before him, the
crowded house hanging on his every word. When he declaimed the
famous line "Thanks to the Gods, my boy has done his duty"—
there was a unanimous shout of "Booth outdone".

What joy that must have brought to Quin's ears, what a tonic
for an actor! And so excited and enthusiastic was the audience that
when he spoke the well-known soliloquy—and playgoers then knew
it by heart—he got an encore. Yes, they actually encored a tragedian
for a speech and demanded it all over again. And Quin gave the
encore, too, with great dignity and lost nothing by so doing.

Quin now stood on the summit. He was unchallenged, even by
Macklin, until an unknown actor arrived and defeated him—but
that was distant yet.

His style of acting was what the public wanted and applauded.
Styles of acting are called forth by public demand and exist by public
support. And Quin's style was elocutionary. He did little in the way
of gesture or movement—he did it almost entirely with the voice.
Today he would be regarded more as an orator than an actor. But
not then: they liked his way, they regarded it as acting *in excelsis*.
Nor did the actors wear costumes of period or nationality—they

wore ordinary clothes. Quin would walk on to the stage wearing a green velvet coat, embroidered with gold down the seams, an enormous full-bottomed periwig, rolled stockings and high-heeled square-toed shoes. With very little variation in cadence, and in a deep full tone, accompanied by a sawing kind of action, which had more of the Senate than the Stage in it, he spoke the lines, rolling them out with majesty and sonority in his magnificent voice—he was like a great organ playing a masterpiece of music. His audiences gave every manifestation of delight—to which he appeared indifferent—he disregarded them and he never seemed excited by the vast applause he gained. But he knew all about it and he knew exactly what force to exert to get that applause. He may have seemed like an orator but he was an actor all through. He was very slow in delivery, but every syllable told. Sometimes he was so long over a big speech that other actors had been known to go to sleep and even fall over! But the public liked it.

His fine voice and splendid elocution caused Frederick, Prince of Wales, to engage him to instruct the Royal children in the art of speaking—and he did so and arranged amateur performances for the princelings at Leicester House—that 'pouting place for princes'—for them to show their paces—or their voices. In later years, when told how well King George III had delivered his first speech from the throne, he smiled with gratification and said, "Ah, it was I who taught the boy to speak." Nor did his Royal pupil forget him—he put Quin on the Civil List.

He was a most self-possessed actor; his seeming indifference to an audience was due to his calmness and control. But nothing escaped him. Nor did he fear any man or anything at all. He would fight the world, if need be. But his temper was hot all the same and his wit often acid. Once when Quin was playing Cato, there was a Welsh actor, named Williams, playing the messenger. When delivering his message to Cato, he said, "Caesar sends health to Keeto"—his way of pronouncing the word. Quin, instead of using the usual line in reply, said, "Would he had sent a better messenger." That nettled Williams but nothing like what was to come, for a few lines afterwards Quin had to say something—the line was "Are not your orders from the Senate?" which made the Welshman get all hot and bothered, for he had to reply "My business is with—Keeto." He could not say it any other way, and as Quin had to use the name too and gave it very clearly, accentuating the long A—the Welshman was furious. And the house laughed uproariously. Later, in the Green Room, Williams attacked Quin for making him look ridiculous. Quin wanted to laugh the matter off; he said there was something the matter with the ears of the audience. But the fiery Welshman was not to be appeased. After the play that night he laid in wait for Quin under the Piazza in Covent Garden, as Quin walked along to a tavern to drink his punch. Williams drew his sword and bade Quin defend himself. Quin, a fine swordsman and experienced duellist, wished the man no harm and told him not to be foolish. Williams lunged and Quin parried with his cane. But that only made the Welshman worse and he attacked so fiercely that Quin was forced to draw his rapier. So hard did the Welshman press him that Quin, in parrying, presented his point upon which the Welshman, still lunging, impaled himself. He fell upon the pavement—dead. Quin was horrified, but nothing could be done. He had to appear for trial at the Old Bailey. The verdict was manslaughter, but Quin was discharged. The jury said that Williams should not have been trusted with a sword.

Other fighting exploits of Quin included a duel with the despicable Theophilus Cibber. Quin, in his capacity of general manager of Drury Lane, had occasion to pull him up pretty sharply and to rate him for his behaviour. Cibber bore malice. Some time afterwards he heard that Quin had spoken roughly about him and used some quite unprintable language concerning his general disposition. He declared he would bring Quin to fight it out. He issued this general challenge in a tavern, not noticing Quin sitting in a corner. Some malicious 'friends' of Cibber's pointed Quin out, who was watching, quite unconcerned. Theophilus made a hasty excuse and beat a retreat. He said he would settle on another occasion. But his friends, eager for the fun, told him that Quin was leaving for Bath the next day and forced him to challenge, which he did with much bluster. Quin invited him to 'come outside' under that very Piazza where he had killed Williams. Theo went with much reluctance. Quin drew his sword and Theophilus had to do the same. Quin, the expert, did not wish to harm him and played with him as a cat does with a mouse. But he had the misfortune to trip and as soon as he was down Theophilus thrust at him, managed to scratch his forehead with the point of his rapier and immediately fled towards St. Paul's Church, where he took sanctuary. Quin did not trouble to pursue.

He had bad luck over another duel, with one Bowen, also an actor. They had been drinking together and making jokes. They got to comparisons of acting and both of them got a bit heated—both with wine and temper. Bowen flung down the money for his bill and stamped off in a rage. Quin sat down again with his friends. But later came a porter from another tavern, the Pope's Head, and whispered a message to Quin, who immediately left the company and went with him. What happened there can only be discovered from Quin's later evidence, but it is pretty clear that Bowen, who resented some of his remarks, forced a duel upon him in a private room. Quin fought in self-defence only. Bowen rushed upon him so fiercely that eventually he impaled himself upon his sword. He dropped, evidently mortally wounded, and Quin rushed back to tell his friends. Bowen, before dying, admitted it was his fault. Quin stood a trial and was formally found guilty of manslaughter, but no punishment was inflicted.

His other public battle was a general *mêlée*. It occurred when he was at Lincoln's Inn, playing Macbeth. A certain earl, of bad character, walked right across the stage during the murder scene, to speak to a friend on the other side of the theatre. Although it was quite customary for people to walk about on the stage then, they usually left the big scenes uninterrupted. Rich, the manager, was furious. He told the earl he would never be allowed back-stage again. The earl's reply was to strike Rich across the face. Rich immediately returned the blow. There was an uproar. The earl's friends leapt on to the stage, drew their swords and rushed at the manager. Quin immediately rallied the actors in defence. He, Walker and Ryan dashed to Rich's rescue, with drawn swords. So well did they use them that they drove the assailants off the stage and right out of the theatre. But that was not the end. Infuriated at being routed by mere actors, the earl and his supporters attacked the front of the house, smashed everything within reach and attempted to fire the building. They would have done so, too, but that Quin, with darting sword, dashed amongst them and fought them off by sheer pluck and skill until his friends came running with the Watch. In the struggle that ensued Quin actually captured some of the ringleaders and they were dragged to the lock-up. As a result of this, Lincoln's Inn had, for some time, a guard placed there at night—as had Drury Lane. There were a sergeant and squad of twelve men to keep order.

Another side of James Quin, mighty actor and expert swordsman, was his love of good food, eating and drinking. He once said that he wished his mouth and throat were as big and wide as the central arch of London Bridge and that the River Thames ran claret. His particular weakness was for John Dories. Those he adored. On rising each morning he sent his manservant into the market to buy some. If none were to be had, Quin returned to bed and told his man to call him in the morning—he would not waste his time on a Doryless day. Yet, much as he loved that fish, he had a horror of

PILLARS OF PANTOMIME

Upper left: Harry Randall *Upper right:* Dan Leno *Lower left:* Harry
Randall and Fred Emney (senior) in the pantomime sketch which grew
into *A Sister to Assist 'er. Lower right:* Herbert Campbell

PRINCIPAL BOY PILLARS OF PANTOMIME

Upper left: Harriet Vernon *Upper right:* Lily Harold *Lower left:* Vesta Tilley *Lower right:* Fanny Leslie

fishing. He regarded it as cruel. "Suppose now, a being who was as much my superior as I am to these poor fish were to say one day, 'I'll go a-Quinning'," he said. "If he were to bait with a haunch of venison, I should gorge. And how should I like being dragged from Richmond to Kingston, floundering and flouncing with a hook in my gullet?" But he never gave up eating fish, all the same.

Quin, the actor, *bon viveur*, good fellow and duellist, had a tongue as sharp as his own sword. He could be amusing and he could be as caustic as occasion served. He did not even spare the feelings of Garrick when they had become great friends. Garrick was a small man, Quin a large one. They were at a tavern together one night, and when they wanted to leave it was raining hard. Only one sedan chair could be found. "Never mind," said Quin, "we can both go home in it." "How?" demanded little David. "Nothing easier," said Quin, "I'll go in the chair and you can go in the lantern." . . . He was dining with a lord who patronized him, a thing Quin would not stand, especially as the nobleman was not renowned for brains. "What a pity, Quin, my boy," drawled the noble gentleman, "that a clever fellow like you should be a player." "Why?" riposted Quin. "What would you have me—a lord?". . . . One night, at Drury Lane, he had to apologize for the absence of a dancer whom he did not like. The audience was in a bad temper. So was Quin. "Ladies and gentlemen," he began, very crossly, "I have to crave your indulgence. Madame Roland has put her ankle out . . ."; a sound of anger reached him from the audience and he added, "And damme, I wish she had put her neck out." A stage-struck young man besought Quin to give him an audition and pestered so much that Quin obliged him. The aspirant chose the famous soliloquy from *Hamlet* and began "To be or not to be . . ." "Not to be, upon my honour," broke in Quin, and the audition was over. He once said that he thought the execution of Charles I might be justified. "By what law?" he was asked. "By all the laws he had left," replied Quin quietly.

He was staying at a tavern in Plymouth and the landlord kept complaining that he was plagued by rats and mice. Quin promised to tell his host how to get rid of the pest. Nothing more was heard of it until Quin had paid his bill—a most exorbitant one—and was getting in his coach to leave when the landlord reminded him of his promise of the cure for rats. "Nothing easier, my good fellow," said Quin. "Just make them out a bill and show it to them. They'll all leave fast enough." He was dining with a gentleman who highly recommended a certain pudding he was serving and strongly advised Quin to taste it. So saying, he put an enormous piece of the pudding on his own plate. Quin looked at his host's plate and then

E

at that on which a fragment of the pudding was left. "Pray, sir, tell me," he said, "which is the pudding?" And one night, when he was lounging in the Green Room at Drury Lane, Peg Woffington dashed off the stage. She was playing Sir Harry Wildair—the male lead in *The Constant Couple* in which she excelled. Peg was noted for the number of her lovers. She gasped out, laughingly, to Quin, "Before heaven, I have played this part so often that half London thinks I am a man." "And the other half knows you are not," said Quin quietly.

But Quin was a man of great heart and kindly nature, for all his sharp tongue and his readiness to fight. He did not like Charles Macklin. He had never approved of Macklin's revolution in acting when he played Shylock, for it was diametrically opposed to Quin's method—yet he conceded that he played it well in his way. But there was no love lost and matters boiled to a quarrel when Quin, who was Macklin's senior in the Theatre, spoke roughly to him and made some very personal remarks. Macklin was by no means a handsome man. His strong-featured face was lined and seared. And Quin remarked to him, "Mr. Macklin, by the lines—I beg your pardon—the cordage—of your face, you should be hanged." He also remarked audibly to a bystander, "If God writes a legible hand, that fellow is a villain." Macklin—who had murdered his man and got away with it—was not the sort to stand that kind of thing without reprisals. It soon happened. One night Macklin came into the Green Room straight off the stage at the end of a scene. As usual, the room was full of visitors, many of them gentlemen of quality, smartly dressed and bewigged. Quin was master there, however. He turned on Macklin and shouted at him, accusing him of putting in gags and business of his own and ruining the other players' chances in the scene. Now Macklin had indeed done this. Everyone stared at Macklin, whose hot temper was known. Macklin appeared to take the rebuke and made some sort of apology. His cue came again. He went on and clowned more than ever. When he came off Quin was in a fury. He spoke to Macklin like a dog, and some of his remarks had such an edge that the onlookers laughed. Quin was just finished eating an apple and he threw the core in Macklin's face. That was enough for the fiery manslaughterer. He rushed at Quin, pushed him down in a chair and punched him in the face. Quin tried to rise, but Macklin continued to rain blows on him. The people in the room scuttled into corners to keep clear of the fight. Macklin made such a mess of Quin's face that it swelled up badly and when he had to go on the stage for his next scene he could hardly speak, and the audience, thinking he was drunk, began to hiss him. He told them he was very ill and could hardly continue to play, which quietened them and he got through somehow. And at the end, he went to Macklin and demanded satisfaction. He said he would be at the Obelisk at Covent Garden and would wait for Macklin there. Macklin said he would be pleased to meet him and Quin left, determined to kill him. But Macklin had forgotten he had not finished, he had to play in the pantomime which brought the evening to a close. He decided Quin would have to wait. But Fleetwood, the manager, who liked Macklin and feared Quin, had heard of the affair. He did not want to lose either and he knew there was every chance of losing one or the other if their swords crossed. He told Macklin that he must not fight Quin, that he, Fleetwood, his manager, ordered it and that he would make it up to Quin somehow. He took Macklin home with him so that he should not keep the appointment, gave him a good supper and locked him in his room. Somehow he smoothed down Quin, but Macklin had to make an apology. He did it with bad grace but Quin accepted it. There was now hatred between the two men, and it was many years before they spoke, other than in the way of business, and then with the distant courtesy of strangers. But years afterwards, they both attended the funeral of a brother actor and after the ceremony found themselves in the same Covent Garden tavern. They sat drinking with friends, and neither was an easy man to put under the table. Dawn came and they found themselves the only two semi-sober men in company. There was still a bottle on the table. They looked at each other. Quin smiled, poured out a glass and drank to Mr. Macklin. Macklin responded by drinking to Mr. Quin. After a short pause, Quin said: "There has been a foolish quarrel between you and me, sir, which though accommodated, I must confess I have not been able to entirely forget until now. The melancholy occasion of our meeting and the circumstances of our being left together, I thank God, have made me see my error. If you can, therefore, forget it, give me your hand and let us live together in future like brother performers." This was a pretty good speech for a man who had been drinking all night, and it appealed to Macklin, who shook hands heartily and they swore friendship. A sleepy pot-boy brought them another bottle. And the reconciliation ended by Macklin, very unsteadily, trying to carry Quin home to his lodgings on his shoulders . . . a very characteristic picture of two of the leaders of the Stage in the 18th century.

Quin lived and died a bachelor but he was a great lover of ladies. He would take a fair charmer away for a week or a fortnight in the country and have her treated in every way as if she were Mrs. Quin.

He would also call her by that name and saw that everyone else did. At the end of the holiday they returned to Town. He would then give the lady a farewell supper at the Bedford Head coffee-house, present her with a well-filled purse and say: "Madam, for our mutual convenience, I have given you the name of Mrs. Quin for some time past. There is no reason for carrying on this farce here, so now, madame, accept this gift, give me leave to un-Quin you and restore you to your own name for the future." He then bowed himself out with great show of courtesy.

He was, however, a very large-hearted and kind man in many ways. He was always ready to help those in distress. A quite obscure actor had been discharged and was in great straits. Quin had interceded for him with success. He found out where the poor man lived, came to his lodging and found him in a state of destitution. He brought the man a suit of good clothes and a hamper of food and wine. He brought good news, too. "Now, Dick," he said, "how is it you are not up? It's all right—you can go back to the theatre. They want you for rehearsal." The actor poured forth his grateful thanks, which Quin brushed aside. "But," said the poor man, "Mr. Quin, sir, I am quite penniless. I don't know how I shall live until treasury day." "Well, I've done all I can," said Quin, rather roughly. "As to money, you must put your hand in your own pocket for that, you know," and he dashed out of the room. The actor thrust his hand into the pocket of the suit Quin had given him—he had pawned his own. In the pocket was a ten-pound note.

It was much the same when he first met Thomson, the poet. That unfortunate man was imprisoned for debt. Quin sought him out, ordered a good supper and a dozen of the best claret from a neighbouring tavern and the two men spent a pleasant evening together. Then Quin rose to go. He laid upon the table a note for one hundred pounds. He said: "Mr. Thomson, the pleasure I have had in reading your works I cannot estimate at less than one hundred pounds. I insist on now acquitting the debt," and rushed away before Thomson could say a word. He hated being thanked. Often he would call upon needy people and hurry off, leaving his purse on the table. On being run after for the purpose of the purse being restored, he would deny that it was his and make off . . . as eccentric as greathearted.

His true colours showed when he was at Covent Garden, as leading man once again for his old manager and enemy, Rich. He was paying him £1,000 a year—an unheard-of salary then. Rich introduced to the Stage a young girl named George Anne Bellamy, aged fourteen—and she was to play a very hard part—Monimia, in

The Orphan. Quin and the company protested. Rich was adamant. She was terrified when the ordeal came and could hardly stand or speak. The audience were sorry for her and gave her a round of applause, but the curtain had to be rung down. But Rich encouraged her and they started again. Now Quin showed himself a real 'Pro'. He gave her every help possible whilst they were on the stage together —he its King and she the most inexperienced of his new subjects, pushed into undue prominence. His kindness melted her fear; she shone out and she triumphed. At the end Quin, then past sixty, seized her in his arms and held her up for all to see, as the audience clamoured their appreciation. "You are a divine creature," he cried. "The true spirit is in you!" From that moment he was her friend. One day, after a rehearsal, he sent for her to his dressing-room. She went, expecting to get the rough side of his tongue. But Quin beamed upon her and spoke like a father. "My dear child," he said, "I hear you have many followers. Now don't let love of finery or any temptation make you indiscreet. You are young and engaging and ought to be very cautious. Naturally you desire nice things. So, if you want anything which it is within my power to give you, come to me and say 'James Quin, I want such a thing' and my purse is at your service." He meant every word he said—alas, that she did not take his advice and help. . . .

It was at Covent Garden that Quin met his defeat, a defeat which tumbled him from his leadership of the Stage which he had held since the withdrawl of Barton Booth. He had resisted two strong challenges: one by Delaine who followed him at Lincoln's Inn, and one by Macklin at Drury Lane, when that actor introduced his more natural style to upset Quin's ponderous oratory. But he had come through and was still leader. Now there arose a young man who had hitherto been a wine merchant but who decided to be an actor. This young man made a start, without rehearsal of any kind, at an outlying theatre in Whitechapel called Goodman's Fields. There he deputized suddenly for his friend Yates, taken ill, and played Harlequin with great success. Gifford, manager of Goodman's Fields, put him on the Stage. He played Richard III and all London went to the East End to see him. The two great Patent Theatres were empty, everyone went to Goodman's Fields. The old actors went too, to see this new menace—whose name was David Garrick. Old Colley Cibber did not like Garrick's bustling manner. He found it inartistic to be natural. Quin went and observed, for he had very good reason to watch a rival. "If this young man is right," he said, "then, damme, all the rest of us have always been wrong." Garrick played in Ipswich to gain experience, then he played at Drury Lane.

But he could not come to terms with Lacy, the Patentee there. He went to Dublin. Quin, determined to scotch such opposition, went over too and played at the rival theatre. Garrick won the battle. Then he returned to London and Rich got him, for one season at Covent Garden. Now he met his great rival on his own ground. It was indeed David and Goliath—David Garrick against the giant leader Quin. It was youth against age—and youth will be served.

They played opposite each other in a play called *The Fair Penitent*, Garrick playing Lothario and Quin Horatio. Quin knew it was a duel for the championship with no holds barred. He was very nervous. Garrick noticed this and commented, "I believe Quin is as much frightened as I am." The play began and the two contrasted actors played against each other—the old style *versus* the new. It was the audience who chose the victor. The verdict came in a scene where Garrick had to hurl a challenge at Quin. He did so, in his quick incisive style. Quin summoned his forces and went into one of his long, impressive pauses. So long was he that a voice from the gallery was heard, calling, "Aren't you going to answer the gentleman?" Quin knew he had lost. He made his reply—in his best manner—"I . . . will . . . meet . . . thee . . . there. . . ." But he knew he no longer led the Stage. David Garrick now wore his crown. The year was 1746.

He bore no malice. He quarrelled with Rich and retired to Bath. After a while, wearying of inactivity, he wrote to Rich: "Dear Rich, I am at Bath. Yours, James Quin." To which Rich replied: "Stay there and be damned. Yours, John Rich." But he had to have Quin back all the same. Eventually Quin went back to Drury Lane and served under Garrick. The two men—the old champion and the new—became the greatest of friends. They loved each other's company, and often on the stage Quin would whisper an invitation to Garrick to sup with him and ask what he would like best to eat. . . .

But age was telling on Quin. And again he retired to Bath. There, although he would come up for one annual performance, for Ryan's benefit, until his teeth failed, he played no more. But his wit held and he was much sought after. Bishop Warburton once argued with him about the man who had executed Charles I—it was when Quin made his remark about the Law—and said that all the regicides suffered violent ends. "I would not advise Your Lordship to make use of that inference," said Quin, "for, if I am not mistaken, that was the case of the twelve apostles also." Allen, Bishop of Gloucester, published a volume of Shakespeare. Quin did not like Allen, who

had been very rude to him. "He had better mind his own bible," he
said, "and leave us to ours." And he once remarked to another
patronizing clergyman who had very dirty hands and finger-nails,
"I see you keep the glebe in your own hands, Doctor." Mistress
Woffington came down to Bath. She told Quin she had come
from mere wantonness. "And are you cured?" said Quin, very
quietly.

His health left him, he grew very ill. The doctors despaired.
They said if they could make him sweat they might save him. "You
have only to send in your bills," smiled Quin. . . . The day before
he died he drank a bottle of claret with relish and he knew quite
well his last exit was upon him. "I could wish that the tragic scene
was over," he said, "though I am in hopes that I shall be able to go
through it with becoming dignity." And he was right. He met his
end calmly and fully conscious at four o'clock in the morning of
21st January, 1766, in the seventy-third year of his life. His last
performance on the stage had been at Covent Garden in 1753—as
Falstaff for Ryan's benefit.

He left a Will—which dealt with a considerable fortune, all
earned by his own efforts—and in that Will he forgot none of his
friends. James Quin was a great man and a great actor. Unlike so
many actors, he knew his own limitations; for when Rich offered him
the part of Macheath in the original production of *The Beggar's
Opera*, he refused it, saying he could not play it. He was the last of an
epoch, of a school of acting which had begun with Betterton almost
a century before. He had conquered many difficulties, his irregular
birth, his lack of means, his lack of influence. He had risen by his
own efforts, his own courage and his own talent. He was a man of
great distinction in many ways and yet of curious contradictions—at
once artistic to a degree and yet sensual and coarse—brutal, and yet
brave and kindly. He mirrored the times in which he lived. He was
essentially of the Theatre and he had pride and dignity in his
calling. He always fought and mostly he won. But when defeat came
at the hands of Garrick, he knew it was decisive and he was big
enough to accept it—and be friends with his conqueror. They named
a street after Macklin but Quin has no such memorial.

James Quin was real Theatre through and through—one of the
mighty ones of his Profession—and although not all his story belongs
to Drury Lane, yet he wrought much there and left something of
himself about it.

He died, as became him, a man of quality and character.
His conqueror, David Garrick himself, who was also his friend,
wrote his epitaph for his tomb in Bath Abbey, and drew a

picture which glowed with the colour which Quin possessed in
his life:

> The tongue, which set the table in a roar
> And charmed the public ear, is heard no more!
> Clos'd are those eyes, the harbingers of wit,
> Which spoke, before the tongue, what Shakespeare writ.
> Cold are those hands, which, living were stretched forth
> At friendship's call, to succour modest worth.
> Here lies James Quin! deign, reader, to be taught
> (Whate'er thy strength of body, force of thought,
> In nature's happiest mould however cast)
> To his complexion thou must come at last.

CHAPTER FOUR

The Actor Who Could Write

IN THAT colonnade which supports the memories of Old Drury
stands a figure which is second to none in interest and talent.
He was beloved of Charles Lamb, the gentle 'Elia', who could
not have enough of him and who had left word pictures of him
which glow. He was a comedian and a comedian of the front rank.
But he had another talent, too—he was a wonderful penman, his
writing was every bit as good as his acting. And that is saying a good
deal. His name was Joseph Shepherd Munden.

Munden was born in Brook's Street, Holborn, in the year 1758.
His father was a purveyor of poultry, dealing chiefly in ducks, geese
and chickens. Brook's Market was quite a short street, but it saw the
end of one genius—the poet Chatterton—and the birth of another,
Joe Munden.

Young Joe was not a good boy. He would not settle down. This
may have been because his father died when he was only an infant.
His mother, an excellent woman, brought up her son with great
care and gave him the best education she could afford. One thing
resulted from that: he wrote a wonderful hand.

The time came when he had to leave school and go into business.
His mother wanted to maintain the commercial respectability of the
family, so at the age of twelve—there were no 'Leaving Certifi-
cates' or searching examinations then—she apprenticed him to an
apothecary. Could anything be more respectable, or more sure? It
was security the lady was after. Joe did not like medicine in any
shape or form. So he left, after a month. His mother discussed his
future with him, and the Law was mentioned. Joe saw no objection,
so he was got into the chambers of an attorney in New Inn. Joe
found the Law very dry. He left it—but not entirely. His mother was
getting a bit desperate. So she bound him for five years to a law
stationer, Mr. Druce, of Chancery Lane. He was in the toils now
and his writing could stand him in good stead. Somehow he plodded
along, mostly because he liked Mr. Druce, but that gentleman died
after Joe had served two years and his successor was not the sort of
man for whom the unwilling apprentice cared at all. They did not
get on. There was something else the matter, too. Master Joe
Munden had become stage-struck. He had sneaked out at nights,
and gone into the gallery at Drury Lane and Covent Garden. But it

73

was 'The Lane' he liked the best—for there he saw the glory that
was Garrick—and that sun of the Stage set him afire. He gave
performances in the office for the amusement of the backwriters,
when his master was not about. Joe had made up his mind. He got
into company with other boys who were also mad about acting and
they gave performances to any audience they could raise, with
vast pleasure to themselves. But still, it was not the genuine thing.
Joe took his courage in both hands. He got into touch with a band
of strolling players and he ran off with them. His mother searched
for him. She had guessed what he would do. She knew he could not
get far—he had no money—so she frequented the little halls and
places where small bands played in the suburbs and within a few
miles of London. Often she saw his coat before she saw her son. For
she dressed him well and the strollers were pretty shabby, so Joe's
coat was often borrowed by the leading man. Her suspicions thus
confirmed, she would catch her son and take him home. But one of
Joe's friends had actually succeeded in getting a real job on the
stage, at Liverpool. He persuaded Joe to follow him and try his
luck; he probably told him that he would get him into the company
all right. And, a week later, Joe turned up in Liverpool. How he got
there must remain a mystery—but there he was. But there was
nothing for him in the Theatre, not even of the most menial kind.
How he lived is not known; perhaps his friend helped. But Munden
was a very persistent young man and at last he got work of a kind.
He got it again by his penmanship. He was engaged to write out
parts for the players, for which he was paid eighteen pence a night.
It was not much, but it was work for the Theatre. But at length he
got on the stage. He had nothing to say and little to do. He just came
on with the crowd and shouted and maybe he carried a banner. But
he was on the 'boards', behind the candles of the footlights—and out
in front was that mysterious thing—the audience. He was, at last, in
the Land of Illusion, and however humble his status, no doubt he
was thrilled. But before he could hope for advancement, the company broke up and returned to London. Joe could not go with them,
he had not the fare. He had no money at all and something had to
be done.

By good luck he got a job, again through his fine penmanship,
in the office of the Town Clerk, and there he made himself quite
useful. But he could not leave the Stage alone. A Benefit Performance
was got up for some local tradesmen in difficulties. He had, of course,
got to know a lot of young men who came to the theatre and he
found they were going to help in the production and play parts. He
volunteered at once. He was accepted. That play was *King Henry*

IV, and now he attained his ambition. He had no less than two parts—one of the Carriers—and as Bardolph. So Munden spoke for the first time on the stage—doubtless in the seventh heaven of delight. To him it must have been wonderful. And, what is more, he made quite a success. To work in the Town Hall was now quite unthinkable. Was he not an actor—a real actor—who spoke lines, who drew applause? It must be the Stage and nothing but the Stage.

He heard of a company at Rochdale which wanted recruits. He went there. He got a job. It was a very scratch affair—which took on almost all-comers. Stage-struck youths and servants would get a chance of playing a part. Munden, young and inexperienced as he was, turned out to be, by his natural talent, one of the best performers there. Odd things happened. They were playing *The Fair Penitent* (a very famous tragedy). The scene came where the fair Calista is seen, seated by the side of the corpse of the gay but false Lothario. Now it so happened that the man playing Lothario was a footman employed at a large house in the neighbourhood who had taken advantage of his master's absence to help himself to an evening out and gratify his Thespian ambitions. His master returned much sooner than expected, and not finding his servant, guessed what had happened. He went to the theatre, and he saw his footman on the stage. He went behind the scenes and had a row with the manager, who was playing Horatio. The raised voices reached the ears of the corpse of Lothario, who heard his master's dread voice demanding the instant return of his servant John. The footman-corpse was in a panic. He rose from his bier, to the delighted surprise of the audience, and fled from the theatre, hotly pursued by his angry master. Poor Calista was dumbfounded and she too ran off the stage. Down came the curtain amidst general rejoicings. Provincial playgoing had a flavour of surprise in those days.

But there is nothing stable in the playhouse and the Rochdale company disbanded. Once again Munden was on his beam-ends. He went back to Liverpool and was re-engaged, because of his excellent writing, by the Town Clerk. He worked there for two years and every day and night he yearned only for the Stage. At length he could stand it no longer. He had saved a guinea, he had met the excellent actor Ned Shuter, who had spoken words of encouragement to him. So he threw up the safe 10*s*. 6*d*. a week he got from the Town Hall and went off to follow an actor's life—the only one for him.

He turned up in Chester. He had now spent all his money, save one solitary shilling. He went to the theatre, read the bills and debated what to do. It did not take him long to decide. He invested his last shilling in seeing the play. He sat entranced, watching the actors and actresses, forgetting that he was now quite penniless. He staggered out of that playhouse, drunk with great gulps of the drama. He sat on the kerb and tried to get his mental balance. He came to a great decision. One day he himself would own or manage that theatre. It did not seem a likely result for the investment of his last shilling. Meanwhile there was no supper, no bed, no roof over his head. He had sat next to a butcher and that man now came along, heard his story and took him home for the night. Next day he went round the town—he tried the theatre first—looking for work. He got it, at a law stationers, because of his writing. But it was very temporary in its nature. Into the shop came a man whom Joe had known in London. Both were pleased at the meeting and Joe told his friend of his situation. His friend wanted to help but he was himself on the rocks. The idea was to get back to London. But how to raise the fare? Joe's friend had a ring. He promptly pawned it and it got them as far as Whitchurch. There they separated. Joe managed to get as far as Birmingham. Here he again found a friend and got a supper and a bed. He was off the next day and reached Woodstock. Now it happened that a market gardener of that town had been in Liverpool some time previously, concerned in a lawsuit, which he had lost. But he had come into contact with Joe Munden and that good-natured young man had shown him some kindnesses, eased his path amongst the lawyers and made himself generally pleasant. He found the man, who was delighted to see him. The bread which Joe had cast on the waters came home. The market gardener gave him, or lent him, his fare to London. So Joe went home to Mother. That good lady treated him as the Prodigal Son, but she put him to the Law again, it was the only thing he knew anything about, and not much at that—but his penmanship stood his friend.

There is a story extant about his enlisting in the Militia and then deserting at Stratford-on-Avon, but it is too fantastic to be true. So Master Munden continued to drive his quill whilst his thoughts took flight far beyond it. It was no good. He must be an actor! He picked up with a theatrical manager in a tavern in Drury Lane. This man had a company then appearing at Leatherhead. Munden joined and his total resources were thirteen pence. It cost him that to get to Leatherhead. He then discovered that the theatre of which his new friend had boasted was just a barn. They all had to set to and transform it into the semblance of a theatre. Munden was the most willing worker of them all. They put in the seats, they erected some sort of a stage by means of planks and they awaited the audience. But not a soul appeared and the company went supperless to bed. It was the same for the next two evenings, but for the Saturday the play had been 'bespoke' by a gentleman of the neighbourhood who had company staying with him. That brought other people, too, and they had a good house. They were on shares and each of them got the sum of six shillings—and two pieces of candle, for it was customary for the strollers to share even the candle-ends which were left over from the stage lighting at the end of the week. It all saved money. The first theatre earnings that Joseph Munden, to be a Pillar of Drury Lane, ever received was six shillings and two ends of candle. He had had his share of the buffetings of fate. He had suffered hardship and privation. He could, by his art of penman-ship, have earned quite a decent living. But that was not for him. Munden was pre-eminently a Man of the Theatre. Nothing else would do. Business slightly improved and the company were to have Benefits. Benefits were doubtful prospects then, and far from enriching the beneficiary, often landed him into debt. Munden could not afford a Benefit. He took a partner in it to lessen the risk—and the profit, if any. He never got the Benefit, for the night before the performance was to take place that barn-theatre was burned down completely and the poor players ruined. Munden flew to his pen. He drew up a beautifully written and worded petition—his legal knowledge helped there—and he trudged about the neigh-bourhood showing it. It worked too, for well-disposed and kind-hearted people contributed between twenty and thirty pounds to help the strollers. The manager, of course, took charge of the cash. He gave each of the company five shillings—there were twelve of them—and he went off to London to buy a new wardrobe and properties. Naturally, he was never seen again.

Joe Munden tramped back to London. He did not go home; he went to the Black Lion Tavern in Russell Street, Drury Lane, which was the gathering place of actors wanting jobs and managers who had them to give. He took the rest of that stranded company with him. Maybe they hoped to find their bogus manager. They did not do that but found another manager who engaged them, lock, stock and barrel. He took them strolling round villages, where they played, and somehow they kept body and soul together. They played at last at Windsor and there they had quite a successful season, if a short one. This manager was not much better than the defaulter. He doled them out shillings at a time, and he worked them like slaves. Munden had pleased the public. He had not much in the way of a repertoire of parts as most actors had then—he had

had no opportunity of learning them. He was told to learn and be completely word perfect in a very long and arduous part within two days. He said he could not do it. He was discharged at once and he was not much worse off than the rest, for the following evening the manager did a bolt as well. Munden walked back to London. Once more his mother put him to the Law. But it was no good—of course it was no good. The Little Theatre in the Hay—now the beautiful Haymarket Theatre—was at that time producing private plays with semi-amateur companies. Munden went there in the evenings and performed. It so happened that he caught the eye of Hurst, manager of the Canterbury Theatre, who offered him an engagement. He was offered second parts in tragedy and comedy. But what Hurst most wanted was a comedian, and a low comedian at that. Munden, of course, who was a born comedian, wanted to play Tragedy. But the chance was too good to be missed. He accepted the engagement. He succeeded. He pleased the Canterbury audiences and he made them laugh heartily. For the first time he really tasted the joys of success in a real theatre. The engagement ended and he had to come back to London. He had become friends with the chief tragedian of the company, one William—or Billy—Swords. They travelled up to Town together in a cart. This amused Swords. "Tap my eyes," he exclaimed, "when you are at Covent Garden and I at Drury Lane— for we shall both be too eminent to be retained by one house—what will the theatrical biographers say when they hear that the great Billy Swords and the great Joe Munden rode from Canterbury to London in a cart?" Well, the record is now inscribed with no comment except to say that Mr. Swords had only one pair of boots to his name, originally in red leather for stage use, but now blackened for general wear, which a cobbler had just refused to mend. He said they were so far gone that he would lose money by the time and materials he would have to expend on them. . . .

Munden's next job was at Brighton—it was now 1780. There he was a big success. He became quite eminent in the town and was patronized by the 'fashionables'. Things had begun to go his way. And now Fate began to work out. It so happened that the leading comedian in the stock company at Chester died. The management, Austin and Whitlock, had heard of Munden and offered him the job. Now he played chief comedy roles in the very theatre in which he had invested his last shilling some years before. He was a great success. He played all round the circuit; he became immensely popular. He got a moderate salary and he began to save. He made a big success in Manchester. He was very popular wherever he went and made friends. A gentleman of means in Chester had taken a great fancy to him. And then the wheel of Fate revolved full circle. One of the proprietors of the theatre in Chester, it was Austin, fell ill and decided to retire. Joe Munden's friend lent the money for the comedian to buy Austin's share. So that vow which Joe had taken whilst sitting in the gutter had come true. He was manager, or at least joint manager (with Whitlock), of the Chester Theatre.

Munden found the duties of a manager were a bit arduous. He had a fine company but a difficult one. Many of them later became great favourites, for they included George Frederick Cooke, a magnificent actor when sober, Mrs. Whitlock, a splendid tragedienne, who might have reached the top if not overshadowed by Sarah Siddons—whom she much resembled—and several more who did very well. Munden found that the difficulty of ruling his crowd and coping with the fickle tastes of the public was a grievous job. He decided to sell out and soon he did so, repaying his patron and having a small profit left over. He decided acting was better than management. It shows he knew a good deal about the Theatre.

He went back to London, now an established provincial star. And he got an engagement at Covent Garden. Edwin, for years the chief comedian there, had died, and Munden stepped into his place.

He made his first appearance there in 1790 as Sir Francis Gripe in *The Busybody* and Jemmy Jumps in *The Farmer*. He had to contend with memories of the departed Edwin and the very popular Parsons, but being a first-class actor he succeeded. He had married whilst at Chester and had two children, both boys.

He played a tremendous round of comedy parts, creating many characters. He had opposition, too, from the established players at Covent Garden.

Quick now reigned there. They were rehearsing *The Road to Ruin* and Munden had been allotted the part of Silky. So well did he rehearse it that Quick decided it was a better part than the one he had, and demanded that it be given to him. His will was law and Munden had to give up the part and begin to study that which Quick was to have played. This was the character of Old Dornton. That attention to detail, that ability to make every bit of him act, caused him to make Old Dornton his *chef d'œuvre*, to the utter disgust and dismay of Quick, who failed as Silky. Thus does chance play a part in the Theatre.

Things at Drury Lane about that time were pretty bad. Many of 'The Lane' stalwarts had gone over to Covent Garden, including Alexander Pope. But they found things at 'The Garden' even worse, where no justice or stability was to be had at all. A few of them banded together and resisted the management. In other words, they

struck. They were led by Pope and Munden. They won. But neither
of those two believed that justice would be done for long. Pope went
back to 'The Lane', his natural home, and very shortly afterwards
Munden followed him there. That was in 1813. His first part there
was Sir Abel Handy. Munden did not only play comedy, although
that was his best line. He was also a first-class Shakespearean player.
His Menenius in *Coriolanus* was outstanding, and as a Witch in
Macbeth he was said to be perfectly terrifying. One of his great gifts
was his understanding of how to dress a part. He got every detail
right, he made his costume fit the peculiarities of the characters he
played, and he wore his clothes to perfection, too.

His career at Drury Lane was long and distinguished. He played
there for eleven years, and rose to be perhaps the finest comedian of
his day. He had a great dislike for Edmund Kean, almost amounting
to hatred. He could not swallow this tempestuous man whom he
regarded as an upstart. Yet Kean had him hypnotized. It is on record
that when they appeared together in *A New Way To Pay Old Debts*,
Kean, as Sir Giles Overreach, was so terrific that he held Munden
spellbound on the stage, staring at him, unable to move—and
having to be pulled off by the other players.

Old Munden was a typical actor of his time—he was steeped in
the Theatre and he took his calling very seriously. He was a man
much respected despite a rather bad peccadillo in his youth, when
he got entangled with a worthless woman—and some illegitimate
children resulted. But what was that, in his day? Nobody thought
the worse of him.

Charles Lamb had the highest admiration for Munden and
devoted a whole essay to him. And a remarkable picture of a
versatile actor, who paid attention to detail, emerges.

"His queer visnomy—his bewildering costume—all the
strange things which he had raked together—his serpentine rod
swagging about in his pocket—Cleopatra's tear and the rest of
his relics—O'Keefe's wild farce and *his* wilder commentary—till
the passion of laughter, like grief in excess, relieved itself by its
own weight, inviting the sleep which in the first instance it had
driven away."

Lamb dreams of him:

"not one Munden, but five hundred, were dancing before me,
like the faces which, whether you will or no, come when you
have been taking opium—all the strange combinations, which

Nellie Stewart, one of Drury Lane's most famous Principal Boys. She came from Australia

PILLARS OF PANTOMIME

Upper left: Mabel Love *Upper right:* Connie Gilchrist (Countess of Orkney) *Lower left:* Belle Bilton (Lady Dunlo) *Lower right:* Marie Lloyd

this strangest of all strange mortals ever shot his proper countenance into, from the day he came commissioned to dry up the tears of the town for the loss of the now almost forgotten Edwin. . . . A season or two since there was exhibited a Hogarth gallery. I do not see why there should not be a Munden gallery. In richness and variety, the latter would not fall short of the former. There is one face of Farley, one face of Knight, one (but what a one it is!) of Liston; but Munden has none that you can properly pin down and call his. . . . He is not one, but legion; not so much a comedian as a company. . . . I have seen this gifted actor as 'Sir Christopher Curry'—in 'Old Dornton'—diffuse a glow of sentiment which has made the pulse of a crowded theatre beat like that of one man . . . but in the grand grotesque of farce, Munden stands out as single, and unaccompanied, as Hogarth. Hogarth, strange to tell, had no followers. The school of Munden began and must end with himself. . . ."

All that is praise indeed of a man who appears to have been the 'complete' actor with a complete understanding of his art—to conquer which he had surmounted difficulties which would have defeated any ordinary man. He was a tremendously popular favourite, and when he came to say good-bye to his public—at Drury Lane—on 31st May, 1824, he took his farewell by playing two characters—Sir Robert Bramble in *The Poor Gentleman* and Old Doxey in *Past Ten o'Clock*—that was a famous part of his, a drunken part. The curtain fell and he came through the proscenium door to say farewell. All his actor's art had vanished—he made his adieu as a simple, ordinary man. He said:

"Ladies and Gentlemen. The moment is now arrived when I have to perform the painful duty of bidding you farewell. When I call to remembrance that five and thirty years have elapsed since I first had the honour of appearing before you, I am still more forcibly reminded that I ought to leave the scene for younger and gayer spirits to mingle in. But it is not easy to shake off, in a moment, the habits of years, and you will, I know, pardon me if I am tedious for it is for the last time. I carry with me into private life, ladies and gentlemen, the deep and indelible remembrance of that kind, that liberal indulgence with which you have at all times regarded my humble efforts to amuse. I feel that I am 'poor in thanks' but your kindness is registered here, and will never be forgotten; and should the recurrence of early association occasionally bring back the veteran comedian to your recollection, he will ask for no higher fame. I thank you most sincerely, ladies and gentlemen, for the

F

patience with which you have listened to me, and I now bid you a respectful, grateful and a last adieu."

He bowed low and walked off the stage to a thunderous gesture of farewell from the audience.

His farewell speech was curious. This very accomplished comedian, who was of the readiest wit and inventiveness on the stage in the general rule, read that last speech of his. He did not memorize it, he read it from manuscript. He was very much over-come with emotion and he did not read it well. His eyes were filled with tears and he had frequently to take off his spectacles and wipe them. Indeed, his speech did border on that tediousness for which he apologized. He who had ever been so quick and ready was lagging in his last public words. But he got a warm-hearted response.

And it was a real farewell. Unlike so many others, he did not make a come-back, owing to great demand, and have several farewell performances . . . in this he would have offended the precepts and rules of the immortal Vincent Crummles. Munden said farewell and meant it. His farewell was not the only one which happened that evening. The other was unforeseen. In that play of *The Poor Gentleman*, a curious actor, a most unreliable although brilliant man, named Oxberry, appeared. It happened so that it was his last appearance on the Stage. He died almost immediately afterwards. His widow wrote to Munden to ask him to appear at a Benefit Performance for her, which his Profession were giving in honour of her dead husband and to help her in her straits. Munden replied regretting that he could not assist. He had, he said, taken his farewell of the Stage and it was final. He added that, if he ever did perform again, he would send her £100. She never got it.

Old Munden excelled in comedy—indeed, in farce and in the gentle art of facial expression, as Lamb has made clear. Occasionally he would clown and be a buffoon but always with artistry. His Shakespearean performances showed his art as an actor outside farce—his Autolycus and his Polonius showed that. If he did, at times, take liberties with the parts he played, he never took liberties with an audience, he never let them down, or his fellow players. He was the best stage 'drunk' of his time—and, if the phrase can be allowed, the most artistic. His drunks were charming, likable fellows, good companions, never repulsive or beastly. Their liquor made them glow and be merry, they were never disgusting or repellent.

He could sing a comic song well, too, although his singing voice was not strong, and again his facial play made the songs most effective.

Joe Munden was a small man, only about five feet three in height. He had a fresh healthy complexion and a most mobile mouth. His eyes were large and effective and he knew how to use them. He always wore powder although it was already old-fashioned in his day, and he was rather stout in body. His walk was all his own, more of a shuffle than a stride, and he often limped when that almost universal complaint of those days, the gout, had him in its clutches.

He was, like so many comedians, a very close man about money. He never spent a copper more than was absolutely necessary. He had known what it was to be penniless, to want food and to want a shelter for the night. He never forgot his early struggles and it made him very careful indeed. He retired from public life when he left the Stage and he went to live in Kentish Town. He had saved money, for although his salary never exceeded £20 a week, his Benefits had always brought him in large sums. In retirement, he entertained his friends and was a good host. But he did his own shopping. He could be seen walking home to Kentish Town, with four or six mackerel, impaled upon a stick through their gills, in his hands. He had walked all the way down to Clare Market to buy these fish, which he loved, because he got them considerably cheaper there.

He had eight years of retirement in which to enjoy his well-earned rest. He died on 6th February, 1832, at the age of seventy-four.

Joseph Shepherd Munden was indeed a Pillar of Drury Lane. He made his impact there and something of his atmosphere can still be felt in that kindly, friendly theatre which, like him, has faced its troubles and overcome them. How many people have heard of him today? Yet his memory should remain. He was a brave man who determined to follow his bent. Nothing deflected him from his chosen course. He meant to be an actor and an actor he became—standing high in his Profession. And when he left it, he did so as Principal Comedian at the greatest of theatres, Drury Lane.

That old actor who had kept him company in the cart coming from Canterbury had spoken truer than he knew. Though Billy Swords himself never rose to fame—Munden ruled at Covent Garden and at 'The Lane' too. He is part of the atmosphere of Old Drury, his work is woven in its fabric, not the least strong link in its chain of fame, and somewhere his spirit still exists to give a touch of kindliness and a smile in that unique atmosphere which graces the oldest theatre in the world.

CHAPTER FIVE

Benefits Forgot . . .

A GREAT deal is often heard about Benefit Performances for actors and actresses, yet very little is known of their origin and how they actually came about. Sometimes, indeed, they benefited the beneficiary—and sometimes they did not, as has been chronicled in the case of Joe Munden. Something about these strange affairs may not be out of place in a book which concerns Drury Lane Theatre, for it was there they really originated.

H. G. Pellissier and his incomparable *Follies* used to do a burlesque which they called 'Everybody's Benefit'. It was magnificent satire. It represented an All Star Matinée on behalf of an old performer. The curtain rose on a clear stage, except for an enormous trestle table covered with a white cloth, almost completely hidden by every kind of drink and refreshment and with Morris Harvey, as a waiter, polishing glasses. To him entered Lewis Sydney as a Theatre Fireman. "Wot's this function for, mate?" he enquired of Harvey, who replied with a shrug: "Oh, it's for another of them improvident professionals." That always got a laugh. Then four men carried a box across the stage from which came wild screams. It was the Escapologist who had failed to get out. The show then proceeded, as such shows usually do, with everyone wanting to get on next and rush away. Everybody, that is, except those stars who had promised to appear, had been billed and then had not turned up. There was an actor-manager who said he had "the entire second act of *The School for Scandal* outside in a motor-bus and simply must be put on next". At the end, when everyone was weak with laughter, the poor old lady on whose behalf the matinée had been held was brought on the stage in an old-fashioned cape and bonnet (Gwennie Mars played her), whilst Pellissier, made up like Sir Squire Bancroft, presented her, with much dignity and more pomp, with "this postal order for sixpence"—to which she could only mutter, "This is most kind—most kind." . . . It was all very funny, very sad—and very true.

That is the sort of thing many people visualize when they read about 'Benefits' in books dealing with the Theatre or hear them discussed. But the real Benefits—when Benefits were part of an actor's living—were not a bit like that. And Theatre people are no more improvident than other classes of the community.

When one of them goes bankrupt you hear about it because he or she is 'news'. Commercial people go bankrupt every day—often more than once—and except in very special circumstances, nobody outside their creditors and the officials at Carey Street hears about it at all, or gives two hoots. Yet theatrical people have a greater and more precarious struggle for their living than most people in this world. Their earnings vary tremendously, they have no certainty of employment. They may have a good year and three bad ones to follow it, in which case Income Tax breaks them. £250 a week as salary may easily mean only £500 in the year. Their goodwill is bound up in their own personal smartness and appearance. They always have to appear prosperous, they must never be shabby—'dress well on and off' was once a clause in the contracts; they must always be about the places where their Profession congregates, and they have to spend money to keep up that level beneath which they must not fall. You will find heartbreaks in the smartest restaurants if you can see below the surface. . . .

Strange as it may seem, dramatists—not usually regarded as poor people but rich and prosperous—had Benefits given them long before the poor players got them. They had them even in Tudor times but they were not called Benefits then, but 'The Author's Night'. Those early playwrights, Shakespeare included, did not command the fat royalties which now accrue. Henslowe, one of the great theatre magnates of the Tudor and Stuart days, considered £8 a lot of money to pay for a play. Later the price rose, as much as £20 was paid down, and the author was given all that was left over after every possible expense had been paid—or charged—on the second time of the play's performance. Later still, this was changed to the third night, which became, as it were, the Author's Benefit, but was still called 'his night'. There was some reason for this, for if a play then lasted for three performances, it was a success. Those short runs had nothing to do with the quality of the play, it should be remembered, but were due to the playgoing public being numbered only in hundreds instead of tens of thousands. But early dramatic authorship was a poorly paid job.

Dryden, the great Restoration dramatist and poet, who is a classic today, seldom got more than £100 out of a play, including his 'Author's Night'. Nicholas Rowe, author of so many successful plays like *The Fair Penitent*, *Jane Shore*, *Tamerlane*, etc., had three Author's Nights—every third night—for some of his plays, and Southern's tragedy of *The Spartan Dame*, entirely forgotten today, produced no less than £500 for him, which was then the high record. Oliver Goldsmith made £400 out of his comedy *The Good-Natured Man*, and promptly spent it all on buying the lease of his rooms in the Temple and furnishing them luxuriously. Was he improvident? At least he got himself a home. How far would £400 go towards that today? The early dramatists were far better off than the actors so far as Benefits were concerned. No player in Elizabethan or Jacobean times would have dared to ask for a Benefit, either from his management or the public. They were mostly poor, downtrodden folk, mere vagabonds and often almost outlaws—and so generally regarded—who took what they could get and were glad of the chance. Yet some of them made money. Thomas Pope, who was a 'clown'—that is to say a low comedian—was a shareholder in the Curtain and the Globe Theatres and did very well by being also on the managerial side. So well, indeed, that he had a monument erected to him in Southwark Cathedral and left a bequest to the poor. But in the main, they were thin times for the players.

The first player to receive a Benefit was the great Mrs. Barry. According to old Colley Cibber, she was, in virtue of her eminence, given an Annual Benefit in James II's time. But the custom of Benefits did not become general until Betterton had quarrelled with crafty old Rich at Drury Lane and gone off to Lincoln's Inn Fields, in the reign of William and Mary.

The agreement which brought about the merger between Drury Lane and the Duke's Theatre, when Drury Lane took over all that had been the Duke's, which shortly afterwards vanished—and under which Charles Hart and Edward Kynaston, of Drury Lane, received certain payments—speaks of "the exclusion of such times as the young men and women of the Theatres play for their own profit". This, however, may have been on a commonwealth or sharing basis and not personal benefits.

When Benefits became general in the 18th century they were a matter of mutual agreement between the management and the players. They were stipulated for in the contracts and were regarded as part of the salaries of the players—they had nothing to do with charity at all. They were, therefore, of vital importance to the beneficiaries and also a test of their popularity—everybody in the Theatre had them, or practically everybody—even the box-office manager. They were usually matters which led to much argument, for there was always dissension between the two parties as to when they were to be taken.

The actors, of course, wanted them on good nights for business and at good times of the year. The managements were desirous of granting only 'off nights' towards the end of the season when business had fallen off.

Benefits often occasioned disputes and bad blood. Christopher Rich, the bad man of Old Drury, swindled his people shamefully over Benefits, and this matter was a prime cause in his downfall, when Colley Cibber, a starving and swindled actor, appealed to Queen Anne.

Popular players, of course, always got a bumper Benefit, and although they had to tout for support and sell tickets themselves, this was not considered beneath their dignity because it was the custom of the Profession. It paid them well, too, because admirers would not only pay more than the ordinary price but make them presents of money as well. Often the house was 'oversold'. A very notable Benefit was that of Thomas Betterton on his retirement. Actually, he had two, one at Drury Lane and the other at the theatre which stood where the Carlton Hotel and Her Majesty's now stand—the King's House, in the Haymarket. Betterton was an upright man of noble character and much beloved. But as Rich was in command at Drury Lane, there was trouble. Betterton got £76 for his share of the house receipts (he was entitled to two-thirds), and Rich accused him of pocketing £450, over and above, which had been given to him as presents. He was fully entitled to do so, the money was given to him in appreciation of his work by a gratified public. Rich had no sort of claim on it—which did not prevent him trying to get a share. Betterton's salary had never exceeded £4 a week. He was one of the finest actors and most upright, honest men who ever lived. He had been provident too, but lost his savings in a commercial venture, recommended by a friend. He bore no ill-will, and although the friend, also ruined, committed suicide, Betterton adopted the orphaned daughter and brought her up as his own. His second Benefit—the one at the King's House—killed him. He was suffering terribly with gout, which had so inflamed his foot that he could not get on his boot. Rather than not appear before his public who were honouring him, he thrust his foot into cold water to bring down the swelling, got into his boots, and played as he had never played before. But the shock was too much at his age (he had turned seventy), and although he got through the performance he died very shortly after. Queen Anne granted his widow a pension. He and his wife were a model and devoted couple and she did not survive him for long.

It was customary for the other players to forgo their salaries on Benefit Nights, thus from the earliest days theatrical people have been in the forefront of charitable work. Beneficiaries would write to all the great players begging them to appear, and seldom got refused. Why Quin and Munden refused has been chronicled.

Those were exceptions. Anne Oldfield was another who was not easy about Benefits. If she appeared in support, she always expected —and got—her salary. It is certain that the players having a Benefit always made more out of the gifts than the takings.

There are some curious instances of the touting for custom. Bickerstaffe, the author, was unable to work for his own Benefit on one occasion. A bill was issued from Drury Lane Theatre which stated "Bickerstaffe, being confined to his bed by lameness, and his wife lying now dead, has nobody to wait on the Quality and his friends for him, but hopes they'll favour him with their appearance". That sad plea filled the house and Bickerstaffe's pockets. He wrote many of the libretti for the operas of Dibdin.

Ryan, the friend and benefactor of Quin, when he was shot in the throat by the footpad, had it announced in the *Daily Post* that "it was uncertain if he could ever act again, and hoped that his friends would excuse him for not making personal application to them". His jawbone was shattered as well as his throat being damaged. They rolled up in their hundreds. But the public liked these personal applications—actors were not respectable in those days, or not considered so—and were therefore doubly attractive. It was quite a thrill to have one come around, to ask for a favour. It gave play-goers a sense of their own importance and they felt like lordly patrons giving of their largesse to these less fortunate people. They reacted according to their natures; but they were always very curious to see the actor and actress and would discuss them afterwards. What the players said about their patrons amongst themselves can be imagined. Those who want a first-hand picture of this soliciting aid for Benefits in the early 19th century, should read Dickens' *Nicholas Nickleby*, where that great man sets it forth clearly and without exaggeration.

Everyone in the Theatre took Benefits. It was not confined to the players, the management had them. That curious character E. T. Smith, who will enter this chronicle later, took Benefits when lessee of Drury Lane. He did not, it is true, go round personally and beg for support but he sent a circular. One of them said:

"I beg most respectfully to intimate that the Winter Season will terminate on Saturday 25th and that My Benefit is fixed for Thursday, March 21st, 1854, on which occasion Mr. G. V. Brooke will appear in one of his great characters, in addition to other Artists of distinction, who have volunteered for the occasion. The honour of your patronage is requested. In order to prevent confusion to my numerous friends, and have them

accommodated, the favour of your informing me at once, by
returning the enclosed, the number of Private Boxes, Stalls or
Tickets you desire to be reserved, will oblige your very obedient
servant, E. T. Smith."

He went in for popular prices for his Benefit. Dress Circle, 4s.;
Upper Circle 3s.; Stalls 5s.; and Private Boxes £3 3s.; £2 2s.;
£1 11s. 6d., and £1 1s. The 'enclosed' referred to was a booking-slip
on which particulars of requirements could be filled in. The prompter
(who was stage manager) had a Benefit, so did the master carpenters,
the wardrobe mistresses and even the box-office managers. Again, it
was not charity, but regarded as part of their salaries—much as the
Easter Offering in churches is the perquisite of the incumbent.
Madame Violetti—or Violette (it was spelt both ways)—who afterwards married David Garrick, had a Benefit on 11th February, 1747.
As it was also a Royal Command Night, she did very well. The
play was *The Careless Husband*, with a cast which included Cibber,
Delaine, Mills and Mrs. Mills, Miss Bennett, Kitty Clive and Peg
Woffington—an all-star cast indeed. Madame or Mlle Violetti was a
dancer, so she had to be accommodated. Nothing easier. In went
some dances performed by Salomon, Cooke and the lady herself, all
of the greatest eminence in their line. The boxes were 5s., that
meant 5s. per seat therein, and the pit 3s.; no stalls existed then, and
eight rows of the pit were railed off to form boxes and servants were
allowed to keep places in the pit and on the stage. Their employers
were asked to have them there by three o'clock in the afternoon.
There was no other way of reserving seats. No doubt Mlle Violetti
did very well. Seats were always sold on the stage for Benefits, and
sold well, also people were allowed to stand thereon and in the
wings. The last time Quin played Falstaff at Ryan's Benefit he had
to fight his way through about 200 of the public before he could
make his entrance.

There was a Benefit at Drury Lane on 27th February, 1747,
which is not without interest. It was on behalf of Signora Padonana.
She was a dancer too. The play was *The Merchant of Venice*, with
Macklin as Shylock and Kitty Clive as Portia. Then there was a
dancing interlude performed by the signora, also Salomon, Violetti
and others. The announcement is interesting:

"Signora Padonana, being utterly unacquainted with the
English language, and without any personal friendships here to
recommend and encourage her, as she has always endeavour'd
to please the Town to the utmost of her power, entirely depends

on the known Candour and Benevolence of this Nation and humbly hopes for the indulgence of the public this night."

Doubtless she got it.

At a Benefit for Kitty Clive on 7th March, 1747—Benefits came thick and fast it will be observed—it was announced that "servants will be allowed to keep places on the stage, which will be divided into front and side boxes and so commodiously enclosed as to prevent the Ladies taking cold". A very wise precaution, as anyone accustomed to old theatres—and even modern ones—will appreciate. Nowadays Drury Lane has special heating arrangements for its stage, but mostly they are cold, draughty places. Sometimes Benefits were taken *en bloc* by the smaller fry, as on 8th May, 1747, at Drury Lane—"for the Benefit of Peacopp, Emberton, Dunbar, Beresford and Steele".

To show how widespread was this Benefit business, on 9th May, 1748, there was one for Gray and Jones (box-office keepers), Beresford (box-keeper), Atkinson (pit door-keeper) and Goodwin (what he did was not specified). Even the musical director, in this case Thomas Arne, had a Benefit. Nobody was left out. On 16th May, 1748, the beneficiaries were Dunbar (box-keeper—there were several of these officials whose job it was to conduct people to their seats in boxes), Warner and Foley (box lobby keepers), Prichard (upper gallery office keeper) and Saunders (stage-door keeper). Prichard had the worst job of these good folk, for the upper gallery was a most unruly place. 'Running footmen' and the servants who kept the seats for the Quality were allowed up there free and always misbehaved until Garrick withdrew the privilege from them. Box-office keepers today deserve a Benefit but nobody thinks of them. Richard Tauber did so, however, for the first thing he did when he came to Drury Lane was to go and shake hands with the men in the box-office. "They take the money," he said.

There was a recognized scale as regards Benefits. There was what was known as a 'Clear Benefit'. That was given to prominent players only. It meant that they had the entire receipts, no charge being made for the theatre or expenses. There was 'Half a Clear Benefit', which meant they got half the takings (and all they got on the 'side' of course), a 'Third Clear Benefit', when a third of the proceeds was theirs. And there was just 'A Benefit', which gave them the proceeds left over after charging rent for the theatre and all expenses. Those charges varied according to the period and the theatre. In the days of the Triumvirate at Drury Lane (in the reign of Queen Anne, the Triumvirate being Colley Cibber, Robert Wilks and Thomas Doggett—the latter replaced by Barton Booth)—the expenses charged against Benefits were £34. Under Garrick they rose to £64 and later they became much higher. For all that time the cost of living was rising and the value of money decreasing. There was often trickery over Benefits but just as often honesty and generosity. Much depended on the character and views of the manager and lessee of the theatre. Robert William Elliston, who once ran Drury Lane, called himself—not without cause—'The Great Lessee'. He had his own ideas about contracts and Benefits and here is a verbatim quotation from one, which may be of interest, if not to the general public, then to Members of Equity:

"The Contract is between Robert William Elliston, of Theatre Royal Drury Lane and William Henry Williams, of 41, Lancaster Street, Burton Crescent, St. Pancras. The term of the agreement is for two years commencing on the 1st October 1822 and the salary payable to the Actor is the weekly sum of Five Pounds and he is bound by all sorts of conditions and penalties. It is agreed that provided Williams shall have done his duty, but *not otherwise*, he

"Shall be allowed the use of the Theatre for One Benefit Night in every season during the said term, to perform there one such play or Opera, and one Burletta or Ballet, or Farce or Musical Afterpiece to be chosen out of the common Stock List of acting plays, except any new Piece or Revised Piece, produced during the Season, in which the Benefit shall be taken, as he shall fix upon such Night, as to the priority and order thereof to be named and assigned by the Manager for the time being of the said Theatre, and according to the usage observed in the London Theatres; the said William Henry Williams first paying to the Treasurer for the time being of the said Theatre, the sum of Two HUNDRED GUINEAS for such use of the said Theatre, exclusive of extra charges for new Dresses, copying, printing, advertising and supernumeraries and other incidental charges, if any there be.

"Providing always in case the said sum of Two Hundred Guineas, and the amount of such extra charges, shall not be paid previously to such Benefit Night, THEN IT IS HEREBY AGREED, by and between the said parties hereto, that it shall and may be lawful to and for the said William Elliston, his Executors, Administrators and Assigns, or the Treasurer for the time being, to stop and retain the said sum of Two Hundred Guineas, together with the amount of such extra charges, out of the Monies to be received on such Benefit Night at the Doors of the said Theatre. And in case the amount of the Monies so to be received shall not be sufficient to pay and defray the same, that then the deficiency shall be retained and made good by and out of the Weekly Salary due or to become due to the said William Henry Williams—and in case the amount of Salary shall not be sufficient, then the said William Henry Williams, his Executors, Administrators and Assigns shall and will be answerable for and pay the Deficiency on Demand to the said Robert William Elliston, his Executors, Administrators and Assigns; or if the said Robert William Elliston, his Executors, Administrators and Assigns shall think fit, give such reasonable security as may be demanded for the payment of Deficiencies that may be due on account of the said charges. . . ."

A lot of good it was going to be for poor William Henry Williams, on his £5 a week, to risk a Benefit! That is why several of them would club together to minimize the risk, and why poor Munden refused a Benefit when a stroller. How could an actor of that standing hope to put up two hundred guineas? How indeed could he hope to draw in even that sum for his Benefit? And what use would his executors, administrators and assigns be to Elliston in the way of security? If he risked a Benefit, he could never pay for its failure.

The actors in those days had a hard life and it is not surprising if they could not save and died in poverty. The rules and regulations which governed them in the Theatre were severe. They were all included as a special clause in the contract. For instance, they got fined for almost everything. The time of rehearsals was that shown by the clock in the Green Room, which timepiece governed their lives. Rehearsals, called for ten o'clock, began at ten minutes past, not another moment being allowed. Extra rehearsals were according to the call given by the prompter (stage manager). Anyone absent from a rehearsal was fined, and if his part consisted of one scene only and he or she missed it, still the full absence fine was exacted. There was a scale:

Salaries of Performers	First Scene in Play or Farce		Other Scenes in Play or Farce		Whole Rehearsal
Up to £1 10s. ..	1s. 0d.	..	6d.	..	2s. 0d.
„ „ £3 0s. ..	1s. 6d.	..	1s. 0d.	..	5s. 0d.
„ „ £5 0s. ..	2s. 0d.	..	1s. 6d.	..	7s. 0d.
„ „ £7 0s. ..	2s. 6d.	..	2s. 0d.	..	9s. 0d.
„ „ £9 0s. ..	3s. 0d.	..	2s. 6d.	..	11s. 0d.
£9 and above ..	4s. 0d.	..	3s. 6d.	..	£1 0s. 0d.

Anyone standing on the stage at rehearsal, unless concerned in the action of the scene, was fined half a crown. Anyone opening the stage door was fined 10s. (by stage door they probably mean the door leading directly from the stage to the corridors, or those leading through the proscenium); and it cost the same amount if they stood about in the wings or impeded the entrances. What is very interesting is that anyone not perfect in the words or music of a part and not rehearsing it without the book at the last or only rehearsal of any old play, opera or farce, was fined the proportion of being absent from rehearsal. Rule 9 was important too: "Anyone refusing to rehearse, study and perform any Character, or Part, or Prologue, or Epilogue or to assist in any Dance, Procession, Chorus, Mask, Pantomime, and other pieces and Entertainments at the appointment of the Manager, shall forfeit for such refusal £30—and nine nights' salary." One wonders what many modern actors would make of that?

Anyone 'off' for the night, when expected to perform, lost a week's salary, unless a doctor's certificate was produced.

Anyone 'drying up'—i.e., forgetting their lines—forfeited a night's salary. Everyone had three weeks' notice in which to advertise their Benefit, but anyone "sending an Advertisement to a Public Print, by any other hand than the Prompter's", forfeited One Week's Salary. That was a wise precaution and should be enforced today. Taking the Prompt Book or 'Harpsichord Book' away from the stage or out of the theatre cost the doer thereof 10s., and if written music was not returned before the close of each season it had to be paid for. Those engaged on a nightly salary—such as the supers—were still bound by these rules.

Rule 16 in the contract laid down a social precedent. It said: "Any Performer, whose salary shall amount to Five Pounds per week, will be entitled to enter the First Green Room." Those below that figure had a small poky room below the stage. And that rule was rigidly enforced. Anyone being away from any cause whatever lost the proportion of their salary for such absence. If the absence exceeded one month, the management had the right to cancel the contract.

And last but not least, was Rule 18, which said: "Any person who shall perform, assist or take a Benefit or any part thereof, at any other Theatre or place of Public Amusement, whether in Play, Opera, Farce, Burletta, Oratorio, Dance, Concert, or otherwise, without previous consent in writing, shall forfeit one week's salary and his or her engagement, at the option of the Management."

That clause, at Covent Garden, nearly got the great clown Grimaldi the sack.

The musicians—the orchestra—engaged in the theatre did not have things their own way. There was no Musicians' Union then, to lay down rules and enforce them, no custom of sending a deputy when playing elsewhere for personal profit. No: hard-and-fast rules were made by the management!

Their rehearsals, too, were bound by the Green Room clock and the prompter, on the same terms as the players. If they missed an entire rehearsal of a musical piece, it cost them 2s. 6d. If, through absence, they missed any incidental music or songs, they forfeited 6d., but if they missed an obbligato, it was 5s. a time. Absence from the First Music of the Evening—the overture—cost 1s., from anything else 6d. per piece, but in the case of opera, missing the overture meant the forfeit of 2s. 6d. and every obbligato, 5s. And absence from a performance, when expected to perform, meant the loss of a week's salary, and the liability to dismissal, unless a doctor's certificate was forthcoming. Discipline was strictly enforced by means of these fines—and fines continued customary in the theatre up to a very recent date.

The status of the player was low and he or she, unless they were great and famous, were under the thumb of the management. Some of the letters asking Elliston for jobs were rather pitiful. John Willmott writes, on 24th October, 1820:

"Sir,
                    Last season I had the honor of an interview with you respecting an opening part in the line of *Country Boys*. I now take the liberty of addressing you on the score of General Utility—for myself and Mrs. W. We should be happy to come a month upon trial—even without salary—as I am certain if persons have merit it will be discovered there, in even so trifling a character—for myself I can only say, I not only *can* but *would* do anything— Mrs. W. has a thorough knowledge of Music and will sing in choruses, etc.—I beg to refer you to Mrs. Ogier and Mr. T. Cooke for a description of our Abilities. I should be happy of an opportunity of an Interview, if convenient,"

and Mr. Willmott remained Mr. Elliston's obedient servant. They got their month's trial—without salary—and they got an engagement at £3—the two jointly. Two years afterwards there is another letter from Willmott, in which he says:

Friday, 14th June, 1822.
"Sir,
I received a note from Mr. Dunn this morning stating
you were willing to retain the services of myself and Mrs.
Willmott on the same terms as the last, for which I thank you—
at the same time I think it a duty I owe to myself not to accept
them. If you will make our Salary £3 10s. we shall be happy to
sign your Articles—less, I cannot take. . . ."

—and he still remains an obedient servant. One is happy to chronicle
that the Willmotts got their £3 10s.

There was a H. Sherenbeck, who had evidently written in for a
chance and been given one, for he wrote from Chatham:

"Sir,
I shall be in Town next week and will (if you please)
do myself the Honor of appearing on your Stage in the part you
have named, Abednigo in *The Jew and the Doctor*. Shall expect on
this occasion *no remuneration* and will attend to *Bell's Weekly
Paper*, and if on tomorrow Sunday I see the Farce advertised for
any night in the latter part of the ensuing week, will most
assuredly attend the Theatre in proper time the same morning
for rehearsal."

He signed himself 'Yours respectfully'. He was not quite so altruistic
as he seemed, for in a previous letter he had stipulated that his fare
should be paid and added "and if on Tryal I should have the good
fortune to meet with your and the public's approbation, we can then,
sir, negotiate for the future". On that occasion he was "with respect,
Yours to command". One wonders what Elliston—and the public—
thought about him.

Another man, poor fellow, wrote begging for a job and offering
himself, his wife and his two daughters—all excellent performers, he
protested—for the small salary of £5 per week for the lot. Elliston,
who always made a counter-offer, suggested £4, and the man took
it and sent a humble letter of thanks. There was a lady who wrote
from Axbridge in 1819, who after a very long preamble, stated that
although now married and comfortable, she had been accustomed
to the stage from infancy and had 'led the business' at some very
good provincial theatres. She was now twenty-three and her husband
was a man of some property. She said there was the sum of £100 for
which neither of them had much use at that moment; she offered it

to Elliston, free of interest, if he would let her 'come out' in 'third or fourth-line business' at Drury Lane. She did not wish to have leads right away, she said, because she had no desire to awaken envy in the other performers, but she might be very handy if any leading lady suddenly fell out. She said she knew that ladies in the lines for which she applied earned four or five pounds a week and Mr. Elliston would have to pay that to somebody, so why not her? She was quite certain of success. One would like to know the upshot; but there is no more about her to be discovered. But it was not like Elliston to refuse money. . . .

Those contracts and those letters show what the life of the players was like in the early 1800s and it was even worse before. What was there to hope for amongst the rank and file when they could no longer get work and could not afford Benefits anyway? Very often nothing but disaster. The Stage, all through its history, worked lavishly for charities. Garrick raised a large sum for the Lock Hospital and an even larger amount for the sufferers in a severe fire. But surely one of the most curious was a special performance in aid of 'a Young Lady, her Father having ruined himself in endeavouring to spread Christianity amongst the Esquimaux', and thousands of other causes—much more sensible than that. Does the Profession do anything for its own poor and needy? It does indeed, and has done for many years. In 1765 all Theatreland was horrified to hear that Mrs. Hamilton, a well-known actress, was, through no fault of her own, in a state of complete destitution. Help was soon forthcoming and Thomas Hull, an actor at Covent Garden, had a fine idea. He did not see why such cases should occur at all and it be left to casual charity to relieve them. He set to work, propounded a scheme, got supporters and founded a fund to meet such cases. He made it exclusive to those who worked at Covent Garden Theatre. Garrick was abroad at the time. When he returned and heard what had happened, he was furious that he had never been consulted. True he had nothing whatever to do with Covent Garden, but he was the undisputed Leader of the Stage. So he founded the Drury Lane Pension Fund. He went one better than Covent Garden. He got a special Act of Parliament authorizing it. He started the fund with £4,500 out of his own pocket and he worked for it unceasingly. The proceeds of his Farewell Performance went to it. It still exists and does splendid work. But it is exclusive to Drury Lane. But there are other theatrical charities now—the Actors' Benevolent Fund, the Actors' Orphanage, the Denville Home, Actors' Day, the Theatrical Ladies' Guild, the Green Room Rags, all run expertly and giving ceaselessly and splendid service. There is the King

Above : William Abingdon, then stage director of Drury Lane and still Secretary of the Drury Lane Fund, cutting the Baddeley Cake. In the picture are G. S. Melvin (Dame, left), Fay Compton (Principal Boy, right) and next to her Jack Edge. Extreme right is 'Jock' Prentice, for years the Drury Lane Musical Director. Top right, Moya Macqueen-Pope—playing Fairy Queen in *Babes in the Wood. Left :* Robert Baddeley in *The Clandestine Marriage*

The Hampstead Heath scene from Ivor Novello's *Careless Rapture*—a typical Drury Lane spectacular scene

George Pension Fund, which maintains pensions for deserving members of the Profession. Nobody works harder or more generously in these causes than Prince Littler, the Chairman of Drury Lane.

The original Covent Garden Fund is now administered by the Charity Commissioners. The income from the capital is given to three theatrical charities, one of which is the only charity of the Theatre to possess a Royal Charter and have the monarch for its patron—a privilege it has enjoyed through four reigns. This is the Royal General Theatrical Fund, founded in 1839. This exists not only for ordinary charitable purposes but to encourage thrift and saving amongst the members of the Profession. They join, they pay in an annual amount—a very modest one and according to their age and medical fitness—and, at the age of sixty, there is a pension for them for life. This Charity fights the failing so often applied to people of the Theatre—it teaches them not to be improvident, to save for a rainy day. It is administered by a small body of directors, which includes many people eminent in the Theatre, who give their services willingly and gratefully for such a cause. There are some curious facts about this fund, for it would seem that people, when they join it, take on a new lease of life and reach a ripe old age. Nonagenarians are amongst its annuitants. Some paid in £200 or £300 and drew out thousands as pension. It makes no great display, but it does wonderful work. It carries on in direct succession to that first Covent Garden Fund. Playgoers who are grateful to the actors and actresses for pleasure given to them by their acting, who cherish in their memories joyful thoughts of lovely evenings spent in that Land of Illusion, the playhouse, might do worse than show their gratitude by a little legacy to the Royal General Theatrical Fund, the oldest and the only Royal theatrical charity—which Charles Dickens worked so hard to help establish and which carries on today in difficult times, doing its best for those who have given so much enjoyment to others. It is really a wonderful cause for theatre-lovers to support and just as a sample of what it achieves: a pensioner who recently passed on had paid in £154 15s., and drawn, as pension, £2,138 9s. 9d. That is sensible, well-thought-out charity—and an encouragement to providence too.

But what of Robert William Elliston, of whom so much has been said? His full, colourful and remarkable career has been chronicled elsewhere. He was an excellent actor—he ran away from home to become one—a most astute manager—as has been shown—a tremendous optimist and a forceful showman. He extended his activities to the Provinces as well as London and did the most remarkable, if erratic, things. His desire for sensationalism often

G

got him into trouble, yet he always wriggled out. Once, at the Theatre Royal, Birmingham, he advertised the appearance of a Bohemian Giant of the most prodigious size and strength and listed a series of seemingly impossible feats this superman would perform. There was no such person, of course, but the credulous public filled the house. The public have always rushed to see (and to pay for the privilege) things which their own common sense must tell them could never happen. The Theatre Royal, Birmingham, was packed to see this entirely non-existent Bohemian Giant. There were other items on the bill, which the public endured, awaiting the arrival of the star turn. There was a nasty pause—and the curtain rose—disclosing not the monstrous Bohemian, but R. W. Elliston. He was nearly in tears; he spoke to them with a broken heart. The giant had let him down—he had not arrived (of course he had not). Elliston assured his now angry supporters that his disappointment was worse than theirs; he had been given the appearance of breaking faith! That, he swore, he never did! In proof of his *bona fides*, he produced an enormous stone with which the giant was said to juggle and a mighty chain which it was the big man's habit to tear asunder. "There, you see them," he said to that audience. "Those are what the giant uses. They could not be here if there was no giant. It proves I speak the truth." . . . And he got away with it!

He exploited Edmund Kean to the top of his bent; but he stood by him when the public would have driven the great actor from the Stage over the scandal of the Cox divorce suit. He had, incidentally, done his best to prevent Kean ever appearing at Drury Lane, before he—Elliston—had that theatre. He spent a fortune in redecorating and improving the theatre. He believed in Quality and in giving the best he could—even if his sense of showmanship ran away with him. He took over Drury Lane Theatre when it was, despite the triumphs of Kean, so far 'in the red' that the amateur committee of management—well-meaning men of no theatrical experience who controlled it—saw no hope at all. Several people were after the chance of running the famous theatre, including Edmund Kean himself. But Elliston got it. His proposal, which the committee accepted, was a tenancy of fourteen years, a promise to spend £7,000 on improvements in the building during that time, £8,000 in rent for the first year, £9,000 for the second and third, and £10,000 per annum for the rest of the tenancy. He got Drury Lane. At once he called himself 'The Great Lessee'. He set about making things hum at Old Drury—and he did. Super-optimistic always, nevertheless he did things well, or as well as a man of his temperament, given to overdoing it, could achieve.

It was a big theatre, so everything had to be big. Eventually he made friends with the disappointed Kean and he stunted him. He was about the only person who was ever able to dwarf Kean on the stage—and he did not do that personally but by means of the extraordinary effects which he introduced into *King Lear*—they were novel and new but overpowering. Even Kean could not cope with the storm as produced by 'The Great Lessee'. Elliston made money and spent it. He lived in great style at Stratford Place, Oxford Street, but he seldom got home before 3 a.m., and it was much more seldom that he was sober. Yet he loved Drury Lane and strove manfully for its success. He had his ups and downs. He made money and he lost it. He faced success and failure with coolness and resource. He fulfilled his obligations about what he would lay out on the place—he spent more than he contracted to do. He lived feverishly and he worked feverishly. Such a life takes a toll. He fell beneath a stroke, actually in Drury Lane in January 1823, but he recovered and fought on. He brought the stars there—like Macready. He brought every kind of show—for he was a true showman. He suffered severely in pocket and prestige when Kean's drunkenness brought about his downfall—but Elliston fought on. Everyone had pestered him, he was dunned for money, but somehow he kept afloat and never lost his confidence. Others let him down badly but still he worked in and for Drury Lane. In 1826 the blow fell. He had suffered many disasters—he was behind with his rent at Drury Lane. He owed them £5,500. He offered them security but the committee believed he had had his day. They dispossessed him of the great theatre. It was his bitterest moment, for he loved the place. He had paid, during his tenancy, over £66,000 in rent, he had spent over £30,000 on rebuilding and improvements—he built the portico over the front entrance amongst other things—he might have turned the corner, but he had no chance. Drury Lane cracked and broke him. But for all that he remains a pillar of the place to which he contributed so much. His cheery personality and smile remain in its atmosphere—his pluck has maybe helped it through many a difficulty since. Robert William Elliston, mercurial, clever, brilliant and erratic, is nevertheless strongly woven into the fabric of Old Drury. . . .

Nobody came forward to offer him a Benefit—he was the victim of Benefits forgot. . . .

CHAPTER SIX

Parlour-Maid and Pastry-Cook

SO FAR this record of those who have served Drury Lane has been almost exclusively masculine. That is because the Ladies of the Lane have had so much literature devoted to them. They are a glittering array—Nell Gwynne, the Marshalls, Bracegirdle, Barry, Woffington, Clive, Mrs. Pritchard, Susanna Maria Cibber, Jane Pope, Anne Oldfield, Mrs. Abington, Sarah Siddons, Mrs. Glover, Vestris—so many more. And this book attempts to chronicle those who are not so well known, but who did their share. There was a woman whose story was perhaps even more remarkable than any of those listed above but is not remembered by the majority. She certainly deserves her niche in the saga of Drury Lane, for there she cut a considerable figure. She came before the days of Elliston who appeared in the last chapter, so a step is now taken back in time—and her story will be unfolded. It should be noted that in her day—and indeed before her and long after—the great ones of the Theatre came from humble origins—they were definitely not ladies and gentlemen—they were not regarded as respectable—and therefore were far more attractive to the eyes of ordinary people. Neither of the two characters which appear in this chapter had any social standing before they came into the Theatre: one of them, Mrs. Powell, was the daughter of a sergeant in the Army and the other a pastry-cook, whose name was Robert Baddeley. Baddeley is remembered through his own shrewd act; Mrs. Powell almost entirely forgotten. May these words bring her some remembrance, for richly does she deserve it.

The Theatre is full of extraordinary people with extraordinary stories, but few of them are more extraordinary than that of Mrs. Powell, the Tragedy Queen. She has been blotted out of remembrance because of the greatness of Sarah Siddons, of whom she was a contemporary. Everyone has heard of Siddons but few of Powell, yet Mrs. Powell stood, in talent and glory, second only to the wonderful Sarah. She came from very low in the social scale and she rose to great eminence in her time. She touched the lowest depths and stood on the greatest heights; she knew degradation and also fame. If her entrance was obscure her exit was glorious. She was indeed a Pillar of Drury Lane.

She was born at Cranbrook, in Kent, and her name was Mary.

Her bad luck started at once for her mother died in giving her birth. Her father, a sergeant in the Army (which perhaps explains her predilection for redcoats), did the best he could for his daughter, which was not much, until she was eleven years old, when he married again. This was the second piece of bad luck for little Mary. Her stepmother disliked her heartily, let her run wild and gave her no schooling at all. The girl became a mere drudge, quite illiterate, but very pretty. This may also have displeased her stepmother, for when the girl was sixteen she was turned out of her home. Doubtless her father was away on service; perhaps he had been killed. He did nothing for his daughter, anyway, and no more is known of him. His daughter was thrown out on to the world to do the best or the worst she could with her life. She found work at an inn. She had no references, but her pretty face and figure were enough. She was a good and willing worker, always cheerful, and for a year she gave every satisfaction to her employer, the lady who ran the inn. Some military were then quartered in the district, and a young officer, coming for refreshment, saw Mary and fell in love with her. His handsome face, gallant bearing—and his red coat—soon made a conquest of the girl—and to her, as to so many more, a uniform was irresistible.

The young couple decided to run away together. His regiment was being moved elsewhere and they could not bear to leave each other. Mary was to steal out of the inn at midnight and meet him. Her mistress got to hear of it and was in no mood to lose such a good servant. So, on the night of the elopement, she took away and hid the girl's scanty store of clothing. When the ardent young thing leapt from her bed to run off, she found that all she had was the tattered nightgown in which she stood—not at all the sort of thing in which she could travel with her soldier boy. She was utterly helpless; being entirely illiterate, she had no means at all of communicating with her lover, then waiting at the tryst. Nor was there anybody who could take a message. So the troops moved off, and she was left lamenting. It brought home to her the iniquity of her stepmother's refusal to invest in her the twopence a week which was then the price of education at the village school. She now realized what it meant to be unable to read or write. Her real strength of character asserted itself. She resolved she would teach herself the mysteries of reading and writing. She got hold of a tattered copy of Milton's *Paradise Lost*, and by means of that she taught herself to read and write. The beauties of Milton's verse so entranced her that it became an inspiration to her throughout life. But that was all later—at the moment the paramount necessity was getting away and finding her lover. She watched her chance, and a month after her romance had been so rudely interrupted she managed to escape. After almost incredible difficulties, and with hardly a penny in her pocket, she managed to reach her soldier. He was overjoyed to see her and they lived together very happily indeed until he was ordered abroad. She never saw him again.

Employment was once more necessary. She entered domestic service and somehow got a situation in Chatham Place, Blackfriars, as a kind of house-parlourmaid. She remained there for two years and during that time something of great import happened to her. She became a playgoer. She got badly stage-struck. She haunted the upper gallery of Drury Lane. To become an actress was now her ambition. When she came back from the play she had learnt it nearly all by heart. She insisted on giving excerpts in the kitchen and she held the other two servants, the cook and the kitchen-maid, spellbound. As she worked about the house she recited great speeches from the drama. Her mistress remonstrated with her but was told she ought to be grateful for the opportunity of listening to Art. Mary must have been a good worker, for she was not discharged, either for her persistent reciting or for impertinence. She acted all the time.

Then, one night, her Fate came upon her again. She had been to Drury Lane and there she had witnessed a performance of *The Grecian Daughter*, by Arthur Murphy. It carried her away—she was transported out of mundane things—she walked in the illusion of the Theatre—she was no longer Mary the maid—she was the Grecian Daughter. She determined her fellow servants must participate in her joy. In the kitchen she staged a makeshift version of the tragedy and she pressed the cook into the part of the villain. The performance was carried on with zest. The kitchen resounded to declamation, yells, entreaties, shrieks and groans. The noise was so great that her master and mistress, alarmed by the racket, rushed down to the kitchen to see what could possibly be the matter.

They found the cook, a tall, brawny Yorkshirewoman, on whom had been thrust the role of Dionysus, lying prostrate on the ground, screaming and groaning. Over her stood Mary, as the Grecian Daughter, brandishing a ladle, which was doing duty as a dagger (it is a good thing she had not used a real knife or tragedy might really have invaded that kitchen). So carried away had she been that she had struck the cook a hearty blow and felled her. The remaining servant, a little kitchen-maid, looked on, torn between fear, admiration and excitement.

There was a first-class row. Both the amateur histrions were told never to do it again. The cook promised willingly enough, and was quite genuine about it. Her first experience of acting had been pretty painful. But Mary had other views. She was right off her balance. She had done with service; for her now it was the Stage or nothing. She 'got her notice'—she did not care, such a slight setback was nothing. Before her lay, she was sure, Drury Lane and all its glory. But of course it did not turn out like that. She had no introduction to the playhouses, and nobody was likely to listen to a discharged housemaid. Her reference would not be a good one. She must live whilst she battered on the gates of the strongholds of the Drama.

So the redcoats came into her life again. She ran off with a sergeant, who was quartered at Coxheath Camp. She took the name of Mrs. Farmer. She became laundress to the sergeant's company. She was so pretty and so attractive that she appears to have wrought as much havoc amongst the redcoats as they wrought upon her. The officers began to take notice of this good-looking, smiling girl. She rose from the ranks. She graduated from the sergeant to a subaltern, and from him to a captain. The captain was mightily smitten. He brought her up to London, and installed her in excellent lodgings, where they lived together in a most expensive and extravagant manner, in a style to which she most certainly had never been accustomed. She had fine dresses and fallals, she rode in coaches, she knew what the feel of silk and satin meant. It was all wonderful to the little orphan. But she never forgot the Stage and very diligently she pursued her studies in reading and writing. She could do both now, thanks to Milton—and was able to buy printed copies of plays and learn much of them by heart. Then disaster befell her again. The captain either ran out of funds or got tired of the persistent reciting indulged in by his inamorata and of being made her 'stooge' in scenes from plays—for he went off without a word and left her without a penny.

She was again thrown on her own resources—which consisted entirely of her pretty face and figure. With no character or reference she could not get back into domestic service, nor indeed did she desire so to do. There was only one course open to her. She became what is known as 'a Lady of the Town', and by that means she lived for some time—indeed, she did well. But she still kept up her reciting.

One gentleman who interested himself in her was struck by her talent in that direction. He thought she would shine on the Stage, and Mary was quite certain that he was right. This man had influence in the Theatre. He introduced her to John Colman the Elder, manager of the Haymarket Theatre. Colman, to oblige his friend, gave her an audition and he was much impressed. He offered her an engagement. Now, with her dream actually dawning into realization, she became panic-stricken. She was no fool, and she knew her own weaknesses: her lack of refinement, her lack of education, her complete lack of experience as regards the Stage. But here was a chance indeed. She reflected that everyone had to make a start—and so must she if her overpowering ambition was ever to be realized. She suppressed her fears and told Mr. Colman she would be very honoured to play at the Haymarket Theatre. So, in the year 1787, John Colman presented her to the public there as Alicia in *Jane Shore*, that famous old drama.

She rehearsed for it—although rehearsals were scant and scrappy then. She was word-perfect in the part. The night came and, trembling and afraid, she went on the stage and faced her audience. She started very nervously and uncertainly, as might be expected. But she warmed up, confidence came to her, and in the second act, in her big scene with Hastings, she was so magnificent that there was immense enthusiasm. Excited playgoers were saying here was a rival to Mrs. Siddons herself. If this new woman was as good as this in an early scene what would she be like when the really big moments came?—and there was a hush of expectancy when those moments arrived. But that was the trouble. Mary had shot her bolt. Her complete lack of technique had betrayed her. She had given all she had far too early—she had expended full force on scenes which did not require it. And when the climax came she could not compass it. She had reached her zenith too soon. The expectant audience was disappointed and chilled. She felt the atmosphere come across to her; she heard the rustle of a crowd she had failed to grip, failed to sway. She did not know how to recover—she began to get nervous again and she almost went to pieces. She fumbled the big moments, she even cut out speeches because of her loss of control. The good beginning was erased in the feeble, tottering end. She even omitted one scene altogether in her panic. It might have been complete disaster for her, but she had done enough early on to show promise and to cause Colman to congratulate her heartily when the curtain fell. That astute man, who knew his business, was satisfied with the début. He could see what this girl would become, given experience and guidance. But she, who had failed herself, who felt that she had betrayed her own trust in herself, brushed aside his praise and would have none of it. She had not satisfied herself; she considered herself a failure. Always frank in all circumstances, she told Colman that she had murdered the part and would never tread the boards again. She left the Haymarket well nigh broken-hearted.

But she was young and resilient. She went over and over that part in her own mind, dissecting her performance, realizing where she had gone wrong, and profiting by the brief experience of even one performance. She was intelligent, she had felt audience reaction —and now she knew where she had failed, of what errors in judgment and attack she had been guilty. She resumed her rehearsing, she resumed her studies of the Drama, and all the time she plied her own trade. That protector of hers who had taken her to the Haymarket must have had considerable affection for and faith in her, for at the end of a year he prevailed on her to see Colman again. She went to see him and found him very pleased to see her and perfectly agreeable to her attempting Alicia again. She screwed up her courage to the sticking point. She worked hard and she remembered what had happened before. She recalled her precipitancy, her loss of power because of over-anxiety. She determined not to make the same mistake twice.

The house was full when, once again, she stepped on the Haymarket stage. This time she made no mistake. She played magnificently—as if she had years of experience behind her. She moved the audience to enthusiasm and she took her success much more calmly than she had taken her defeat. She was a woman of character, even if she had not one which would get her a job.

She played regularly at the Haymarket and gained useful knowledge. Her gentleman friend was delighted with her and his own judgment. He never rested until he got her an engagement at Theatre Royal, Drury Lane, itself. And there she was a very successful actress. She became a 'Lane' favourite—especially popular when Sarah Siddons was not playing. Indeed, as tragedienne, she ranked second only to Sarah herself.

John Philip Kemble, star and manager of Drury Lane and Mrs. Siddons' brother, saw her value too, although he may not have been too pleased at her close approach in popularity to his sister. He was interested in the theatre at Liverpool, and he sent her there to play leading roles for a season, at a time when Powell, who was Prompter (stage director) at Drury Lane, was in charge of the stage there as well. It was a summer season, 'The Lane' was closed, so Powell was free to go and take control and report back to Kemble of what happened, how things went, who was playing well, who not giving satisfaction. Powell fell in love with Mary and she returned his affection. But, being a very straightforward and honest woman, despite her period of street-walking, she told him the whole of her past life, keeping nothing back at all, making not the slightest reservation. Instead of being disgusted, Powell was filled with admiration for this pretty and talented woman who had such candour and honesty of purpose. He considered that hers was a strong character and likely to make a good wife. He swept aside her past and they married. For years they lived in perfect harmony and happiness. She had left her old life entirely behind her. She was now Mrs. Powell, Tragedy Queen of Drury Lane, second only to Siddons in public estimation. She and Powell separated after many years and she divorced him. There was no bad blood. It was a question of financial difficulties which had arisen, and his was the fault. They never bore each other any animosity—indeed they remained friends. She married again, a Mr. Renard, but she kept the name of Mrs. Powell.

She was now a beautiful woman of majestic figure and bearing. If her face was not classical in feature, it was expressive and full of charm. She had a lovely, mellow voice, not very powerful but flexible, capable of many tones and full of music. Her diction was perfect. As an actress, her great gift was sincerity. She always appeared to feel and to mean what she said, as if expressing her own emotions. She was especially good as Portia and as Euphresia in *The Grecian Daughter*—what a thrill she must have had when she first played that part professionally and remembered that performance in the Blackfriars kitchen which had been the start of so much. She was excellent as Milwood in *George Barnwell* and one of the best Queen Gertrudes in *Hamlet* the Stage has ever seen. Many actresses dislike this part, but Mrs. Powell liked to play it—and performed it as it should be performed, as a lustful, sex-ridden trollop—which is what Shakespeare meant her to be. She was one of the first women to play Hamlet—in which she succeeded. She always played it at her Benefits. Charles Lamb, no mean judge, leaves us a picture of her as Olivia in *Twelfth Night*: "She touched the imperious, fantastic humour of the character with nicety. Her imperious person filled the scene."

Indeed, she was a curious woman and had a most eventful life. Her second marriage, to Renard, was a very happy one. This woman, whose early life had been so irregular, yet made an excellent wife. She and Powell had been happy until financial disasters overtook him in which he did not wish to involve her and let her have the marriage dissolved—which shows in what esteem he held her. Renard was not in 'The Profession' but they got along very well. Whether she told him all about her early life, as she had told Powell, is not on record. But she probably did for there would have been many ready to do so if she had not.

In the fullness of time she retired from the Stage. She was an excellent hostess and loved to entertain. Her invitations were sought for eagerly. She was a brilliant conversationalist, far removed from that illiterate girl at the inn, for she could talk on any subject with intelligence, wit and understanding. She died in 1831, and her age was believed to be seventy. She had travelled a long, rough and eventful road from the outcast orphan to the Tragedy Queen of Drury Lane—but frankness, sincerity, concentration and courage had brought her through.

Hers was an extraordinary career, full of incidents hard to match in fiction. But perhaps the oddest of all happened to her at Drury Lane one night when she was playing there. There was a full and excited house. People of the very greatest distinction and importance were 'in front'. Not only the audience but the players were agog— for this was even more exciting than a Royal Visit. The play began and on to the stage swept Mrs. Powell in all the glory of her theatrical queenship. She glanced at the Royal Box which the distinguished visitors were occupying. And what she saw made her gasp. For sitting there was the nation's darling, Lord Nelson, and beside him —yes—the little kitchen-maid who had watched Mrs. Powell in that kitchen at Blackfriars on the night she got the sack. That kitchen-maid was now Lady Hamilton. There she sat, like a queen, beside her beloved hero, and there on the stage was Mrs. Powell, a Queen of Old Drury. What a meeting for two domestic servants—for whom the years had brought about such changes—one of the strangest things which have ever happened in the history of that ancient theatre, which is full of odd things. . . . And what was the play on this occasion? Why—*The Grecian Daughter*. . . .

One hopes that, to make it complete, the cook was sitting in the gallery.

Mrs. Powell deserves her niche in the colonnade of Drury Lane.

Her companion in this chapter is not less remarkable, for he too shows what courage, a firm conviction and determination will do.

When the memory of many famous actors has passed away, one Thespian will still be remembered every year, on Twelfth Night, the 6th of January. A few paragraphs will appear in the newspapers, a picture or two, of a man in evening dress cutting a cake, whilst around him stands His or Her Majesty's Company of Comedians, the company playing at Drury Lane at that particular time. It has happened now for 160 years, and unless an atom bomb wipes out Drury Lane, or the theatre falls so low that Covent Garden Market absorbs it, as once it nearly did, a man in evening dress will carry out that ceremony for many centuries to come; he will cut the cake, and tell the company the story of Robert Baddeley, who will thus have his moment of remembrance. It was what he set out to get for himself and he has succeeded. His idea was that he should always be remembered by succeeding generations of players at Drury Lane. Perhaps he did not realize that his name would be 'news' for centuries. Or did he? There is no knowing, but Robert Baddeley was a remarkably astute publicist in his own lifetime and was probably determined on some form of immortality. He got it. A very good actor, but not a great one, he would have been forgotten long ago—his name just lingering in certain books, on some old playbills as the actor who created the part of Moses in *The School for Scandal*. Even then he would have struck no resounding chord. But Mr. Baddeley desired to be remembered. He was consumed by two great forces—his intense love of Drury Lane Theatre and his just as intense love of personal publicity. He wedded the one idea to the other and he got his heart's desire. Pretty good for a man who started life as a pastry-cook and ended up a leading actor and a wealthy one at that.

He was born in London, although the exact place of his birth is unknown. Nothing about his parents is on record but he makes his entrance as a pastry-cook in the kitchens of Lord North, that sleepy statesman of unhallowed memory who succeeded in losing the United States of America as part of the British Empire. Evidently Baddeley did not think much of his service for he left him and was employed in a similar capacity by Samuel Foote, the English Aristophanes, that man of mordant wit and superb mimicry, who cared little for the feelings of his fellow men but who loved the Theatre and made the gracious Haymarket Theatre famous and got it a Royal Charter. As pastry-cook to Foote, Baddeley was naturally much about the theatre. He spent his leisure behind the scenes; like many another man he got stage-struck. He wanted to exchange the floor-boards of the kitchen for the more public boards of the stage. So great a hold did his desire get upon him that one evening he presented himself before his employer and asked to be either raised or lowered in status (the choice can be taken) from that of cook to that of actor. This momentous interview took place at Drury Lane, where Foote was playing for a season, as he often did when the great David Garrick was away. The interview can be imagined. The respectful bowing figure of Baddeley the cook, asking his unusual favour, soliciting the chance of being a mummer from the lolling, impertinent figure of Foote, seated in temporary majesty in Garrick's dressing-room. One can imagine the acid, biting comments of that master of sarcasm on his servant's request. But that cook was a Cockney, with all the determination and tenacity of that race.

He stood his ground, as sticky as his own pastry, as hard of purpose as his piecrusts were light. His own mind was made up. Anyone who has ever endeavoured to turn a would-be actor from his ambition will realize that even the barbed shafts of Foote's bitter tongue fell blunted from the armour of Baddeley's high resolve. So Foote tried another course. "All right," he said, "I don't understand you. You are a good cook—why do you want to be a bad actor? Think it over, Baddeley, my boy, think it over, for a year. If you are still of the same mind then, come back here and I'll give you a job. But at the moment go back to the kitchen and see that I have something good for supper."

Baddeley bowed, and went out. He returned to his kitchen for the last time. Foote's remarks rankled a little. He would not be a bad actor, of that he was certain. But he decided not to do anything in a rush. He would take that year—and gain experience—he would wipe out the pastry-cook and become something else. He would enlarge his mind by travel. He saw an advertisement from a young gentleman about to make the Grand Tour of Europe, who wanted a valet. Baddeley applied. He had never been a valet but his manner and address were such that he got the job. He went abroad with that young gentleman and was a very good valet indeed. He probably gave a performance as a valet. He is said to have had a small business of his own, which he sold. It is likely, for he was a good man of business. Abroad with his new employer he made the best use of his time. He found that he had the gift of tongues and he picked up a very useful smattering of French, German, Spanish and Italian. He spoke them with a perfect accent—there showed the actor—and he had the actor's retentive ear and keen observation.

Shortly before the end of that year for reflection he returned. He had money in his pocket, he was well dressed, and his manners were perfect—perhaps a little too perfect, perhaps slightly more of the 'gentleman's gentleman' than the gentleman himself. But he was always dignified and impressive. He was waiting for the actual day when he must present himself and again request permission to be an actor. He strolled around the Town, he visited the playhouses and the resorts—and he fell in love. He met a young lady, very pretty, very charming, very gay, extremely good company and gifted with a delightful singing voice. She was Miss Snow, daughter of a State Trumpeter to His Majesty King George III. Baddeley was a man of resolution and action. He laid siege to the fair one, he swept her off her feet, and in a remarkably short space of time she surrendered. They were married. His joy was almost complete—not quite: for he still had to become an actor.

The fateful day came round. Punctually at the end of the year Robert Baddeley presented himself at the stage door at Theatre Royal, Drury Lane, and sent in his name to Foote, who was playing there again. He described himself as Mr. Robert Baddeley, an actor of foreign parts, being perhaps the first actor deliberately to type himself. Foote remembered all about it, saw him, laughed at him and, for a joke, engaged him. But the laugh was on Foote, for Baddeley turned out to be a good actor. He specialized in parts requiring a foreign accent and in Jewish parts, though he was not a Jew. He did so well that when Garrick returned Baddeley became one of His Majesty's Company of Comedians. He then brought along his wife. Her charm, beauty and voice soon convinced the management that this was a discovery. Both of them now appeared at Drury Lane. But Baddeley showed his business acumen. By this time he probably had an inkling of his wife's character. He contracted with the management that her salary should be paid to him. Mrs. Baddeley soon became a favourite with the Town. Some adored her singing, some her acting, but most of them thought she was the loveliest person they had seen for many a year.

The lady had not a strong power of resistance. Her surrender to Baddeley had been pretty quick, but her surrender to the joys of being one of the main Toasts of the Town and all that it meant was even quicker. Gentlemen of title competed for her favours and found them easy to come by. She had no lack of admirers—and would confer her smiles and something more exciting on the male members of the company if no noble lord, marquis or baronet happened to be about. Meanwhile Baddeley made steady progress in his various roles. He was aware of what his wife was up to and was also aware that there was little he could do about it. She was, it appeared, of the very easiest of easy virtue. He had made a bad bargain, it seemed, so he must make the best of it. He was not going to be the loser. There were rows in the Green Room over his insistence on receiving her salary. That and the fact that his wife's goings-on were a Green Room scandal led to their dismissal from Drury Lane. But not for long. Baddeley was too good and sound an actor for that. His wife, too, by her notoriety, brought much money into the theatre. The management decided, as many have done before and since, that the private affairs of the Baddeleys were no concern of theirs. So the couple were re-engaged.

Their bickering stopped. Baddeley took on a new pose. He now became the defender of his wife's honour—and of course of his own. At the mere mention of his wife's name in connection with another actor he would at once challenge that man to a duel. It was known that he and his wife were very self-detached; but Baddeley decided that in the theatre at least he should keep his honour unsmirched. It was no use his challenging a gentleman or a nobleman. They would not have fought such a low rank of life as an actor. The actors, knowing Baddeley to be a man of his word, now began to give his wife a pretty wide berth. But one did not—no less a person than George Garrick, the great David's brother, who went in fear of his mighty brother but was his faithful servant. Imagining that he would be secure, he did indeed dally with Mrs. Baddeley. Instantly the pastry-cook actor called George Garrick 'out'. What could George do but accept? He appealed to David, who washed his hands of the affair. Consequently one morning at dawn they repaired to Hyde Park. Baddeley was no mean swordsman, George Garrick, trained as a lawyer, had little liking for cold steel or chill, fresh morning air. But there he and Baddeley stood, in their shirts and breeches, the guilty lover and the outraged husband. The swords clashed, there was a scream, and from the bushes dashed the beautiful Mrs. Baddeley. Her disordered dress, her flowing hair, her air of alarm and terror only added to her charms. She threw herself on her knees before her husband, dashing aside the swords, probably to George Garrick's immense relief. Passionately she begged pardon. She exonerated Garrick—it was mere idle chatter, she maintained, spread by malicious people. She knew she had often erred and been guilty, but not this time. Would Robert have the blood of an innocent man on his hands because of her former escapades? She wept and she wailed, there were floods of tears—and a very good performance. Robert Baddeley was touched. He extended his hand and raised his wanton wife to her feet. He kissed her brow in forgiveness. Then he extended his right hand to the now perspiring but hopeful George, who grasped it eagerly. There was a general reconciliation. It was chocolate—or something stronger—for three. Everyone was in happy and friendly mood. Somehow this all got into the public prints and redounded greatly to the credit of Robert Baddeley. That was not the only occasion on which such a thing happened. And the newspapers always got the story.

But Baddeley tired of this troublesome wife of his and she left him. He did not care. She got into debt and became too pressing and insistent in her demands on her male friends. Her admirers began to shun her. She was reduced to poverty. Arrest for debt was imminent. She fled to Scotland to evade it, and there this fair but frail woman died—of an overdose of laudanum. It may have been an accident. Or she may have preferred the quick way out of a life of hopeless poverty. . . .

Baddeley steadily pursued his career. He was now a regular member of His Majesty's Company of Comedians at Theatre Royal, Drury Lane. The old privilege of their wearing the Royal Livery, granted by the Patent, had died out—except in respect of the footmen of the theatre. Baddeley revived it. He always wore the Royal Livery and was the last actor so to do. Today, however, the footmen at 'The Lane' still wear it.

He was a very painstaking actor and always in work. When Drury Lane closed for the summer he played at the Haymarket. And often he would appear in Marylebone Gardens, then a popular pleasure resort, where he gave a one-man show, a running commentary on current events enlivened with excellent mimicry of celebrities. He called it 'The Modern Magic Lantern'. But it was Drury Lane that Baddeley loved, as does everyone who works there. There he was a person well esteemed. His salary was £12 a week, a considerable sum then. His knowledge of business and financial affairs caused Garrick to place him on the Committee of the Drury Lane Fund when it was first founded in 1774. Baddeley loved that job.

He was a popular performer and his character studies were first-rate. Perhaps he was at his very best as Canton, the Swiss doctor, in *The Clandestine Marriage*. It was said that his shrug of the shoulders was the most eloquent on the Stage. But his creation of Moses in *The School for Scandal* is his best-remembered part. It was a *tour de force*. It was when he was making up for that character at one of the many repeats of that immortal play that he was stricken down in the dressing-room by his fatal seizure. They carried him to his house in New Store Street off Tottenham Court Road, but he died before reaching there. In that house he had established a 'lady friend', Catherine Strickland, who passed as Mrs. Baddeley, but he never married her. He died that November night, in 1794, one of the old school, and another link with Garrick was severed. He was buried in the Church of St. Paul, Covent Garden, the Actors' Church.

But that was not the end of Robert Baddeley by a long chalk. He left a will, a lengthy document of some seventy pages. He had a good deal to leave and there were many bequests. One was "to my faithful friend and companion, Mrs. Catherine Strickland, generally called and known by the name of Baddeley, a life interest in my house in New Store Street and in my freehold messuage, garden, etc., at Moulsey, in Surrey". After her decease, "the above estates, with certain monies to arise from the insurance of an annuity, to go to the society established for the relief of indigent persons belonging to Drury Lane Theatre. The house and premises at Moulsey to be used as an asylum for decayed actors and actresses, and when the net

A scene from Ivor Novello's *The Dancing Years* during its original production at Drury Lane. Ivor Novello is at the top of the steps

ROYAL VISITS TO THEATRE ROYAL

Above: Queen Mary, The Duke of Kent, King George V, Duchess of Kent, Princess Alice *Below:* A Happy Picture of the present Queen Mother, the late King George VI, the present Queen and Princess Margaret

produce of the property amounts to £360 per annum, pensions to
be allowed. Especial care to be taken to have the words 'Baddeley's
Asylum' in the front of the house." His executors were to publish,
every year, his letter setting forth his disagreement with his wife, "so
that posterity should view my character properly and not be swayed
by certain scurrilous books and pamphlets on the subject". And
then came the clause which matters most, "that One Hundred
Pounds, three per cent consolidated bank annuity, which produced
three pounds per annum, be left to purchase a cake, with wine and
punch, of which His Majesty's Company of Comedians appearing at
Drury Lane are requested to partake every Twelfth Night in the
Great Green Room, so that I might be remembered by them".
There was another little bequest. Certain trees on his Moulsey (or
Molesey) estate were to be felled and their timber used somewhere
in that great theatre he loved so well.

Those bequests were carried out. They did not all work well.
The Asylum affair failed. The actors and actresses did not like being
labelled as decayed and did not like the word 'asylum'. So, although
it was given a trial and contained his collection of pictures and his
bust of Garrick, the estate was merged into the property of the
Drury Lane Fund—and old Robert would have approved of that.
But the timber of his trees is still in the fabric of Theatre Royal.
It escaped the fire in 1809.

But the Baddeley Cake goes on. A separate fund administers that.
It has its own Master; at the time of writing he is that excellent
actor Austin Melford—an Old Druriolanian himself. He it is who
cuts the cake annually and tells the story. The Secretary of the
Fund is William Abingdon, stage director of Drury Lane for over a
quarter of a century before he left to go into business for himself.
The ceremony has undergone certain changes of venue. In Gus
Harris's time it was cut on the stage and made the occasion of a vast
party and dancing. That was not Baddeley's idea. Now it has returned to its old simplicity. It is no longer cut in the Green Room,
for the Green Room, although still there, is no longer used as such. It
takes place in the lovely foyer—a masterpiece of Regency architecture.
There the company gather, hear the story, eat their cake and drink
their punch and remember the donor. It is a purely private affair. The
company in costume and make-up—but nobody below the rank of
understudy by rights—the management, the heads of departments
and a few highly honoured guests. And maybe the ghost of Robert
Baddeley too, who smiles with pleasure as he hears his name uttered
and remembered and watches the waiters—in the Royal Livery, as he
himself wore—pour out the punch and hand round his cake. Ever

H

since 1795 that has gone on, with the exception of a single break in
the First World War, when, owing to a sugar shortage, the cake
could not be made. The money was given to charity—of course it
costs much more than £3 today. And during the Second World
War, it could not be carried out, because, owing to the occupation of
Drury Lane by ENSA, there was no Company of His Majesty's
Comedians to fulfil the will. It was revived again in 1947 and an
emergency arose. Rationing was in force and to get the ingredients
for the cake things called 'B.U.s' were needed. Nobody had any to
spare. But a member of the public, entirely unconnected with
Drury Lane, but who loved the place and knew its traditions, came
to the rescue. She gladly surrendered her precious 'B.U.s' for two
successive years and the cake was made and eaten by her generosity.
Her name is Mrs. Middleton, and she may be sure that, when she
and her family attend the ceremony nowadays as special guests of
honour, they get a special smile and greeting from the ghost of
Baddeley.

So that ceremony goes on and in it Baddeley is remembered.
Quite recently his legacy and his story got even wider publicity than
he had ever dreamed of or newspapers could accomplish. The
writer of this book, himself a Druriolanian, and bound to that
theatre by ancient family ties, was allowed four and a half minutes
to tell the story of Robert Baddeley by means of Television one
Sunday evening at 8.25. He was told—and believes—that about ten
million people saw and heard him. How Baddeley would have
revelled in that. . . .

That determined actor, that pillar of Drury Lane, still plays his
part in the playhouse he so adored and where doubtless his good,
genial spirit wanders, although he is not its official ghost. And it is
comforting to know that as long as Theatre Royal, Drury Lane,
stands—and may that be for centuries to come—so long will Robert
Baddeley, pastry-cook, actor and expert publicity man, be remembered therein. He got immortality for the sum of One Hundred
Pounds—in itself, no mean feat. . . .

CHAPTER SEVEN

He Saved Drury Lane

THE tens of thousands of people who flock to Drury Lane Theatre, and the even vaster crowds who pass it daily, connect that great playhouse with Nell Gwynne, David Garrick, Richard Brinsley Sheridan, Edmund Kean, Sarah Siddons, Grimaldi, Dan Leno, Herbert Campbell, and, more recently, with Ivor Novello and Rodgers and Hammerstein.

Yet there is another name which gets no mention, save from a handful of Theatre historians, a name famous in itself but somehow ignored where Drury Lane is concerned—which is most unfair, because but for him there would have been no Drury Lane Theatre today. His name was Samuel Whitbread, brewer and Member of Parliament, and he saved Old Drury. Had he been an actor or even a dramatist his name would glow! But he was only a great-hearted, public-spirited man who, when the theatre was burned down in 1809, made Drury Lane rise again, and it endures today much as he left it. He saved that treasure-house of the drama but at the cost of his own life. His name should be on those walls in letters of gold.

Samuel Whitbread was the son of the founder of the famous firm of brewers, and he represented Bedford in the House of Commons from 1790 until his death in 1815. Therein he followed in his family's footsteps, for a Whitbread had sat for Bedford since 1768.

He had no theatrical blood, no theatrical background. Born in 1758, he had a very strict upbringing. His youth was spent in very different surroundings from the glitter and romance of the Stage, his manhood was concerned with his great firm and his parliamentary career. Yet he made it his special business to save a theatre with which he had no previous connection, save a very slender one through Richard Brinsley Sheridan, Drury Lane's brilliant Patentee —and also its worst enemy.

Samuel Whitbread was a Whig, and a Radical Whig at that, standing always for reform, an upholder of causes in which he believed. He fought beside Wilberforce for the abolition of slavery— Freedom was everything to him—and he worked on plans for the establishment of proper wages for our own agricultural labourers, whose conditions in his day were deplorable. He stood for the oppressed against the oppressor, an Englishman of the best kind, during a very troubled period of English history.

He was occasionally headstrong, letting his heart rule his head. He never spared himself and that was what eventually killed him. Yet in matters of finance he could be very cautious indeed. Sheridan, when defeated at Stafford, blamed Whitbread for withholding funds at a critical time. But Samuel Whitbread knew what he was about.

His interest in Drury Lane arose through his connection with Sheridan, politically and socially. He had stood a firm friend to that erratic genius on many occasions. He had kept him out of a duel. He was also trustee for Sheridan's second wife and there was some connection by marriage as well. Samuel Whitbread, whose word was his bond, knew all about Richard Brinsley Sheridan, whose word and bond alike were valueless.

So long as Sheridan was Patentee of Drury Lane, he had something upon which he could take a stand, some tangible asset, no matter how mortgaged and complicated his position might be, something which, as its Patentee, gave him a standing beyond that of his talents in and out of Parliament. But the night came when he stood in the House of Commons, about to make a speech, and the sky of London blazed a dull red. Word came that Drury Lane was on fire. The Speaker offered to prorogue the House, but Sheridan, always something of a showman, replied: "No. The nation's business comes first." He made his speech and then he hastened to Drury Lane, to find it worse than he had feared. That enormous building, which he had rebuilt at vast expense—nobody quite knows how much, but he certainly exceeded the estimates by the matter of over one hundred thousand pounds—it probably cost well over a quarter of a million. None of that troubled Sheridan very much, he had not the slightest intention of paying for anything that he could wriggle out of. But he had called it his Grand National Theatre, he had done all sorts of plays in it—he had even installed a safety curtain, the first the world had ever seen, and boasted that there could be no fire— and now . . . fire was consuming everything. The story goes that he pushed his way through the great crowd to the very front, where the watchmen stopped him. To them he said: "What? May not a man warm his hands at his own fireside?" Another and more likely version is that he sat at the tavern just across the way, from which he could see the fire (it was bombed in the Second World War) and the Duke of York was his companion. After all, this was Theatre Royal. Sheridan was in a state of tremendous anxiety and almost paralysed by nerves, but he summoned his fortitude, and when they tried to lead him away said: "What? May not a man be allowed to drink a glass of wine by his own fireside?"

Theatre people are notoriously superstitious and many had

prophesied bad luck for this new theatre of Sheridan's, which he had opened in 1794, because he had turned it round the other way. Its front was not in the street which is now Catherine Street—formerly Bridges Street—as it is today and as had been the first two theatres, but in Russell Street. Old actors and actresses had said, with a shake of their heads, that no luck could come of the alteration. Well, they were right. Another thing which displeased the seekers of omens was that he opened it with *Macbeth*—another 'unlucky' play. Well, that superstition turned up again. Did any of those thoughts cross Sheridan's mind as he sat watching all he had go up in smoke and flames? Did he remember the players who had not received their salaries yet who worked on because it was 'The Lane'? Had he a thought of Jane Pope's letter saying that if it was necessary for the sake of the beloved theatre she would play for £2 a week and wait for it if it was not convenient to pay her? Or was he rather thinking of those creditors of his own who were always flocking around him, and feeling already the touch of the tipstaff's hand on his shoulder, now the armour of Drury Lane was no more?

Many irreplaceable treasures went up in smoke that night, little indeed was saved, except the Charter itself and a few oddments. And when dawn came there was a heap of ruins, a few walls and, underneath, the sturdy indestructible structure of Wren's arches— but no theatre. Strangely enough the room in which Sheridan had written *The School for Scandal* escaped—and so did the Green Room and one small portion of the wall of the first theatre—maybe rendered immortal by the wonderful play and the Immortals amongst the players who had frequented those places. But to the general eye that proud theatre, so old and so famous, was an unsightly heap of ruins.

The date was 24th February, 1809. Sheridan knew he must rebuild his only asset. He had no money and no credit. What was he to do? He turned to Samuel Whitbread. The gambler, risking another throw with Fortune, turned to the man of business.

Samuel Whitbread appreciated what Drury Lane Theatre meant. It was part of his country's history. He undertook the job. He did not realize what he was taking on, but he knew the task was difficult and he was undaunted. If he did not understand anything about the ramifications of a theatre's business, at least he knew all about Sheridan and his ways. He knew that man's nature, his recklessness, his disregard for money and figures. He knew all about the slapdash manner in which the new building, now destroyed, had been constructed, when estimates were swept aside for a whim. He knew all about the masses of unpaid bills, actors and actresses with salaries hopelessly in arrears, and the many other scandals of the

Sheridan regime. That must never happen again. There must be a clean start for the new theatre, if indeed it could be rebuilt—and he, an Englishman to the backbone, put his faith in that truly British institution—a committee.

Drury Lane must be rebuilt—upon that he was determined. A huge sum had to be raised. Whitbread enlisted Lord Holland, Douglas Kinnaird, Lord Byron and other great names of the time to help him in this effort. They—and the public—trusted Samuel Whitbread. So did the actors and theatre folk in general. The appeal was made and money came rolling in. He raised £400,000, an enormous sum in those days of high purchasing power.

Fire had twice consumed Drury Lane. This time that must be prevented and some sort of a fireproof building contrived, if possible. The place must necessarily be very big, but the auditorium must not be too vast and cavernous, as had been the case with the destroyed theatre. Whitbread put his faith in Wyatt as architect, and so much energy, force and drive did the Member for Bedford display that the first stone was laid in October 1811. And the new theatre— the playhouse which stands today—was able to open a mere twelve months later.

But there was a grave danger still to Drury Lane, as great as that of fire, and Whitbread was fully aware of it. That danger was Sheridan. If the new Old Drury was to succeed, Sheridan must have no part in its management. Now Sheridan held the Patent—the Charter—a trump card. He had farmed some of it out, mortgaged it to get money—he had done the same with other parts of the property. It was a complicated position and negotiations with him were long, troublesome and protracted. The great dramatist but bad manager had hung millstones of debt around the theatre's neck by selling seats and boxes to private owners for a small capital sum. He had done this to 'raise the wind' when in low water. The people who purchased had what amounted to debentures. That meant that even when Drury Lane was packed to capacity, only a proportion of it represented cash to the management, the rest of it had gone into Sheridan's pocket, in advance, and could not be recovered. Whitbread tackled the task of unravelling the labyrinthine twists of the knot of Sheridan's tortuous theatre finance and finally got a clear—if alarming—picture.

Drury Lane was rebuilt—and reopened. And Sheridan was shut out. Not only out of Drury Lane but out of Parliament as well. What is more, he was under arrest. Now he turned on Whitbread, whom he accused of withholding funds justly due to him. But Samuel Whitbread was within his rights. He was protecting Drury

Lane and paying off its creditors. Sheridan wrote him one of his famous letters, which might have melted a heart of stone. It failed with Whitbread, who knew he was doing his duty—and who knew Sheridan.

Sheridan was eventually paid off with what was legally due to him. But he never forgave Whitbread, nor Whitbread's wife, Lady Elizabeth, although when the end came he professed to be profoundly shocked.

Samuel Whitbread had won. He had rebuilt and reopened 'The Lane' and he had removed Sheridan after tremendous difficulties. Had he but known it, those were the least which he had to face. That was business, straightforward business, which he understood. What followed was theatrical business, which is not, and never can be, business at all. There is no doubt that what he had to do to Sheridan worried him very much indeed and caused him some compunction, all of which told upon him before long.

The new Drury Lane was controlled by the committee. They had the very best of intentions but they were amateurs. True, they had a professional manager to guide them, named S. J. Arnold. The committee did what most committees do, put in a tremendous amount of work without really knowing what they were driving at. And, of course, little cliques appeared. Whitbread belonged to none of them. He tried to apply business principles to the control of the building for which he had been responsible, and Arnold did what he could to help and advise.

In charge of the stage was Tom Dibdin, whose title was 'The Prompter'. Today he would be known as 'Stage Director'. He was an actor, producer, a writer of lyrics and pantomimes and a dramatist. Also, he was the son of the famous Charles Dibdin, the composer of over 1,000 songs, and he had inherited a full share of his father's obstinacy and belligerence. It was not long before there was inevitable and open war between the amateurs and the professionals. Arnold, the manager, was nearly always at arm's length with the committee. Dibdin had constant clashes with them. On one occasion he crossed swords with Whitbread. Dibdin was away from rehearsal for a short time, whilst somebody else 'held the book'. Naturally, that was the occasion on which Whitbread asked for him. It appears to have been nobody's business to tell Whitbread the real truth as regards Dibdin's very temporary absence, or maybe the underlings wanted to see Dibdin in trouble. Anyway, Whitbread wrote to Arnold complaining that the executive always seemed to be absent when he called or wanted them. Arnold passed the letter to Dibdin, who sent a stinging reply, stating the facts. Whitbread took no offence, he was too big a man. Instead he sent a most courteous and understanding answer which Tom Dibdin prints at length in his *Memoirs*.

Whitbread had his troubles and pinpricks outside Drury Lane as well as inside. The wits, the lampooners, the writers of broadsides, all made great game of the brewer turned theatrical manager. His political opponents made capital out of it. He was mercilessly lampooned and Drury Lane was spoken of as 'the New Brewery'. The question of the competition for an opening address to be delivered on the first night of the new theatre caused lots of fun and 'Rejected Addresses'—a splendid piece of mimicry—is almost a classic. It was not the only thing of its kind. There was quite an elaborate production issued—an address to be delivered by one 'Peter Puncheon'—nobody, it appeared, was quite sure if the theatre was a tavern or a playhouse. This was quite a long affair, full of all sorts of political and social satire. But it was more pro-Whitbread than many. It dismissed Sheridan thus:

> Well, Gentry, welcome to our new-old Inn;
> Well stock'd our cellars, full is ev'ry bin;
> Old port, old hock, old cider and old perry;
> But none of that neat article, *Old Sherry*!
> Although well cork'd, and seal'd in quarts and pottles,
> It bounc'd, too frisky, and broke all the bottles . . .!

And it gave full mention of Whitbread—who is called 'Whitebread'.

> Now let not our friend Whitebread be forgotten;
> I'll drink his porter till my bones are rotten;
> For mind me, Gentlefolks, (I do not frolick)
> I'll tip his stout although it give the cholic.
> Whitebread—nice name—a name of fair renown;
> May never turn to black or brown!
> Whitebread superior to the Commons on his legs,
> As tuns of hogsheads, quarter casks and kegs.
> Porter and Whitebread act two glorious parts;
> One charms our palates and one charms our hearts;
> So soft his manner, such persuasive notes;
> Should boobies doubt me, ask his Bedford votes.
>
> By this blue apron, and this porter mug,
> Which to my breast with gratitude I hug,
> I swear his head upon my sign I'll put,
> A quartern loaf, a drayman and a butt;
> On this the world, the gaping world will stare
> And wonder Whitebread never was Lord Mayor.

Mere doggerel, of course, and the substitution of Whitebread for Whitbread considered extra funny—but a sign of the times. And later in the same work, when the actual so-called address is spoken, this occurs:

> E'en now from tow'ring walls thy Lares greet
> Their kindred deities of Chiswell Street;
> They in their turn, their mantling goblets drain
> And send their greetings back to Drury Lane;
> Amidst his stock of politics and ale,
> Thy Drama's patron cons his scenic scale,
> With varying talent each occasion hits
> Is Patriot, Brewer, Manager by fits.

The reference to Chiswell Street is to the Whitbread brewery, which still stands there. Whitbread was 'news' all the way round—a thing he did not really want to be. He just wanted to do his duty and his job. Things were not good at 'The Lane' anyway. A new play was wanted very often. And on one such occasion, there was more trouble. Dibdin had one in preparation, a musical farce, which he had concocted. The state of the box-office made its presentation imperative. Arnold the manager was away ill. Dibdin had plenty of troubles himself, for the man who was to have played the lead had also fallen sick. Whitbread stepped into the managerial breach, anxious to do his best. He pressed for immediate production, but the time was too short, even for Dibdin, the lightning playwright and producer. He had now another problem. A Mr. Phillips, who had been given the lead in place of the original actor designed for it, was making a lot of fuss and threatening to walk out. That was the unfortunate state of things at the moment when Whitbread demanded production. Dibdin wrote him a strong letter, telling him all the truth. At once Whitbread gave way. The amateur stepped down for the professional. His letter to Dibdin, written in 1813, is worth quoting, for it shows the man:

> "I am a very incompetent judge of the length of time necessary for preparation and only named Thursday because I know it to have been Mr. Arnold's confident hope and expectation that the farce would be produced that very night. I do not presume to give any directions, and I must beg that my wishes may be put quite out of the question when they clash with the interests of the Theatre or the author."

It is quite remarkable to find a man controlling a theatre who has

the slightest regard for the feelings of a mere author! But there is a
delightfully human touch in the same letter, as follows:

"Of all the things which have struck me since I became con-
versant with the interior of a theatre, the most extraordinary
has been the refusal of performers to take parts allotted to them,
of which we have now a signal instance in the case of Mr.
Phillips. I do not understand how salaries can be paid if performers will not co-operate to render pieces attractive."

Poor Samuel Whitbread! Many before him, and after, have marvelled at the same thing which struck him as being extraordinary.
The complex and—to the layman—crazy life and methods of
theatre managements must have bewildered him and worried him
incessantly. He tried to get things done in an orderly and businesslike
manner, only to find that he was usurping somebody's brief authority, or breaking theatrical etiquette. With his unruly committee on
one side, and the temperamental professionals on the other, and with
money pouring out much faster than it came in, his life was anything
but smooth. One wonders if he ever regretted that love of Drury
Lane which had made him save it. Added to all his theatrical
troubles, he had his parliamentary duties to perform and his great
business to control. The strain was beginning to tell.

For the committee was driving fast downhill. Unlike Samuel
Whitbread, they were given to interference in matters which they
did not understand. In that they did not resemble the House of
Lords, as depicted by W. S. Gilbert. Despite the enormous success
of some plays, there were costly and terrible failures. They had had
a piece of gigantic good luck. Edmund Kean had appeared and he
could and did pack the great theatre. Whitbread, who had done
much to secure Kean, rejoiced at the triumph and success which
came thereby. On one occasion he called on Kean and, on departure, slipped a fifty-pound note into little Charles Kean's hand.
Yet, by their incompetence and constant interference with the
professional management, whom Whitbread always supported, the
committee managed to turn what should have been a profit made by
Kean's attraction into a big loss. Everybody blamed everyone else.
Whitbread stood firm and tried to rule the storm. Dibdin wrote a
letter—he was always writing letters—to the committee and stated
that from 10 per cent to 15 per cent more than need be was paid
by the amateur management at Old Drury for articles required in
the house, and he added frankly that in his opinion the whole cause
of the woe lay in the ignorance of affairs theatrical amongst the

committee of management, a truth which did not make honest, forthright Tom Dibdin too popular amongst the men whom he was really trying to help.

There are some reports extant of the meetings with the shareholders. There was a meeting on 20th March, 1817, with Lord Essex in the chair. The meeting was called for the purpose of considering the state of the exchequer generally and the possibility of letting the theatre (it should be noted that this was after Whitbread's death, but the spirit of the committee was that with which he had to contend).

"As regards the question of letting, an Ironmonger was of the opinion that it should be sold. Mr. Cocker violently opposed that. Mr. Trent then spoke warmly in favour of the committee. Lord Essex remarked the sub-committee were quite willing to retire if anyone could be found competent to conduct the theatre as well as themselves. Somebody remarked that nobody could have conducted it worse. Mr. Holland objected to the affairs of the house being made so public and doubted if a tenant could be found. Mr. Grenfel asked that time might be given for consideration. Mr. Robins promptly moved a hasty decision. Mr. Grenfel then moved three resolutions.

(1) That the T.R.D.L. be let upon a lease provided that adequate rent and valid security be obtained.
(2) That a general meeting take steps accordingly at the end of the present season and that it be empowered to give publicity to such reports as in their opinions may be for the interest of the proprietors.
(3) That the further proceedings be reported at the next annual meeting in May.

The Hon. George Lamb objected to the manner in which the sub-committee had been spoken of, but seconded the resolutions, which were carried."

That was the exact spirit of the people with whom poor Samuel Whitbread had to contend, although that report was almost the last concerning the committee. But the amateurs outnumbered the professionals. Arnold, the manager, was out-voted and out-manoeuvred. In self-defence he published a pamphlet addressed to the proprietors. In this he printed a letter which he had received from Whitbread, who pays him a tribute but who also puts into words the worries which were hastening his tragic end.

"You know how I have been drawn into this whirlpool of business, and that I could not say 'Here my duty ends' when the theatre opened. The work was not half done; but I have been lucky in the persons with whom I have been connected in building and managing. . . .

Yet I have had to fight the battles of each against the multitude and in respect of the architect and builder, sometimes against each other: but they have all done me the honour to confide in me and supported me. Should I not have been bad, to have forsaken any one of them? . . ."

It is all in those few words. Whitbread had never wanted to help in the management, he had wanted only to save Drury Lane, rebuild it and give it a fair start. But he was too deeply involved and he would not desert those who looked to him. The strain was too much, the whisperings, the intrigue, the appeals from aggrieved parties, the constant flow of letters of complaint, of entreaty, the whole vicious circle of that small circumscribed world that makes the Theatre what it is. The old professional takes it all in his stride; he knows its value and treats it accordingly.

But Samuel Whitbread was a man unused to such things. He was serving three masters—his business, Parliament and the Theatre Royal—and of the three the latter was the most troublesome.

It was too much. He had long been suffering great pain. And, one day, a blackness came over him. He took his own life. . . .

Drury Lane closed, as a gesture to his memory, for one evening. Then the life of the theatre went on as before.

A post-mortem showed that a fragment of bone had been pressing on Whitbread's brain. The worry of the place he had saved had killed him. For there is no doubt that the strain of the theatre, the constant broadsides and lampoons connecting him with the playhouse, with which his political opponents persistently assailed him, brought about his tragic, sorry end. No tragedy ever enacted on the boards of 'The Lane' was more poignant. This man was killed by what he had saved from oblivion. He sought no reward, no gain, no thrill of excitement, no publicity from his connection with the Theatre. All he had desired was to see that Theatre Royal, Drury Lane, went on.

So, after all, that great and good life has not been lost in vain. It was given for a cause. That cause was the world's most famous theatre, which stands today as steady and sure as when he caused it to be built.

Very recently, another Samuel Whitbread, a schoolboy, was

taken over Drury Lane to gaze wide-eyed at the theatre which is his great-great-great-grandfather's true monument. The name of Samuel Whitbread still goes on—so does his work. So does Drury Lane. And there, in the great circle lounge, stands his bust, the work of Nollekens, for all to see who care to look upon the man who sacrificed his life for their continued pleasure.

And so long as Drury Lane stands, so must Samuel Whitbread be remembered. He must stand alone in this book, with nobody to share his chapter with him. For he is more than a pillar, he is one of the creators of Drury Lane—and his good work endures.

CHAPTER EIGHT

He Defeated the Critics

THE complaint is often heard today, even from actors and actresses: "Ah, we have no dramatic critics now. If only we had such men as there used to be. . . ."

Well, it is doubtful if those who complain know what they are talking about, for if they were subjected to such attacks and plain speaking as were the players of yesteryear, the air would be full of writs for libel and the lawyers would all make fortunes. The newspapers would not have room for full reports of the cases, either.

It is not so much the standard of criticism in the old days which is remarkable but the method by which it was expressed. Attacks of the most violent nature, jeers and sneers at personal appearance, terrific 'sloshes' at their mannerisms and technique were the rule rather than the exception. Yet the players of the old days stood up to it. Sometimes they answered back—in which case they mostly lost the battle. Sometimes there was real war and they would run counter-campaigns, not only against the critic but the journal he represented.

But one man, and one of the most assailed, especially by a most eminent critic, ignored the whole thing, took not the slightest notice, just went on acting as well as he knew how, always doing his very considerable best—and left the public to judge him. He won. He beat his most redoubtable opponent, who was no less a man than Leigh Hunt. The actor's name was Alexander Pope. He used the weapon of indifference, and a critic has no armour which can turn that deadliest and sharpest of points.

All the critics were not against Alexander Pope. Many of them praised him. That only added fuel to the fire of wrath in the heart of Leigh Hunt, who had evidently sworn the actor's ruin. Here is what he wrote, on one occasion, in a book of his:

"When I place Mr. Pope immediately after Mrs. Siddons, everyone will see I do not criticize actors according to their rank. But it is for the sake of contrast. If we have just had an example of almost perfect tragedy, we have now an instance of every fault which can make it not only imperfect but disgusting. Mr. Pope has not one requisite to an actor but a good voice, and this he

uses so unmercifully on all occasions that its value is lost and he
contrives to turn it into a defect. His face is as hard, as immovable
and as devoid of meaning as an oak wainscot; his eyes, which
should endeavour to throw some meaning into his vociferous
declamations, he generally contrives to keep almost shut; and
what would make another actor nearly serious is enough to put
him into a passion. In short, when Shakespeare wrote his description of 'a robustious fellow, who tears a passion to tatters' one
would suppose that he had been shown, by some supernatural
means, the future race of actors, as Macbeth had a prophetic
view of Banquo's race, and that the robustious phantom was
Mr. Pope.

Here is an actor, then, without face, expression or delivery,
and yet this complication of negative qualities finds means to
be clapped in the theatre and panegyrized in the newspapers.
This inconsistency must be explained. As to the newspapers,
and their praise of this gentleman, I do not wish to repeat all
the prevailing stories. Who does not know their corruptions?
There is, however, an infallible method of obtaining a clap from
the galleries, and there is an art known at the theatre by the name
of clap-trapping, which Mr. Pope has shown great wisdom in
studying. It consists in nothing more than in gradually raising
the voice as the speech draws to a conclusion, making an alarming outcry on the last four or five lines, or suddenly dropping
them into a tremulous but energetic undertone, and with a
vigorous jerk of the right arm—rushing off the stage! All this
astonishes the galleries; they are persuaded it must be something
very fine because it is so important and so unintelligible, and
they clap for the sake of their own reputations. . . ."

Leigh Hunt goes on for a long time, tearing Alexander Pope to
tatters, just as he says the actor tore his passion. It will be observed
by the careful reader that Mr. Hunt attacks not only Mr. Pope but
the audiences as well, whom he accuses of lack of understanding and
of ignorance, because they failed to see eye to eye with him in his
dislike of Mr. Pope. Also it will be observed that he attacks his fellow
scribes and critics and is darkly suggestive of bribery and corruption
—well, perhaps he himself knew something about that, if another
author is to be believed. . . .

But with all his violence and bitter invective, the critic did no
harm to the actor, who continued to play leading parts, to be a
star of his day, to play opposite Mrs. Siddons and Edmund Kean—
and to be able to fill Drury Lane, and also Covent Garden, on his

own account when the mighty planets were invisible. Not so bad for a robustious fellow, a master of claptrap. He took no notice publicly of the disgruntled critic, and he was, alas, dead before he was avenged. For avenged he was, by no less a person than Charles Dickens. In *Bleak House*, under the guise of Horace Skimpole, Dickens drew a picture of a man whom all the world knew to be Leigh Hunt. He flayed him alive, as Hunt had endeavoured to flay Pope. How the shade of the old actor would have chuckled, if he were aware of it. . . .

Who was this Alexander Pope, a leading actor of his day, and what sort of man was he? It is obvious, from the space that Hunt devotes to him, that he had importance. And so, indeed, he had. Yet very few have heard of him, so ephemeral is the art and fame of the poor player, who struts his hour upon the stage.

Alexander Pope was a man with generations of the Theatre in his blood. He was born to his business. His actual birthplace was Cork, but he was no Irishman. His father, also Alexander Pope, and his mother were in occupation of the Cork Theatre with their own company when the baby boy was born there. He was christened after his father—and also after his grandfather. That grandfather—the first of that family which has served Drury Lane since 1720—had made his first appearance at the Theatre Royal on 6th January of that year—Twelfth Night—and had been so good as Hastings in the old drama of *Jane Shore* on that occasion that although he was a tragedian the audience recalled him and made him speak his great speech all over again. He shares with James Quin the honour of being the only two tragedians ever to get—and take—an encore.

Our Alexander's father was also a good actor who 'played The Lane'. He was also very skilled in wigmaking, and produced wigs of such quality and beauty for his own wearing that when old age came upon him he made it his business and did well. But he would go back to 'The Lane' from time to time, and also take provincial theatres for seasons. He was a popular without being a famous actor. His sister had the fame. She was the great Jane Pope, who started at Drury Lane as a child in one of Garrick's pantomimes, eventually succeeded Kitty Clive in all the comedy parts, was leading lady with Garrick and later created Mrs. Candour in *The School for Scandal* and Tilburina in *The Critic*. She served her beloved Drury Lane faithfully for fifty years. Her story is told elsewhere. So Mr. Pope's breeding was all Theatre.

He had another talent. He was an excellent artist and his pictures were greatly esteemed. He could have become famous with the brush and palette, but he preferred the wider canvas of the stage and

The stalls and circle of Theatre Royal, Drury Lane, the morning after the bomb hit the theatre during the Second World War

Gracie Fields joins Ensa and is greeted by the chiefs. Miss Fields stands at the top of the table with Basil Dean on her left.

Also in the picture are many famous people, including Alec Rea, Sir Kenneth Barnes, E. P. Clift, William Abingdon, Thorpe Bates, Henry Oscar, Dame Lilian Braithwaite — and even the author

painting living portraits of the great dramatic characters. He liked his art of painting, however, and did very well at it. His judgment as an art critic was much respected and he was in great request in that capacity. He was asked by the nobility to visit their picture galleries and inspect their new purchases and make his assessment of them. He liked doing that too, for it may be that he was a bit of a snob.

Despite his talent for painting, he decided to become an actor. He had very little choice. He always had a soft corner in his heart for the city of his birth and actually went there to make his début. He could have gone straight to Drury Lane where his family connection would have secured him an immediate opening. But Alexander Pope was a man of spirit and independence. He wanted to make his own way and see if he was worthy of 'The Lane'. Consequently he went to Cork and he played *Oronokoo*, that Othello-like drama so beloved of actors of the 17th and 18th centuries. He made good. It so happened that Covent Garden was in sore need of a tragedian. He applied for the engagement, young as he was. He got it. Again he played *Oronokoo* and London acclaimed him. He remained at 'The Garden', and there were family rows as to the superiority of the two theatres, always rivals at that time.

In 1799, wanting fresh fields to conquer, the young Alexander went to Edinburgh and was a great success in that city of culture and high judgment. But Covent Garden wanted him back—and on his own terms. He returned there, and remained there until 1802. He drew the crowds, he filled the house, he became a great popular favourite, and a leading tragedian of the day—whatever Mr. Leigh Hunt might think or feel about it. But in 1802 there was trouble at 'The Garden'. The management were oppressing the actors— according to the actors. There was a desperate fight and Pope threw himself into the forefront, championing his brother performers, standing shoulder to shoulder with them. He did not start the fight but he was not slow to join in. He was a very loyal friend. He might have stood aside and reaped the benefit. He was always for freedom and against aggression. So he fought—and won—and left Covent Garden. He did nothing by halves. He had already been married twice, first to Miss Younge, who had been one of Garrick's leading ladies, and then to Miss Chapman, who became a celebrated actress—Mrs. Pope.

Shaking the dust of Covent Garden from his feet, Alexander now went to his natural home, always the Mecca of his desires. He went to Old Drury. His family probably said, 'I told you so.'

I

Elliston was his manager there and there was great friendship
between Pope and 'The Great Lessee'. When Elliston was treated
so badly by the greedy committee of Drury Lane and had the
theatre taken away from him, Pope, his loyal friend, went too. He
had reached his greatest heights at 'The Lane'—he had played all the
leads on his own, and he had been the 'opposite number' to Mrs.
Siddons and Edmund Kean. He had helped 'The Lane' when it
needed help. But now he disapproved of the way it had treated his
friend—who had also done great things for the old theatre. So he
went back to Covent Garden, where they welcomed him with open
arms. He remained there, one of its foremost players, until he died
in 1835, at the age of seventy-two. He acted right up to the very end.
His first two wives had predeceased him. He had one child only—a
boy—by his second wife—and he also became an actor. He married
for the third time, the widow of an artist friend named Wheatley.
The third Mrs. Pope outlived him. But she never shared his grave. He
had bought one in Westminster Abbey, and there he put Mrs. Pope
the first and Mrs. Pope the second—and there he subsequently
joined them—a *ménage* of death *à trois*, as it were.

He bought that grave in the Abbey because only the best was
good enough for him. That was his motto and he lived up to it. He
considered he was one of the best actors of his time and many people
agreed with him. He considered that Covent Garden and Drury
Lane were the two best theatres, so he played there. He wore the
best clothes, he acted with the best players, he mixed with the best
people. He considered Westminster Abbey the best place in which
to be buried—and he brought that off too.

There were evidently two schools of thought about Alexander
Pope's acting—which is quite usual. There were two strongly
divided schools about the art of Sir Herbert Tree. Not that Pope
was in Tree's class, even at his best. But, as regards both, you either
liked them or you did not.

What Leigh Hunt thought and said about him has been chronicled. Other critics, too, complained of his lack of facial expression
and of a whine in his voice, but they agreed that he was a handsome upstanding man and that he knew his business as actor
despite those two defects. There is a little poem written by a
critic of that time who—like so many critics of today—appeared
to like nobody or anything and so 'sloshed' them all indiscrimin-
ately. One is always sorry for the man who cannot find pleasure
where others find it. But this man imputed grave defects to all
the leading people, so maybe Alexander Pope was no worse than
the rest.

Here is the poem, and it can be judged, as can the critical faculty of its author. It is called *Prayer of a Playgoer*:

> From Farley, with his brazen, roaring throat
> From Fawcett, with his harsh ill-omen'd note
> From Elliston, in highflown, lofty scenes
> From Glover, when she murders Tragic Queens
> From Conway, tearing passion into rags
> From Sacchi and all such ill-favour'd hags
> From Pope, with vacant phiz and whine tremendous
> Angels and ministers of grace defend us.

Imagine a thing like that being printed today! What a first-class row there would be! But the old players put up with it. They pursued a policy of 'live and let live'. "The man's a critic," they said, "he has to say something." Personally they were content with the applause they drew from their faithful public. All the names mentioned in that poem were famous. Mrs. Glover was the best actress of her time.

There is another view on Pope which seems to prove that he did lack facial expression.

> "His figure is in every way well formed, but his features, though regular and pleasing in a private gentleman, are not well calculated for the stage. By the constant contraction of his brows, his eyes cannot emit that variety of passion necessary for great professional excellence. The playfulness of the eyes, the dilation of the brows, together with judgment in their use, constitute one of the great properties of the actor. Mr. Pope, however, compensates for this physical defect, in possessing good natural talents, which are under the regulation of a well formed judgment and a cultivated taste. His personification of Henry VIII claims our particular notice and approbation. He imparts every appropriate feeling to the character which he renders, by his excellent performance, more than commonly prominent in that drama. Othello, Lord Townley and a great variety of other characters meet with a very able representation in this gentleman."

He was also a very excellent Ghost in *Hamlet*, an outstanding Jaffier in *Venice Preserv'd* and a fine Tamerlane.

It will be noticed what a very high standard was demanded, physical as well as artistic perfection was looked for. Of course it was never attainable. If they had not possessed that real dramatic fire, apart from physical attributes, almost all of the great actors would have failed. Betterton had a small head and short arms, Colley Cibber a high-pitched and affected voice, Garrick was a very small man, so was Edmund Kean. Macklin was gnarled and ugly, Quin was fat. Irving had so many physical drawbacks that one wonders what the critics in the earlier part of his century would have made of him. Yet they had genius which transcended all. Pope laid no claim to genius but the 'notice' quoted above shows he was a good actor. Unless, of course, it was one of the 'puffs' which, according to Leigh Hunt, he bribed the critics into writing. If indeed he did so, then the price of a dramatic critic must have been very low indeed, for actors did not earn big salaries in Pope's day. Perhaps his sideline of painting supplied the money for his corruption of the Press. And perhaps not. Perhaps he was a pretty good actor and all the public thought him so—for in their eyes he stood very high indeed. Kean did not suffer fools around him. Mrs. Siddons was pretty careful with whom she played. Whine and vacant phiz notwithstanding, he suited them—and he suited the public who paid to see him.

Alexander Pope was also famous apart from his painting and his acting. He was, in his day, the outstanding authority upon food. There his word was law. At the opening of every oyster season it was customary to await Mr. Pope's verdict on the crop. This he would pronounce with great solemnity. Not only did he deliver his judgment in London, he travelled down to fashionable Brighton for that purpose as well. His approval or disapproval was final. There was no appeal.

His understanding of and his reverence for food and the manner in which it was cooked and served often made him enemies and struck terror into the hearts of those who offended against his high standards.

Once he, Edmund Kean and Madame Catalini were guests at a most important dinner party. The meal was well in progress when Pope suddenly broke off his conversation with his partner and a horrified look came over his face. It was by no means a vacant phiz at that moment. He asked Kean, who was seated opposite to him, for what time the carriage had been ordered. "For eleven," Kean replied. "Send for it now," demanded Pope, in a voice which brooked no argument. Kean, who treated Pope with great respect, a thing which he showed to few people, obeyed him at once, without question, which says a good deal for the power of Mr. Pope. As soon as its arrival was announced, Pope took Kean by the arm and marched him from the room. "Let our cloaks and our hats be brought," he demanded of the servants. The two men left the house in silence and drove away. Once in the carriage, Pope sat bolt upright and spoke not. Kean, who was mystified at this sudden exit from what had seemed to him a good dinner, waited for some explanation, but it was not forthcoming. Finally he said, "Alex, why did we leave like that?" "Why, did you not see what occurred?" demanded Alexander. "No," said the puzzled Kean. "No?" said the horrified Pope. "Did you not observe what that monster Catalini did?" "I did not," said Kean, now full of amazement. "Why, sir," said Pope, in a voice of anguish, "she cut a fricandeau with a steel knife." And he threw himself back in the carriage in a state bordering on collapse, further words failing him. "Well, what of it?" queried Kean—and then wished he had not spoken. "What of it?" roared Pope, in a voice of thunder. "What of it? Why, she should have used a spoon. I will never sit at table with a woman who does not know how to treat a fricandeau." Kean, who might well have made the same mistake himself—and knew it—was suitably abashed, and impressed.

Pope was asked to a ducal castle, to inspect and report on the pictures. He went and made a great impression. Dinner was served. The fish course arrived. Pope surveyed the huge silver dish on which it lay. He started from his seat in anger and dismay and rushed to where it was being served. He said to his ducal host: "Damnation upon your cook, Your Grace. He—or she, and I suspect a woman— has served a very fine Torbay turbot and ruined it by smothering it with capers. One cannot eat such desecration. It is unpardonable." And he began to scrape off the offending capers with a spoon. He was not asked there again. Nor would he have gone.

One night, seated in the Green Room at Drury Lane, he was musing on a brace of partridges which were awaiting him at home and savouring their flavour in his imagination. So wrapped in this beautiful dream was he that he failed to comprehend the constant questions and chatter of a young actor, who had an important part entrusted to him on the following evening, and was bothering everybody for advice as to what costume he should wear—as to how he should 'dress' the character. So full was he of the subject that he imagined everyone else was interested, too. He approached the thoughtful and silent Pope, immersed in his gastronomic dream, which the young man had mistaken for attention to his discourse and queries. "Mr. Pope, sir," he said, "how would you dress it?" "Dress it?" replied the actor, his mind intent on his partridge supper. "Why, with red wine sauce, of course. How else?"

And yet one more story of him. Incledon, the great singer, had been on a tour in America. There was some concern to know how he had fared, for it was only just after the War of Independence. So, almost as soon as he was home, Alexander Pope, his friend, went to enquire. Incledon, glad to see him, told of his enormous success. He had been received with the utmost friendship and good fellowship. Also, he had made a lot of money. "You ought to go over, Alexander," he said, "they have not seen a great tragedian like you. They would give you a great welcome and you would make a lot of profit." But there remained one question of the utmost importance in the mind of that tragedian. "That's all very well," he said, "but how do they feed you? What's the food and the cooking like?" Incledon went into raptures. "The finest in the world," he said. "I had the most wonderful food, the choicest wines, and there are dishes they serve which would be new and extremely palatable to you. Don't be afraid on that score." He paused, and looked at the gastronome actor. "There is, certainly, just one thing," he said with some hesitation. "Oh, and what is that?" demanded Pope. "Well," said Incledon, "they don't use any oil with their salads." Pope the tragedian started back, his eyes well open this time and staring. "Don't use any oil with their salads?" he shouted, as if unable to believe his ears. "Don't use any oil with their salads? Why did we make peace with them?"

A man like that is worthy of remembrance, though he is almost forgotten today. But not quite, for his descendants still serve Drury Lane. But, remembered or not, Alexander Pope was no small figure in his day. He steered his own course, he maintained a sturdy independence, he ignored the venomous criticism of his enemy, Leigh Hunt. He played on and he filled the theatres. He got his applause, claptrap or not. He set himself a standard from which he never fell; he liked the good things of this world and saw no harm in that. If he would only have the best, he would only give the best. He kept his bond and he upheld his reputation. He loved the Theatre and he loved Drury Lane. Having achieved it, he only left it because he considered it had betrayed his friend. If he had a whine in his voice, there was none in his soul. If there are good restaurants in whatever Paradise he found when that soul left his body, be sure that he will be there, keeping up his own standards, making certain that the chef does so too, and keeping a watchful eye for any solecisms in the matter of eating. A good actor, a good artist, and a good friend, Alexander Pope deserves his place as a pillar—a small one, but nevertheless a Pillar of Drury Lane. And if by the world he is forgotten—there is a great-great-grandson to remember him still. . . .

It must not be imagined that only Pope and those mentioned in that 'Playgoer's Prayer' came under the lash of vindictive criticism. That was applied to most of them, not only during Pope's time, but before and for long afterwards. Those who complain of the critics of today should delve in old volumes. The sort of thing from which people of the Theatre, not only the players but the managements, too, suffered is very well illustrated in a periodical called *The Idler and Breakfast Table Companion*. It believed in free speech, it never minced matters and if it could hurt feelings, it was, one is sure, well satisfied. An extract or two from 1838—only just after Pope's death —will be found both instructive and illuminating.

"St. James's—Mr. Braham's nightly losses (estimated at from £60 to £65) seem to have almost deprived him of the exercise of a cool judgment; for on Monday last he allowed his theatre to be appropriated to the uses of that musical charlatan, Pilati, whose concerts (!) were first announced to be given at the Colosseum. The 'bill' put forward on this occasion was one of the most impudent and disgusting of any we ever beheld—not excepting those of Bunn—the whole affair purporting to be 'for the gratification of the public, with the pit covered in and no advance in prices'!!! We need hardly say that Pilati and his 'eighty performers' took very little by their motion. Never was there a more ridiculous exhibition made within the walls of a respectable theatre. The audience were 'in amazement lost'. The concert (!) was preceded by 'Is She His Wife?' and followed by 'The Young Widow'. After this debasement what can we say but Alas, poor Braham."

Braham, the great tenor, put his life's savings into building and running St. James's Theatre—and lost the lot. The Colosseum referred to was in the Regent's Park district.

Here is another nice little titbit of criticism—evidently the writer had not been corrupted in this case and perhaps that is why it was written.

"The City of London has, this week, rather declined in popularity; Mrs. Honey having engaged—we know not why— Mrs. Franks to play Clari! Perhaps the fair manager owes a grudge to the last-named lady, and takes this mode of revenge. If so, she has succeeded to her heart's content. When Mrs. Franks is singing 'Home, Sweet Home', we can compare her to nothing but a frisky young frog, who, after clearing his husky throat, attempts to warble 'The Light of Other Days'. The effect is sublime!"

The City of London was a playhouse in Norton Folgate, and very popular, too. A little later this theatre was under the lash again:

"Had Mrs. Honey still the reins of government here, we should have said much to compliment her. As it is we can but lament that so pretty, and, until the present time, so well conducted a theatre should have fallen into the hands of Osbaldiston. Its fate may now be fully predicted. Small beer and ardent spirits will be handed round the dress circle, and pipes and tobacco will be in request all over the house. In short, no decent people will visit it, lest they should be robbed or poisoned."

The Idler did not like Osbaldiston, who was a most successful if robustious actor-manager of his time, who catered for popular tastes and was not much concerned with the Upper Classes, to which *The Idler* obviously belonged—for it took a shot at him further down the same page, under the heading of 'Sadler's Wells':

"This unfortunate establishment, rendered doubly unfortunate by having lately been in the hands of Osbaldiston, 'The Mountebank actor', is again in the market. It is in a most filthy state, and requires a second Hercules to cleanse it from its impurities. The smell of porter and tobacco has penetrated the seats of the dress circle to the depth of three inches—but the said seats are about to be fumigated."

It may be wondered why no mention is made of the stalls. They had not yet come into being.

Not only the smaller fry and the outlying theatres came under the whip of *The Idler*. Such giants as William Charles Macready, the 'eminent tragedian and leader of the stage', felt the sting of the cat-o'-nine-tails. Here is an extract which, in the light of what followed, shows the judgment of *The Idler* at its own worth, for the play so dismissed became a classic of its kind. But then—what *The Idler* did not care for *The Idler* did not like:

"Covent Garden—The new play of *The Lady of Lyons* turns out, after much mystery, to be the production of Mr. Edward Lytton Bulwer, whose merits Mr. Macready has eulogized, we are sorry to perceive, in the most fulsome and childish manner—

not only in the public prints, *usque ad nauseam*, but on the stage, over the footlights! We allude to the whining address he delivered last week, respecting Mr. Bulwer, and the political opinions contained in his new play. It was not only not called for, but quite out of place, and caused us, in common with others, to pity Mr. Macready for making himself so thoroughly ridiculous —to say nothing of his unparalleled egotism. As for Bulwer's kindly presenting his play to Covent Garden—it is mere moonshine—something like Stansfield's *kindness* in painting the panorama for the Pantomime; both are well paid for their *kindness* and well 'puffed' to boot. What more would they have? Of a verity, our theatrical managers are all going mad, outright."

And Theatre Royal, Drury Lane, did not escape the eagle eye and the castigation of *The Idler*—who when it came to scandal, libel and utter biased viewpoints, certainly belied its name. There was in charge of Drury Lane one Alfred Bunn, and *The Idler* held him in particular detestation. It was after him day and night—he pervaded its pages, you could not escape from him and his 'misdeeds'. Something will be said of this gentleman later. He was, it is true, a curious character and not always above suspicion, but even Bunn cannot possibly have been as black as *The Idler* painted him. He had, as star in the theatre, Charles Kean, the son of Edmund, and *The Idler* liked young Mr. Kean hardly any better than it liked Mr. Bunn. Here is a sample:

"Drury Lane—Mr. Bunn has been amusing himself during the week, trying to gull the public with Mr. Charles Kean's Hamlet, but the cry of 'stinking fish' has now little attraction; and the manager and his 'expensive toy' have (with the exception of those who were ushered into the theatre by 'orders') been left comparatively alone in their glory."

This marvellous paper began its 'notice' of Charles Kean's Hamlet with a nice attack upon Bunn:

"The principal novelty of the week has been the appearance on Monday, of Mr. Charles Kean, in the character of Hamlet. Bunn, prince of quacks, having covered the walls of the metropolis and its vicinity, with preparatory puffs, and secured the valuable services of some few hundreds of claqueurs, the house was filled in every part long before the rising of the curtain—all present being anxious to catch a glimpse of the 'greatest actor of the day'. The discussion as to his merits or demerits, during the performance of the overture, was such as to drown all the beauty of the music, which was performed on this occasion for the sole amusement of the gentlemen of the orchestra. When the curtain rose, the greatest anxiety was observable amongst the spectators to see 'the lion of the evening', and it was curious to observe the *paid* functionaries applauding every actor as he appeared, supposing it *might be* Kean. We will venture to say that Baker, H. Cooke, etc., etc., were quite unused to such agreeable sounds."

The dramatic critic then gives his opinion of Kean and a pretty poor one it is—ending up by saying:

"Our opinion, thus candidly given, we will abide by; and if, a month hence, or even a fortnight—nay, even a week—the house can be respectably filled without the issue of some hundreds of 'orders', we will readily acknowledge ourselves to have no judgment whatever."

Nor are other actors in this production accorded much praise. Here and there one gets it but this is much the general style:

"The Ghost, played by Mr. Cooper, was a 'very good ghost' and said what it had to say with proper emphasis and correct expression. It took, however, prodigiously long strides and looked as if it were hungry. . . . Compton, as the First Grave-digger, was, as he always is, an uninteresting buffoon, and delivered his dialogue in a most horrible chuckle, which he mistook for humour. Hughes, as the Second Grave-digger, made amends for his brother sexton, and was much applauded. Baker as the King, and King as Laertes, divided the applause; the former, when stabbed, falling down dead as a doornail, and the other being laughed at and derided from beginning to end. To us, he looked like a long, twisted walking stick, painted black. If not a walking stick, he was evidently taken for a stick of some sort. The rest were all 'leather and prunella'."

That was the sort of criticism which actors had to endure. Also managers who ran not only the minor but the Royal or Patent Theatres. True, *The Idler* was scurrillous and had its favourites, which makes it wonder if Mr. Leigh Hunt had not some reason in saying what he did about the corruption of the Press. And Mr. Bunn, when he takes the stage, will have some remarks on the subject, too. In the early days of newspapers, they had paid the theatres for their news—they had not charged for advertisements but paid to get them. And Garrick wrote many of his own paragraphs and probably his own notices.

Yet amidst it all were critics of the stature of Hazlitt. Perhaps the best thing to do was what old Colley Cibber had done—and what Alexander Pope did—ignore the men who attacked them. Certainly nothing annoys a critic more.

CHAPTER NINE

A Blaze of Glory

THIS is the story of Alfred Bunn, Esquire, sometime lessee and Patentee of Theatre Royal, Drury Lane, and of Covent Garden, too—stage manager, impresario and poet—and of all those titles, perhaps he was proudest of the last, to which he had the least right. In his day he made theatrical history. He was the first man to control, single-handed, the destinies of the two great Patent Theatres and by so doing to be virtual dictator of London's Theatrical World. There he exceeded Killigrew, who shared his realm with Davenant. Bunn proclaimed his intention of restoring the prestige of the Drama, which he found at a low ebb, yet he quarrelled with and oppressed its greatest contemporary exponent, William Charles Macready, even, at one time, to the point of fisticuffs. He said he would make Drury Lane the Temple of Shakespeare, but he filled it with performing animals.

Yet Queen Victoria came to see those beasts four times in one month. He waged eternal warfare with the actors and the Press— he made money from concerts and light opera and lost it with the Drama proper. All of which goes to show that things have altered very little since his day. He served Thackeray for a model of Dolphin in *Pendennis*—"A tall, portly gentleman with hooked nose and a profusion of curling brown hair and whiskers; his coat was covered with the richest frog-braiding and velvet. He had under-waistcoats, many splendid rings, and jewelled pins and neck chains" . . . all of which is exactly Bunn, except for the height.

The most-talked-of man of his day and often the most decried and criticized, he is now almost forgotten except for the fact that he was a librettist and as such wrote the libretto for Balfe's opera *The Bohemian Girl*, which he also produced . . . yet he gave London the matchless Malibran and engaged Taglioni to dance on nights when the diva was not singing—and it was through him that Michael Balfe got his first chance with opera in this country.

A man of pluck, courage, enterprise, extravagance, showmanship, strange meannesses, deep hates and odd loyalties, optimism and an indomitable will to triumph over difficulties—he was, in other words, a theatrical manager. In his way he loved Drury Lane—and it twice brought him to bankruptcy.

His story is too long, too diffuse and too widespread to tell it all in the space allowed. It is best to concentrate on his methods and what led up to that achievement which he always felt was just round the corner, in which he always believed and which, when it came, he savoured to the full—the one thing which has survived him and which gave him, towards the end of his career, the sublime moment to which he had always looked forward—his Blaze of Glory.

He was not originally of the Theatre. He married an actress. He is said to have owed his introduction into the Theatre to a certain noble lord, who was acquainted with Elliston and recommended Bunn to him. Anxious to oblige, Elliston made Bunn his stage manager. He seems to have been quite good at the job. He was pompous but he impressed—he seldom took responsibility—unless he was flattered into so doing. He did not have an easy task, for he had to cope with that flame of fire which was Edmund Kean and to do so in Kean's later and drunken days. Furthermore, he had to try and keep the peace between two leading actors—the old champion and the young challenger, Kean and Macready. They first appeared together when Bunn was stage manager. Kean, the old 'pro', outmanœuvred the more gentlemanly, less experienced and better behaved Macready. Macready appealed to Bunn and got little satisfaction. Kean added fuel to the fire, for already they disliked each other.

Bunn had met, during his stage-management days, a young man who played in the orchestra, and was sponsored by Tom Cooke, the genial Irishman who presided over Old Drury's music. Bunn patronized the lad, heard his ambitions and said that if he applied himself diligently to his work and studies, who knew that one day he might even compose a score to a Bunn libretto. And that day was to come.

Poor Elliston fell. A certain Captain Polhill took an interest in Drury Lane and he had money. He also had a strong interest in a lady friend with stage ambitions. Mr. Bunn therefore took an interest both in Polhill's lady friend and Polhill's money. He became manager, nay, partner with Polhill, risking no money himself but putting in what he pleased to call his experience, and whilst all London laughed at his postures and his pompous manifestos— Bunn adored issuing manifestos—it suddenly became aware that this Poet was no fool. The day dawned when London rubbed its eyes and discovered that Alfred Bunn was Patentee not only of Drury Lane but of Covent Garden as well.

Mr. Bunn made the world aware of this by another manifesto— in his usual overblown, flamboyant style. But he controlled both the theatres, making his poor players perform at both and run between the two to do so. They had little choice—he held the whip hand and they wanted work. He misused his power shamefully and the dual control did not last for very long. But during that time he had Macready as his star—and he was now Leader of the Stage at 'The Lane' and he brought to Covent Garden no less a person than the amazing Madame Malibran, the world's greatest soprano. He did that as a gambler's throw when, at last tired of pouring money into what appeared to be a bottomless pit, Captain Polhill withdrew what was left of his money from what Alfred Bunn was pleased to call 'The Grand Junction of the Theatres'. That junction had not joined up for him. He had lost £50,000. Bunn took a chance to save his face. He brought Malibran to Covent Garden at a fee— then unheard of—of £125 per performance. Bunn banked on novelty backed by the necessity of Society seeing the great singer so as to 'be in the swim'. He claimed that when he played Shakespeare —even with Macready—he lost money. When he staged opera, he made it. And, as final surprise, he engaged Taglioni to dance on evenings when Malibran did not sing. It was wild, it was extravagant, but it was tremendous publicity. And then Bunn, who spent money like water, nearly spoilt the whole thing by refusing to allow La Malibran to have four pairs of stockings with every dress when he decided three would be enough. He had trouble with his tenor, Templeton, who fell out with Malibran, but the lady had a sense of humour and overlooked it. But the real battle was over the extra stockings—and Bunn won the fight. Having won it, he lavished valuable jewellery on the singer, worth hundreds of times what the stockings would have cost.

Malibran sang at Covent Garden. She packed the house. They took £312. Bunn thought it was his blaze of glory. Then he got the 'return' of the takings at Drury Lane That was a mere £52. 'La Somnambula' had beaten Shakespeare.

So Shakespeare and Macready were turned out of Drury Lane and Bunn ran opera and Malibran instead—for a much boosted limited season.

Perhaps Shakespeare and Macready had not been quite turned out of 'The Lane'. They were there on sufferance. They played as curtain-raisers and after-pieces to the opera, which did not suit the 'eminent tragedian', Mr. Macready. Shakespeare and Macready filled the bill—as after-thoughts to opera, and Macready's temper grew steadily worse. Who shall blame him?

But without Malibran, opera was not such a sure card. Bunn was in financial trouble again—he had to find a novelty. Malibran had

mentioned to him a young composer whose name he had caught as
Balphè. He had not paid much attention. But now, in his trouble,
came Tom Cooke with a suggestion. Arnold, down at the English
Opera House—now the Lyceum—was in trouble, too. He could not
produce a new opera he had acquired—and Bunn could have it if
he wished. Bunn asked who had composed it. Said Tom Cooke,
"None other than Michael Balfe." It rang a bell. "Balfe? Balfe?"
said Bunn. "Madame Malibran mentioned a Balphè or Balfi to me
—I did not think—could it be the lad who was here?" "It most
certainly is," said the blarneying Cooke, "and 'twas yourself who saw
his talent and said that one day maybe he could compose an opera to
a libretto of yours. Now he is famous on the Continent and only needs
his chance for fame here—and much money will pour in. Will you
give him that chance?" Bunn, flattered at his supposed foresight,
did so. The result was a big success with *The Siege of Rochelle*. Balfe
was grateful. Bunn got his claws into him.

Bunn still gave seasons of drama and Shakespeare and he still
had Macready. That man was getting worse and worse in temper
and disgust. The 'eminent tragedian' found himself playing the first
three acts of *Richard II*, and to follow there was what Bunn described
as a grand Chivalric entertainment called 'Chevy Chase'—an example
of the equine drama, a mere glorified stage circus. Macready could
stand it no longer. He went to Bunn's room. The men quarrelled—
and the men fought. If, indeed, it could be called a fight. They
scrambled and struggled, they fell on the floor; there does not seem
to have been a decent blow struck from start to finish. They were
dragged apart by a scandalized staff. Macready shook off the dust
of 'The Lane'. He was terribly ashamed of himself, this upright,
pious, honest man of most gentlemanly instincts and behaviour.
This was the only time he had lost control of himself. Bunn had no
such scruples. He pretended to be badly hurt—the air was filled
with rumours of lawsuits—the papers were full of the scandal of
the fight—Macready was horror-stricken, Bunn enjoyed every
moment of it. Finally, the rather disgraceful affair was settled, but
Macready never forgot what he considered his shame. He always,
all his life, bitterly regretted that moment of anger.

Mr. Bunn wrote a book and it is most revealing. He gave his
character away completely and unconsciously. Whilst he thought
he was rolling out fine sentences and pulverizing his rivals, he was
showing his own mind and methods. Yet at times one must feel sorry
for him, for he was above all things, a 'tryer'. He never surrendered
—he always bounced back—until the final knock-out. He fought
many battles, quite a lot of them in the Press and with the Press. His

particular detestation was the 'Free List'. In his day this had indeed become quite unwieldy. And all the deadheads who took advantage of the free admission were ready to turn and bite the hand which had distributed 'the orders' if these were withheld. Bunn knew quite well that the greater portion of those who came in free were no use, but for a long time he could do nothing about it. But when he took over both Drury Lane and Covent Garden he was in a very strong position indeed. He dealt remorselessly with the 'Free List' and a howl of rage went up to Heaven. But he thought he was secure. Then his Covent Garden venture failed and he had to fall back upon Drury Lane. This made it awkward for he had antagonized many of the very scurrillous scribblers of the day. To add to his troubles, after his scuffle with Macready, the 'eminent tragedian' took over Covent Garden and went into management there—in Bunn's words, 'opened against me'. It was to be a battle *à outrance*, no quarter given or asked. It was fought very largely in the Press and the strategy of both throws a remarkable light on the Theatre of those days.

Bunn adored issuing manifestos. Macready took a leaf out of his book. He announced his opening at Covent Garden in one which was long and prolix. He dwelt upon his own unworthiness but he felt that something had to be done to 'save the Theatre'. Which goes to show how little times change:

"The decline of the drama, as a branch of English literature, is a matter of public notoriety. The distressed state and direct losses of those whose profession is the stage, if less generally known, are more severely felt. Under these circumstances he has become lessee of Covent Garden Theatre with the resolution to devote his utmost zeal, labour and industry to improve the condition of that great national theatre and with the hope of interesting the public in his favour by his humble but strenuous endeavours to advance the drama as a branch of national literature and art, it will be his study to accomplish this object by the fidelity, appropriateness and superior execution of scenic illusion."

Macready, who dealt in the 'third person', went on to say he had been promised influential support, had got co-operation from able and distinguished authors and that he spared no expense or pains in forming an efficient company. And then came a blow to Bunn.

Above : London Carries On. The Famous Drury Lane Wartime Broadcast Programme which ran for two years. Jack Leon is on the conductor's stand, and grouped round the microphone are Stephen Williams, Margaret Harper-Nelson and the author. *Left :* Harry Leggatt, theatre fireman, hauls down the banner of Ensa, to mark the close of the wartime occupation

Prince Littler, Chairman and Managing Director of Theatre Royal, Drury Lane, Ltd.—the present strong and successful Pillar of Drury Lane

"As English opera has become an essential part of the amusements of a metropolitan audience, he has been anxious to procure the aid of native musical talent and trusts he has succeeded in his engagements with composers, singers and instrumental performers."

Here was the great Shakespearean deciding to stage opera which had been Bunn's trump card. Macready further announced certain improvements in the auditorium—"made with a view to consult the convenience and the respectability of the audience"—and announced changes in prices—he did not lower them, he put them up slightly. His reason for that was another cut at Bunn: "In regulating them, a mean has been taken between the high scale of former seasons and the reduced scale, which the experience of the last two seasons has proved wholly inadequate to the proper maintenance of the establishment." That was a shrewd one for Bunn, but worse came: "It remains for him to add one thing more. Instead of announcing the reception of new performers by outrageous exaggeration in the playbills, he will trust to the impression carried away by the audience and to the voice of the public Press." . . . All that, and lots more, was issued on 23rd September, 1837.

That proclamation must have made Bunn writhe. He read it word by word and analysed every syllable. He found scores of poisoned thrusts at himself. The cap fitted and he wore it. In his book, he derides the whole thing—but the bitterness is apparent. He had to do something about it. The century-old feud between the two theatres was on again, strengthened by the personal feud between the flamboyant showman and the great actor-manager. There was a feud within a feud and double bitterness. Sitting in his room at Old Drury, in his ornate clothes, his three waistcoats, his spy-glass, his innumerable gold pins and chains, he dipped his quill in the inkpot and issued his thunderous reply.

"Theatre Royal, Drury Lane—The lessee begs most respectfully to announce that this theatre will open for the winter season on Saturday next, October 7th, 1837.

It has been the custom, and very properly so, for new managers to make new professions and boast of new regulations. The Lessee of Drury Lane Theatre feels that any such course would be at once useless and unbecoming on his part.

It is a matter of notoriety that the distressed state of the national theatres owes its origin to the exorbitant demands made

K

by certain professors, to the prejudice of the whole community; yet, with this difficulty to contend against, the lessee has upheld the legitimate drama in a far more effective way than it can possibly be represented at the present moment; but if he has almost invariably sustained a heavy nightly loss by the performances of such plays as *Macbeth, Othello, Richard III, Hamlet, Every Man in His Humour, School for Scandal*, etc., while the representations of such novelties as *Gustavus the Third, The Jewess, The Siege of Rochelle, St. George, King Arthur*, etc. (each played about one hundred nights in the season it was first performed), has been productive of great nightly gain. It is obvious that by this selection public pleasure and private enterprise have been equally consulted.

Mr. Garrick delivered in a prologue, on the stage of Drury Lane Theatre in 1747, the following opinion of Dr. Johnson, with reference to legitimate or illegitimate performances of the stage under the management of that eminent tragedian.

> Ah, let not censure term our fate our choice
> The stage but echoes back the public voice
> The drama's laws the drama's patrons give
> And we who live to please must please to live.

It remains for the lessee to add but one thing more. Notwithstanding he has had to combat the rivalry of an almost annual succession of managers, instead of announcing any outrageous exaggeration respecting himself, he will simply state a determination to continue his humble exertions for the promotion of public amusement, and to sustain the character Drury Lane has long enjoyed of being the FIRST THEATRE OF THE EMPIRE."

That statement of Bunn's is noteworthy, quite apart from its open attack on Macready, but because that was the first time that Drury Lane had been proclaimed 'the First Theatre of the Empire'. It has always—and rightly—considered itself the most famous theatre in the land. But Mr. Bunn went further and made it lead the playhouses of the Empire. A lesser showman would not have thought of that, for the Empire was in those days very dimly comprehended by the British people—it is doubtful indeed if they ever had any clear view of it at any time—but—the First Theatre of the Empire—how majestic it sounded and how Bunn must have enjoyed writing it!

Bunn, in his book, launches an attack on Macready's methods of

Press publicity. He says that prior to the actor's going to Covent Garden as manager, he had often been slated, but when he opened as actor-manager,

> "he became the idol of most who write concerning him; for while the sentiments of the established journals remained unchanged and were not to be changed by any venal means, a host of others sprang up that were to be influenced only by such means. I firmly believe that Mr. Macready put upon the free list of Covent Garden Theatre almost every metropolitan publication—reviews, magazines, journals, penny pamphlets, halfpenny squibs, and so on—and I will tell the reader WHY I believe so—because, for the first time during my long management, scores of writers in such productions, of whom, until that moment, I had never heard, applied to me for the freedom of Drury Lane Theatre, alleging as a reason why they ventured to apply, and why I ought to comply, that Mr. Macready had obligingly placed them on the Press List at Covent Garden."

Bunn also attacks Macready for the "employment of Forster as a whipper-in". That made Forster, if true, the first accredited Press Agent. He was, of course, Dickens' friend who wrote his biography and Dickens was a great friend of Macready's. Actually, Forster embarrassed Macready by his friendly efforts, to a considerable degree. He wrote in his diary recording him as "the most indiscreet friend that ever allied himself to any person. I cannot sufficiently condemn the officious folly of this Marplot Forster, who embroils his friends in difficulties and distress in this most determined manner. It is quite too bad." . . . Forster was indeed an over-zealous supporter.

Those halfpenny squibs and the like to whom Bunn refused admission to Drury Lane never ceased to vilify him. But always his worst opponent was that periodical *The Idler*, already mentioned. They had the entrée but they did not like Bunn. They attacked him mercilessly and they mostly upheld Macready, giving him a back-hander now and again to make it look fair. But what would the manager of a theatre say to this? *The Idler* pretended to have found a packet of papers which set forth the qualifications needed to be manager of Drury Lane. It was a terrible libel.

> "To be manager of a national theatre requires few qualifications, but those few are absolutely necessary. For instance a man must be essentially a blackguard, a swindler and a liar.

Being a blackguard he is safe from being called out by any of his male performers when insulted; being a swindler he has no character to lose, and being a liar, his word is estimated at its precise value."

It went on for over half a column and ended:

"As for the supernumeraries and members of the ballet, these being generally poor, you must fine them on every possible occasion, or deprive them of two-thirds of their salaries, and if they grumble, you must threaten to turn them adrift at a moment's notice. Signed A. B——n."

There is no disguise as to whom is meant.

In comparing the methods of Bunn at Drury Lane with those of Macready at Covent Garden, *The Idler* said:

"The degraded state to which Drury Lane Theatre is reduced may be readily seen by comparing the playbills of that establishment with those of Covent Garden. Bunn's playbills are filled with the most impudent falsehoods, disgraceful puffs and unmeaning nonsense that can be conceived; whilst those of Macready simply announce without any comment what are to be the entertainments of the week, leaving the public to use their own discretion in selecting their favourite plays. . . . Bunn sinks to the degrading situation of a strolling mountebank who placards the walls of every stable door he can find, with a bill of the performance to take place at his barn in the evening."

Those were strong words, as applied to Drury Lane and its manager. *The Idler* never let up on Bunn and Drury Lane. Here is a pleasant little paragraph. "Drury Lane. The performance at this nondescript establishment seems devoted principally to the amusement of Mr. Bunn and his latest new toy—Mr. Charles Kean."

For all the attacks on Kean the younger, he was destined to write a wonderful page of theatrical history later on, at the Princess's Theatre, and to raise the whole level of the drama and production. But *The Idler* knew nothing of that and they kept up their attacks; not content with their own adverse views, they reprinted every unfavourable comment from any other paper.

True, Bunn was a charlatan. Yet he engaged Macready at Drury Lane, he brought the matchless Malibran, the wonder singer, to this country and he sponsored Balfe here. He wrote the

libretto for *The Bohemian Girl,* of which of course Balfe composed
the score, and between them they managed to produce the British
Opera which is most tenacious of life and is still played. If Bunn did
reduce the status of the First Theatre of the Empire to that of a
booth by engaging the celebrated Van Ambergh and his menagerie
of wild beasts to appear there—what was the result? The rank and
fashion of the land, including the Duke of Wellington, rushed to
see the animals. And Her Most Gracious Majesty, Queen Victoria,
no great lover of the Theatre, visited this wild beast show no less than
four times in one month. Of course, the beasts were, by virtue of
appearing at Drury Lane, Her Own Company of Comedians, but
four times in a month for a Queen is pretty good going. On the last
occasion she went 'behind' and watched the animals being fed.
Bunn and Van Ambergh, showmen both, had kept the wretched
beasts without food for thirty-six hours, so that the Queen should
see a really good feeding time. They ran a risk, for during the actual
performance, Van Ambergh had all he could do to prevent a lion
and a tiger from falling upon and eating a lamb which was placed
in their cage—this being one of the high spots of the show, a lion,
tiger and lamb lying down in amity together. On this occasion he
was forced to "lash them into the most abject and crouching sub-
mission". It is to be hoped that the Queen was pleased with this
edifying spectacle. Bunn wrote his own story of that Royal visit
backstage and got it in the papers.

"The first portion of food thrown amongst them, seized by the
lion as a matter of priority, was enough to convince any sceptic
of the fearful savagery of their nature . . . the rolling of the tiger's
eye, whilst he was devouring the massive lump of meat and bone,
clutched between his forepaws, seemed to possess the brilliancy
as well as the rapidity of lightning; and was only diverted by a
tremendous and sudden spring of the lion, who, having demol-
ished his own portion, seized upon what was left of his ferocious
neighbour's fare. The dash against the sides of the den sounded
like the felling of huge trees and was enough by its force and fury
to shake the strongest nerves; but it was a positive fact that,
whilst the boldest hearts of the Royal Suite speedily retreated
at this unexpected plunge of the forest monarch, the youthful
Queen never moved either face or foot, but with look un-
diverted and still more deeply riveted, continued to gaze
upon the novel and moving spectacle."

That is Mr. Bunn at his very best.

Bunn always claimed to be a poet and liked to be called 'The Poet Bunn'. But his verse was pretty bad and his lyrics worse. Balfe, when asked by Malibran for his opinion on Bunn as a lyric writer and poet, said he was forceful—and when she asked him what he meant by that he said that Bunn forced his rhymes. He quoted as an example:

> My heart's with anguish wasted
> Fresh hearts this will supply
> My lips have nothing tasted
> 'Twill wine the brightest but
> And cafés in plenty are nigh.

Bunn made the word 'cafés' of one syllable and had the accent on the 'ty' of plenty. Anyway, it does not seem to make sense . . . yet he got away with it. Bunn soared to the heights and he fell to the Bankruptcy Courts. He produced his accounts and made such a showing that the Official Receiver was sympathetic to him. Drury Lane and Covent Garden broke him—and Drury Lane was to do it a second time. Still, he believed in his star, the incurable optimist, and he fought on—he was sure that, one day, he would have his Blaze of Glory.

He lived in Brompton and there in his garden he had a walnut tree. Under that he would sit and evolve his plans, his stunts, his ideas for showmanship. One night he entertained Malibran and her husband there—very late indeed; in fact he had gone to bed when the volatile Prima Donna knocked him up. Nevertheless, he served the party with cold chicken, salad and wine. But Malibran did not want food—she wanted to walk round the garden and smell the flowers—she said she seldom had the opportunity. So she and the Poet strolled in that London garden which held the scents of the country. Suddenly she shivered. Bunn was concerned. "Are you cold?" he asked. "No, no," said Malibran, "quite deliciously warm. I shivered, it is true, but not with the cold, no. Perhaps, as you English say in your so cheerful characteristic way—someone was walking over my grave." Bunn pooh-poohed the idea—that grave was very far away. But Malibran was not so sure. "Sometimes I hope it may not be too far away. I do not think I could bear to get old—to lose my voice, to be a silent nightingale or skylark. Have you seen them, those aged Prima Donnas? I have. It is terrible. They sing no more or they have sung too long—ashes in mouths once filled with golden notes. . . ." It may have been premonition—for Malibran died not long afterwards, passing in her prime. But she cheered up that night. She found some onions growing in the garden. She made Bunn pull up a

lot of them straight out of the earth and also fetch her some beer.
"Onions and beer under the moon," said the Prima Donna, "and
beneath the boughs of a walnut. A supper for a Queen. . . ."

They turned Bunn out of Drury Lane after an acrimonious
committee meeting at which one member said : "The boards upon
which the plays of the immortal bard have been represented for
nearly a century have been disgraced by an exhibition worthy only
of Bartholomew Fair—wild beasts, monkeys and horses and asses,
have polluted the fair fame of that once classic temple". But he had
not yet done—the picture was not completed—for it had been
visited by an additional indignity of becoming 'The Shilling Theatre'.
All the riff-raff of London let loose to congregate in Drury Lane
Theatre—but to no purpose." It was stated that Covent Garden
had made a profit of £22,000 and that "a minor theatre" (the
Haymarket) "was actually paying £4,000 a year and making
profits"—yet all Drury Lane had had from Bunn was £6,000 in
three years. The figures quoted were rentals. Yet, they had to have
Bunn back.

Bunn went on in his own sweet way, over-riding everyone,
quarrelling with everyone and getting money in by any means he
could. He found that promenade concerts were quite popular—
that accounts for the reference to The Shilling Theatre. But
always in his mind was the fact that one day he could conquer, one
day the Glory would blaze. He had had in his mind for some time
past the story for an opera and he wrote the libretto. He had been
bankrupt, he had been thrown out of 'The Lane', but he was back
again, full of hope. He had got Balfe to compose the score to his
opera. But he was a very sick man indeed. His 'old complaint'—the
gout—had seized him. But there he was in Old Drury, full of hope
and prepared for another tilt at Fortune. He had sent his libretto
to Balfe two years before—and now the score was complete and ready
for rehearsal. Short of money, in constant pain, beset on all sides, he
still believed in his luck. He had called his opera *La Bohemienne* but
had changed the title to *The Bohemian Girl*. He had a belief in Balfe—
they had had success before. This time it should be a triumph.

Bunn was a martinet at rehearsals where his own work was
concerned. He resisted any alterations in his book, he argued about
the lyrics, but he never stopped away. He had done his best to give
this opera what he called a 'sumptuous setting'—he was quite convinced that everything he did was in the very best of taste.

Balfe would have been delighted to be rid of him at rehearsals
but Bunn struggled down every day. This was his masterpiece, he
believed, and he was not going to be cheated out of a minute of it.

He had decided to produce on 27th November, 1843—and nothing must stop that. So, although hardly able to walk or stand, he was there, dealing with every detail of the multifarious matters of production, smoothing out arguments, being cajoling or overbearing, according to the status of the person with whom he dealt, always full of confidence and hope.

The night came. Bunn sat in his box, gazing at the full house, drinking in the music, finding exquisite pleasure in his own words as they were sung. He heard the growing enthusiasm of the audience, he swelled with pride at the thunders of applause—the encores drove him nearly drunk with joy. . . . "Success, success," he muttered. "Listen to them. . . . Ha, Bunny, my boy—they may assault you, they may kick you, they may libel you, they may make you bankrupt, but they cannot beat you. This will run a hundred nights—a hundred nights, I say . . . at last, at last . . . my Blaze of Glory. . . ."

And Bunn was right. After a most enthusiastic reception the opera waned and then, as happens in the Theatre, it soared up to splendid business. It ran its hundred nights—to the glory and memory of Bunn and Balfe. It also became legendary, for one of the most popular songs in *The Bohemian Girl* has become an unlucky song in the Theatre—one always considered to have a jinx, a hoodoo on it. That did not work in the case of Bunn nor of Balfe. Now the name of Balfe is remembered. His statue in marble stands in the rotunda of Drury Lane, erected at a cost of £480 by admiring friends. It keeps company with Garrick, Kean and Shakespeare. There are those who grudge it the space it occupies and think that others have a better claim. But Balfe in his day was the most popular composer and he was a Pillar of Drury Lane.

Bunn lived on another seventeen years after his blaze of glory. He died on 20th December, 1860, at the age of sixty-four. For all his short-comings, his vulgarity, his shameless showmanship, he was still a man of the Theatre—he was perhaps the first eminent manager to belong to 'show business' as against being a Member of the Theatrical Profession. He has no statue at Drury Lane—nor does he deserve one. His name is on the mahogany tablet in Drury Lane's vestibule, where all those who have held the Patent or Charter are inscribed. Nobody notices it. He is almost entirely forgotten—and yet he deserves his place in Old Drury's colonnade.

He was a real specimen of showman—of theatrical manager—with all the faults and all the qualities. He was never completely beaten until his health finally failed. He took the slings and arrows of outrageous fortune—and came back to do more outrageous things. Alfred Bunn, Patentee of Old Drury, Manager, Librettist and

Poet, deserves his meed of remembrance. He was no worse—if no better—than many more. His end was not happy. He failed miserably the second time he came back to Drury Lane. He went bankrupt again and he fled to Boulougne. There he existed until his death, living mainly on the charity of friends. But we may be sure he did his best to keep his shabby, ageing clothes smart and to assume a dauntless, hopeful air—as he warmed himself in the glow of his one real Blaze of Glory.

CHAPTER TEN

Odds and Ends, Earthly and Unearthly

W HEN old Prompters' logs and records are examined, with
reference to Drury Lane, odd facts often emerge as regards
customs and happenings. It had been the usage of the
Theatre for many years, indeed from Tudor times, to allow people
to sit on the stage whilst the play was in progress and walk about
there. This custom was specially prevalent at Benefits, where the
idea was to get as much money into the house as possible. But attempts
were made to check it—and Garrick finally succeeded in doing so.
There is an entry in a Prompter's Log of the 1746 season which
records:

> "By Particular Desire. *The Merchant of Venice.* The part of
> Shylock to be performed by Macklin. Boxes 5s.; pit 3s. Places
> for the Boxes to be taken of Mr. Hobson at the Stage Door of the
> Theatre. By reason of the many inconveniences that have arose
> by Gentlemen being admitted behind the scenes, it is hoped it
> won't be taken amiss that no money be taken there."

That phrase 'By Particular Desire' crops up constantly. 'By
Particular Desire of Several Ladies of Quality' and also 'Gentlemen
of Quality' shows that there was a personal interest in the Theatre.

The old prompt book is illuminating in many odd ways. This
entry, for instance:

> "The Widow Turbutt begs leave to inform her friends that
> she has removed from the Swan in Smithfield to the Foundling
> Hospital Coffee House in Red Lion Street, Holborn, where she
> begs the continuance of their favours. She has provided herself
> with the best of liquors of all sorts and Punch is made immediately
> as good and as reasonable as anywhere in London."

That notice had probably been on the theatre's call-board. One
hopes the Widow Turbutt succeeded.

The first appearance in London of a very famous actor—
Spranger Barry—is recorded very quietly. Barry, a handsome man
with a voice of silver, eventually challenged Garrick himself—but
lost the battle. That is what the old book says.

"On Saturday night last, 4th October, 1746, Mr. Barry, from the Theatre in Dublin, performed the part of Othello in the Theatre Royal, Drury Lane, before a numerous and polite audience and met with as great applause as could be expressed."

A nice touch about the polite audience—audiences could be most impolite in those days.

On Monday, 3rd November, 1746, there is a most illuminating entry.

"No play. A man in the gallery was carried before a Justice of the Peace on Saturday for throwing an apple on the stage with the intention of hitting some person who was peeping through the curtain but by mistake struck a lady of Quality in the face who was sitting in the stage box. On his begging pardon and promising not to repeat the offence, he was discharged."

That opens up the question of the underlying force which drags most British audiences to a theatre. They regard a theatre as a place in which to eat or drink. That is the main object for going. They cannot endure the two or two and a half hours' traffic of the stage without constant refreshment. That has been true of the Theatre since the days of the Tudors and it is true today. Drury Lane, when it first opened, had the first professional refreshment contractor in Mistress Mary Meggs—Orange Moll—who employed the famous orange girls. But she was not allowed to sell her wares in the topmost gallery, for the very reason which got that man into trouble in 1746, nearly a hundred years afterwards. That man had not taken the apple to the theatre to throw at an actor—he had taken it there to eat. Its use as a missile was an afterthought. And if anyone doubts the truth of this statement about eating, let them read this and ponder. It comes from a most respected periodical which still comes out and the date of it is back in the 1870s.

"An incident occurred the other evening, at Drury Lane, which should not be left unrecorded in theatrical annals. During a performance of *Richard III*, a hungry spectator, occupying a seat in the front row of the gallery, felt inclined to enjoy his supper and the performance together. Removing from a paper parcel the savoury nourishment he had brought with him, it was his misfortune to drop a small pork pie over the gallery railing; and his shrieking ejaculation of horror and woebegone look, as he saw the rich repast he had contemplated with such expectant delight lodge in the centre of a dress circle chandelier far below, first called the attention of the audience to the circumstances. Presently, as the pork began to frizzle in the gas jets, a most appetising odour pervaded the house, and, a few fragments of crisp piecrust dropping through the convenient apertures in the chandelier among the persons in the pit, there was an evident scramble for the succulent morsels, which were devoured with manifest relish. In a short time attention became more directed to the flavorous fumes of the frizzling pork pie and to the pursuit of the oleaginous morsels occasionally falling into the pit than to the description of the 'devouring boar' on the stage. Everybody began to feel hungry, and the eager looks of the supernumeraries forming the contending armies of Richmond and Richard centred, not on their opponents on the field of Bosworth, but on the chandelier exhaling such delicious fragrance. The fun reached its height when, on a call for the manager, a wag in the pit cried out, 'Mr. Chatterton, is that a real Melting Mowbray pork-pie?' "

That story, printed elsewhere, now takes its place, as its original chronicler requested, in these annals of Drury Lane. And it proves about the eating. The Mr. Chatterton mentioned in connection with this incident was a splendid manager of Drury Lane who strove manfully to keep the prestige of Drury Lane upon the level of what Bunn called 'The First Theatre of the Empire'. He was a man of great integrity who took the Theatre seriously. He always gave the best. He paid, as rent, £6,000 a year, plus £10 extra for every performance over 200 in any season. The theatre still had seasons then, and closed in the summer. A few years before, E. T. Smith had paid only £3,500. Theatre values were going up. Chatterton staged Shakespeare, Byron and Old English comedies. He had such front-rank players as Samuel Phelps, Walter Montgomery, Barry Sullivan, John Ryder, Helen Faucit, Mrs. Herman Vezin and Miss Neilson. He was a pioneer, too, for he produced the first of those great spectacular melodramas for which Drury Lane became so famous under Augustus Harris and Arthur Collins. It was called *The Great City* and was presented in 1868. A cab, drawn by a horse, was driven on the stage and the audience applauded vigorously. They did not know that real horses had appeared on the stage at Drury Lane, in a play called *Hide Park*, as early as 1665. Chatterton started those melodramas and, as usual, those who followed him reaped the benefit. He had a most unusual fate. He was broken by

Pantomime, usually the safest card to play in the whole theatrical pack. But the Vokes Family, who appeared in his Pantomimes almost to the exclusion of everyone else, had outworn their welcome, and one sad night the theatre closed down in the middle of the Pantomime season. Chatterton had lost £36,000. It is only fair to say that Drury Lane alone was not wholly responsible. He was also running the Adelphi and the Princess's—and neither was proving profitable. He left his famous dictum—that Shakespeare spelt ruin and Byron bankruptcy. . . .

Royal Commands are chronicled in the old log book:

"3rd December, 1746. By His Majesty's Command. *The Refusal*, Macklin, Delane, Mills, Cibber, Mrs. Macklin, Kitty Clive and Peg Woffington (what a cast!). In Act 4 The Original Cantata by Lowe. With entertainments of Dancing by Sig. Salomon, Madame Violette (being the first time of their appearing on that stage), Muilment, Mechell, Madame Mechell, and others."

There is quite an intriguing entry on 6th February, 1749:

"Never Acted Before. A new Tragedy called *Mahomet and Irene*. The principal parts to be performed by Garrick, Berry, Barry, Harvard, Sowdon, Blakes, Usher, King, Mrs. Pritchard and Mrs. Cibber. 'Tis hoped that no Gentleman will take it ill that they cannot be admitted behind the scenes."

This was the play by Dr. Johnson. It was not a success but Garrick did what he could for his old friend. It was repeated on the 7th February and on the third evening—February 9th, for the previous day had been Ash Wednesday, when the theatres closed— the author took 'his night', his Benefit. The great doctor did not condescend to sell tickets himself but they could be obtained from Mr. Mitton in the Strand, Mr. Dodsley in Pall Mall, at the Half Moon Tavern near Holborn and of Hobson at the stage door of the theatre. It was given again on 11th and 13th, and Johnson had another Benefit on the 14th—the sale of tickets as before but this time also of Mrs. Payne in Paternoster Row. It was also performed on 16th February, with *The Anatomist* thrown in and some Scottish dances, and again on the 18th, also reinforced by Scottish dances. Then the play was published under the title of *Irene* by Mr. Samuel Johnson, as acted at the Theatre Royal, in Drury Lane, price 1s. 6d.

But the play was not a success, although a long letter, unsigned, appeared in *The General Advertiser*, extolling its merits and probably written by Garrick. It is mentioned in this letter that the play 'had not been so favourably received of others' and the writer of the letter declared that "Poetry is caviare to the multitude who desired whining of lovers, complicated murders and bloody plots." Yet, apparently to boost the printed version, it was staged again on 20th February and the author once again took a Benefit. Nobody can say that Garrick, for all his meanness, did not do his best for his old friend.

There is a record in the log book of a nice little row between two leading actors, Woodward the celebrated comedian and harlequin and old Samuel Foote, who made the Haymarket famous and dodged the Patent Rights of Drury Lane and Covent Garden by advertising not a play, but an Auction of Pictures in his Auction Room in the Little Theatre in the Hay. The 'pictures' were a succession of supreme bits of mimicry of celebrities by Foote. You paid —but not for the play, you paid for a cup of chocolate, and got the play thrown in. Woodward had a Benefit at Drury Lane on 18th March, 1749, and he also was a fine mimic. He wanted to score off old Foote. He advertised it as follows: "*The Stratagem*, also a Savoyard Dance by Matthews, Mrs. Addison, etc. By particular desire, Mr. Woodward will present his *very good friend* The Auctioneer with *Tit for Tat* or One Dish of His Own Chocolate."

A letter appeared in the Press:

"To Mr. W . . d . . . d. Oh, ho! is it come? What, at your *Irish* tricks again? No, my Dear, they won't do. I am too well established here. Do you think we have so soon forgot your Harlequin Puffs? You defeat me in Ireland? Very likely, as if we did not know you. But what you—or the whole Town—could mean by propagating such a report, the Devil take me if I know, unless you have taken an antipathy to the Irish and found out this method to damn their judgment at once. Which, by the bye, Hal, would be a little ungrateful, considering how you profited by their ignorance. But let what will be the motion, if it produces a piece of Dullness equal to your last, I shan't quarrel at the means, or be more uneasy *Now* than *Then*. Yours, F.

From my Auction Room, March 9th, 1749."

This brought a disclaimer from Foote, who wrote saying:

"In justice to the many obligations I have received from the Gentlemen of Ireland, I think it necessary to inform the Publick that the advertisement in yesterday's paper signed F. is not mine, but is, I suppose, the production of the Comedian whose benefit it is calculated to promote. 11th March, 1749. Samuel Foote."

What was the upshot? This is the public report:

"Last Saturday, *The Stratagem*, with *Tit for Tat* was performed at the Theatre Royal in Drury Lane for the benefit of Mr. Woodward when there was the greatest audience that ever was seen there. And the *Dish of Chocolate* was received with uncommon applause."

That was in *The General Advertiser*. Knowing what the Press of the day was like, it may not be true—for Woodward although a good actor was not likely to draw such a vast audience as that. On the other hand, so many people had suffered from Foote's mimicry that they may have gone along to see him put in the pillory himself.

And whilst back on the subject of Benefits, two more instances are not without interest. Two sterling performers, Mr. and Mrs. Mills, took one on 21st April, 1750. They were in trouble and issued the following announcement:

"To the Public. Gentlemen and Ladies. I am very sorry that a long, sharp and severe fit of illness prevents me the satisfaction of making my personal application to my friends, as usual, against my Benefit; but finding myself every day rather worse than before I hope you will be so kind as to take this notice that *The Stratagem* will be performed on Saturday 21st April, the part of Archer by Mr. Garrick, for the Benefit of Mr. and Mrs. Mills, with a new farce and all other usual entertainments. From your most obliged Servant, William Mills.

Mr. Mills hopes that the friends who intend to honour him with their company will be so kind as to send to him for places, Tickets, etc., or call upon him at Mr. Gardiner's Printing Office in Russell Street, Covent Garden, or at Hobson's at the stage door."

There was a quite unusual Benefit on Thursday, 5th April, 1750.

"For the Benefit of Mrs. Foster. Grand-daughter of Milton and his only living descendant. *Comus*. The part of Comus by Harvard, Bacchanal by Beard. The character of Euphrosine by

Kitty Clive, Sabrina by Miss Norris (with the song of 'Sweet Echoes') and the part of The Lady to be performed by Mrs. Pritchard."

It is to be hoped that Mrs. Foster benefited handsomely. That Mr. Beard got himself into the log book, too, but not for a performance. It was on 17th January, 1750:

> "Yesterday morning, about two o'clock as Mr. Beard belonging to the Theatre Royal in Drury Lane was going home, his chair was stopt in Drury Lane by four or five fellows who took from him his watch and money but did not otherwise treat him ill."

Maybe Beard, a good actor, consoled himself with Iago's statement that 'Who steals my purse, steals trash. . . .' He lived in New North Street, Red Lion Square. All those old players lived near their work. Quin lodged at the Sign of the Sun, a druggists, in Bedford Street, Covent Garden, Kitty Clive in Cecil Street, Strand, Delane at the Golden Bull in Exeter Court, Strand, Macklin at 12, Wild Court, Lincoln's Inn Fields, Mrs. Pritchard at 8, Craven Buildings, Drury Lane, Woodward at a peruke-makers next to the Swan in Vere Street, Clare Market, and Ryan, Quin's friend, 3rd House in Gt. Queen Street, from Drury Lane. Garrick at that time lodged first in Mansfield Street, in 1741, and in 1747 in James Street, Covent Garden. After his marriage, of course, there was first the house in the Adelphi and then the one which still stands in Southampton Street, Strand, next door to the famous theatrical publishers, Messrs. Samuel French.

Nobody will deny that Drury Lane is full of atmosphere and people often expect it to be full of ghosts. Well, it has its quota of them, too. Some can be vouched for, others not. There is one superior ghost who must take precedence over all others—for he is now world famous—The Ghost of Drury Lane—The Man in Grey. His story has often been told, but perhaps it is fitting to include it here once more. For this man was probably not an actor at all. Indeed, who he was is wrapped in mystery. Nobody knows and nobody will ever know. But that he is there and can be seen is fully authenticated. There are theories about him but they can be no more than theories. And there is the story.

Just over 100 years ago, some workmen employed in the main walls of the theatre in the Russell Street side, where they are old and very thick, came across a portion which sounded hollow.

The exterior of Theatre Royal, Drury Lane, as it is today

Scenes from *Pacific, 1860*, by Noel Coward
Above: Mary Martin and Graham Payn *Below:* Mary Martin and
Sylvia Cecil

Puzzled by this, they reported to their foreman who reported to his master, who spoke to the management. A decision was taken and the men broke through that portion of the wall. They found themselves in a little room. In that room was a skeleton and in the skeleton's ribs was a dagger. Somebody had been murdered and bricked up there. Nobody knows when, why or how. It was a male skeleton and there were upon it some pieces of cloth with a corded edge which crumbled at the touch. There was an inquest, an open verdict and the bones were interred in the little graveyard, now—like so many of its kind—a children's playground, at the corner of Russell Street and Drury Lane. It is the graveyard Dickens mentions in *Bleak House* on the steps of which Lady Dedlock died. That is all that is known. There was no clue. The dagger was of an old pattern but it might have been used as a theatrical prop.

But perhaps that murdered man is still at Drury Lane, for it is from the wall adjacent to that old room that the Ghost comes. He walks right through a room, now the upper circle bar, turns left, goes right round the back of the upper circle, and vanishes through the wall of the room which balances, on the other side of the theatre, the one from which he comes. He is very well behaved. He makes no noise—there are no groans or eldritch screams, no moans or jingling of fetters—he does not even carry his head tucked underneath his arm. He just does his walk and interferes with nobody. He has a peculiarity—although this is by no means so rare in apparitions as might be thought—he is a daytime ghost. He can only be seen between the hours of 9 a.m. and 6 p.m., never at night time. Perhaps he belongs to a union and those are the hours. The writer of this book, who has spent very many years in Drury Lane and by virtue of being its Chief Air Raid Warden in the Second World War, was about the theatre at all hours of the night, never caught sight of him during the hours of darkness. But by day, many times. What does he look like? He is just over middle height, he wears a three-cornered hat, his hair is either powdered or he wears a powdered wig—one cannot be quite sure of that—and he has a long grey riding cloak of the early 18th-century period draped about him. Beneath it can be seen his riding boots and the end of his sword. He is perfectly visible provided one does not get too near—then he is out of focus and vanishes. Even his features can be seen, a rather square, strong, good-looking face. He is not nervous of company although he never takes any notice of them. Sometimes he will take his walk when a matinée is in progress and the house full. He has been seen by many members of the public. Whether he can be seen or not depends on the possession of that special sense, which quite a lot of people possess, of being able to see such things. Often a crowd of people have been there when he was passing by. Some have seen him, others not. The late King and Queen Elizabeth, the Queen Mother, were most interested in him when they came to Drury Lane to inspect Ensa. It fell to the lot of the writer to take them round and he told them, at their request, all about the Ghost. But, although they waited quite a while, he did not show up. What made that all the more exasperating was that he was in full sight twice during the following day. He is popular at Drury Lane. Recently an offer was made to exorcise him, which was rejected with scorn, because he is regarded as a mascot. It has been noticed over the years that if he is seen just before the production of a new play, it will be a success. If not, it will fail. And that has always worked out.

When the writer conducts parties round that great theatre, as he does from time to time, there is always the liveliest interest displayed in the Ghost. He never fails to take them up on the Ghost Walk and tell them the story and gets much amusement out of watching the facial expressions of his listeners, which always include a large proportion of scoffers. Not so long ago he had the most disbelieving party he has ever taken round. As he told them the tale he observed they were openly derisive, touching their heads and nodding to each other, between pity and amusement at this poor fellow's state of mind. He did not mind, he is used to it. And he can believe his own eyes. But on that occasion, when he reached the climax of the story —entirely unsuspected and unknown to him—through an archway on his right came a workman in long grey overalls, wearing rubber shoes. You should have seen that disbelieving crowd of people run! They could not get out of the door quickly enough! Nobody believes in ghosts, of course, but everybody takes a good deal of care when they think one might be about.

Anybody can put it to the test. All that has to be done is to buy tickets for a matinée in the upper circle and preferably in the centre block. Then keep an eye on the big doors on the left. You may see him. There is no extra charge. Perhaps the best thing is to come twice—watch the show the first time and then watch for the ghost the second. He is worth seeing and one can guarantee that nobody will be frightened at all.

The theory about the apparition is that the murdered man was a young fellow of some substance who came up from the country to London in the reign of Queen Anne. He would naturally gravitate to the Theatre. At that time, the public had access back-stage and maybe this young man got very friendly with a girl employed in Drury Lane. Perhaps her lover was jealous and he killed that gallant.

If this is right it must have happened during the time when Christopher Rich, the Bad Man of Old Drury, ruled the theatre. He had an obsession that what mattered in the theatre was the number of seats it could hold. That idea persists today—what really matters is what happens on the stage to fill the seats. Anyway, Rich was constantly altering the theatre and pulling down walls to get in more seating accommodation—he had to be stopped eventually because he was endangering the structure. Workmen and builders were never out of the place. What more easy than for a stranger to be knifed, bricked up and quite forgotten? There was no police force, news travelled slowly, disappearances in London were a common event. And there perhaps the man lay for over a century. There are records of his visitations for nearly two hundred years.

There is said to be a tall, thin, emaciated and very ugly wraith which stalks across the theatre in front of what used to be the pit. That might be Macklin—but it cannot be authenticated. Strangely enough, Hallam, whom Macklin slew in the Green Room, does not walk, so perhaps Macklin's peregrinations are part of his eternal penance.

There is a story of a screaming woman in the Green Room and back-stage. That sound can certainly be heard—or something very like it—but it is a trick of the wind. When poor Clifford Heatherley died with tragic suddenness in *Crest of the Wave* many of the company swore they saw his ghost on the stage that night. He played The Ghost of *Henry VIII* and many were certain they saw him.

There is another Ghost Story of Drury Lane which has considerable authenticity. Some years ago a lady living in Birkenhead wrote to the author and said that she had seen a ghost in Drury Lane. It was not the one so often described. It appeared that she, her sister and her brother had attended a matinée there during the Boer War period. It was in the old theatre, prior to the auditorium reconstruction of 1921–22. There were, in those days, three blocks of seats in the dress circle, and those at the side reached right to the wall, so anyone entering had to come from the gangway. The party had three seats in the front row of the dress circle, on the left-hand side of the house, gangway seats, and there happened to be nobody else in the row at all. During an interval the lady glanced along the seats and was astonished to find a man sitting there. This seemed odd to her because nobody had passed them and nobody had been sitting there when they took their seats. It was all the more strange because his dress was very old-fashioned, it was that of the early part of the 19th century and his hair was longish and altogether he seemed very old-fashioned indeed. She drew her sister's attention to the man and the sister saw him, too. They discussed this rather odd happening until the brother asked what was the matter. They told him. He looked along the row. "What's the matter with you?" he said. "There is nobody there." The two ladies insisted they could see the man plainly. But the brother could not, and made jokes at their expense. When the curtain rose again, they still took occasional glances and he was still there. Gradually, the show absorbed their attention and when they looked again—he was gone! Nor had he passed them and there was no other way out. Despite their brother's sarcasm, they were both perfectly certain of what they had seen. The lady sent a description but it was not very clear. It might have fitted so many people. Then *Theatre Royal* was published—and a letter came almost at once. That lady now knew whom she had seen sitting in the dress circle at Drury Lane on that afternoon. It was Charles Kean. There was his photograph in the book, exactly as she and her sister had seen him. . . .

Stanley Lupino, when he played in pantomime at Drury Lane, always claimed that the ghost of Dan Leno came to him in his dressing-room—it was the one Dan had used—and gave him counsel and advice. Nobody else, however, has ever seen the shade of that superb comedian.

And now there is perhaps the most curious phenomenon of the lot and perfectly authenticated. This is not an appearance but a ghost of contact—and there are such things. You never see old Buckstone at the Haymarket but you hear him and see the things he does. This contact ghost at Drury Lane is a kindly, beneficent creature. He is there to help those in need and help indeed he does.

During the long run of *Oklahoma* there were many changes in the cast—practically every part had several performers. It so happened that a young actress came over to play the comedy role of Addo Annie who was not very experienced. She was young in her profession and she had never played in such a vast place or on so huge a stage as Drury Lane. Now 'The Lane' is notoriously hard on comedians. It has been the grave of many comic reputations. This girl found that her scenes were not getting over, she was not getting her laughs, she was getting no response at all. She was most upset because she was playing it exactly as shown and on the lines which had, by that time, become traditional. But still, she was not succeeding. Then suddenly, one evening she was conscious of two hands on her shoulders. She was gently impelled down-stage, and twisted to a certain angle. She felt also a pat on the back. She looked around, wondering what had happened, thinking that one of the two men on the stage at the same time was doing this to her. But they were right out of reach, as the business of the scene demanded. The hands kept a firm but friendly grip and again there was the little pat. She played the scene from that new position and she got her laughs. She got her comedy over. She succeeded for the first time. Then again, she felt the pat on the back and on occasions through the rest of the show those unseen hands guided her. She surrendered herself to them. This happened for three nights until she was quite certain as to what was meant and how to stand and how to speak. There was absolutely no more trouble for her. She came to see the writer of this book and told him her story. She expected he would laugh at her, but he did not. He listened with close attention. He had heard rumours of this before, but never met an actual case. She wondered who it could be, this good-natured soul who was so helpful to her. That he could not tell her. And that was that.

Then came the production of *The King and I*. In that successful play was a young actress named Doreen Duke. She had played a good selection of parts, she had an excellent singing voice and she wanted very much indeed to get this part and play at Drury Lane. Like everyone else she had to attend an audition. That is a rule. She went down to 'The Lane' scared and frightened. Nobody likes giving auditions anyway and to walk on that stage and sing to an empty auditorium in which sit only one or two people—the men who hold the fate of the players in their hands—is a shocking ordeal. But she did long to 'play the Lane'—it was her ambition. She went through the stage door, having shown her audition card, in fear and trembling. She went through the big doors leading from the passage on to the stage. And instantly she was conscious of two hands on her shoulders and a most cheerful feeling of helpful guidance all around her. The hands, gently laid on, never relaxed. Her name was called, she went on the stage and the hands guided her to a certain portion of it. There was a reassuring pat on the shoulder. The accompanist played the introduction. She received another pat as she began. And when she had finished, she was again patted on the back. She had got the part, not at all an easy one, for it requires skilful singing, and expert acting and splendid diction. Well, she can do all that. But throughout the rehearsals she felt that friendly guidance, right up to and including the first night, when she scored success. Then there was another pat and her unseen mentor left her, his job done. But she has been conscious of him at times since. Miss Duke is quite sure about this and it tallies with the *Oklahoma* story. It tallies with what has been heard before.

Who is this unseen friend who helps young players? It could be so many people, although such people are far more scarce in the profession than most people believe. It must have been a man of gentle character, upright and honest, who had had troubles himself and fought his way up and now was around the scene of some of his battles to help others on the upward path. It would seem that he was a comedian, for he knew exactly how that *Oklahoma* girl should play her comedy scenes. He must have known about singing, too, and also about drama. There is one person who fits all that and he is Joe Grimaldi, the great clown, a good, honest, kindly soul who helped people in his life—and he would do it again—as often as he had the chance. The author knows that many people will sneer at what he has written in this chapter. He does not mind that. He is not a spiritualist but he has the gift of seeing ghosts, not only in Drury Lane but elsewhere. These things are not phantoms, not spectres, they have a scientific explanation, they are linked with radio, television and radar. It has something to do with imprints on the ether and nobody really knows what the ether is. They know it is there but that is about all. One day, when scientists have given up inventing methods of destroying the world and everything in it—if there is any world left—maybe they will turn their attention to these phenomena. Then by twiddling a knob . . . But meanwhile, there are more things in heaven and earth than are dreamed of in our philosophy. . . .

CHAPTER ELEVEN

London Was Unlucky for Him

ALTHOUGH he earned fame elsewhere, there was a tragedian who was a Pillar of Drury Lane in his time—the 19th century—who was one of the strangest characters who played there. Yet, today, how many people will know anything about him? The fame of an actor is always ephemeral, only a few reputations live on. Yet there were some, who in their day were stars of the first magnitude, who are quite forgotten by the general public and remembered only by the historian. It is a pity, for many of them deserve their niche in memory and such a one was Gustavus Vaughan Brooke, the tragic tragedian, who in his time had international fame and whose whole life was one long, exciting adventure of triumph and disaster. But none of the great tragedies he played on the stage—and he played them nearly all—was stranger or more tragic than the story of his own life.

In many ways his career resembled that of Edmund Kean, who was a supreme Pillar of Old Drury. He lived dramatically—he died dramatically.

Not only did Brooke's career resemble Kean's but he was hailed as Kean's successor—nothing less. And as the story unfolds the similarity will become apparent. It is not pretended that he earned his fame at Drury Lane, but he played there with great success— one of his few bright patches—and he can be regarded as a pillar of the place. It is his due.

Gustavus Vaughan Brooke was born in Dublin on 25th April, 1818. He came of a distinguished family. His grandfather had served as an officer in the army of Gustavus Adolphus of Sweden, the Lion of the North—from whence the boy derived his name. He received a good education. There is no trace at all from whence his great theatrical talent came, yet he showed it early. As an infant, he would recite to his father's guests, using the dining-table as a stage. After hearing a ventriloquist for the first time, he mastered that strange art at once and scared his sister out of her life with his new achievement. His charm and vivacity, always his greatest asset, he inherited from his mother, whom he loved all his life. He did not like school but shone at athletics, especially fencing. He came into his own at the school entertainments. At one

167

such he played Young Norval—delivering those then well-known speeches:

> "My name is Norval; on the Grampian Hills
> My father feeds his flocks . . ."

and "Ye crags and peaks, I'm with you once again" with great gusto and to much applause. At a school production of *William Tell* he was so successful that he decided to become an actor and the ambition was fostered by his elocution master. His family had destined him for the Bar and he might have become a great advocate —but an event occurred which altered all that. In 1832 Macready, the 'eminent tragedian'—with triumphs from Drury Lane and Covent Garden fresh upon him—came to Dublin.

Young Gustavus begged his Mother to let him see the great actor. He had never been in a theatre. Eventually he gained permission and he went. He sat entranced. He saw a vision. This—and no other —was the life for him. 'The boards' could be his only highway.

The next morning, this hopeful, enthusiastic and very stage-struck lad had the courage to call upon the great Macready and what is more got an interview with him. He poured out the yearnings of his young soul to this very respectable, rather pompous and gentlemanly actor and got the advice which actors have been giving to aspirants since acting began—'Don't'. Gustavus thanked the great man politely, but did not take his advice. It was their first meeting but by no means their last. Macready had not daunted him then—and in the battle which followed he never succeeded in doing so, either.

Brooke's mother, very naturally, did not approve the stage ambition of her son. To be an actor then meant practically social ostracism. People in Brooke's class simply did *not* go on the stage. But she could not break the boy's firm resolve. Finally she said he could see what could be done about it. She expected he could do nothing.

He wasted no time. At the mature age of fourteen Master Brooke called upon Calcraft, the manager of the Dublin Theatre, and proposed an engagement. He was a handsome lad, with dark grey eyes, golden brown hair and a most persuasive manner. Something about him made the busy manager—and theatre managers were very busy men then—spare time to give him an audition. Gustavus spoke the big speech from *William Tell*. He impressed Calcraft, who made a vague promise that he 'would do something about it'. Young Brooke went home triumphant—only to learn that managerial promises take longer to cook than the piecrusts they resemble. The months passed by. And then, something happened. Edmund Kean was billed to appear. As often occurred, he failed to materialize. Calcraft, at his wits' end for an attraction, suddenly bethought himself of the local prodigy who had called upon him. A boy of good parentage—well known locally—it might do. . . . Gustavus was sent for and, to his delight, told he could play William Tell. Calcraft was taking a pretty big risk. The part was one which taxed mature tragedians, but young Brooke was not dismayed. His family were, however; they were horrified and his mother was stricken with remorse. Nothing stopped the impetuous boy. He had soon absorbed the part thoroughly and the announcement was made:

THEATRE ROYAL

Extraordinary Novelty

This present evening, 9th April, 1833,
Their Majesty's Servants will perform
Sheridan Knowles' Historical Drama
of

"WILLIAM TELL, THE HERO OF SWITZERLAND"

William Tell, by a Young Gentleman of
under fourteen years of age
Emma . . . . . Miss Huddart
A *Pas de Deux* by Master and Miss Harvey

The Entertainment will conclude with (second time these
seven years) *The Forty Thieves.*

Master Brooke had a good deal with which to contend, not the least being his leading lady. She was a good actress, who afterwards rose to fame as Mrs. Warner, but she was massive, and whenever she had to faint in the hero's arms, which occurred frequently in the action of the play, she completely overwhelmed the lad and 'got a laugh'. But Gustavus Vaughan Brooke triumphed over that. He followed his first success by playing Virginius, an even more mature part, and then Young Norval, to which he was better suited. In all of them he succeeded—as he also did in *Lover's Vows*—and his Benefit drew an enormous house. He was now certain that it was an actor's life for him.

So despite family opposition and the demands that he should at least take another name, he went off on tour—and his mother went too. He played tragedy and he played comedy and each was as good as the other. He played all over Ireland, and then he went to Scotland—and his mother went too. What she must have endured, that gently bred lady who had always lived in sheltered comfort, beggars description. Life on tour then was more rough than ready.

He opened in Glasgow for twelve nights and remained for twenty-four. Edinburgh acclaimed him next and so greatly did the playgoers of Dumfries admire him that they named a street after him—and called him 'The Second Edmund Kean'.

London heard about him. So he went to London—and London was always to be unlucky for him. In 1834 he made his début at the Royal Victoria Theatre—now the Old Vic. He played Virginius with the celebrated Miss P. Horton as his leading lady. He shared the bill with the famous Looking Glass Curtain, for the announcements read 'before which the celebrated Ramo Samee will go through a variety of extraordinary and novel tricks' (one would like to know more of that act), and additional items were *The Man With the Carpet Bag* and *Court Courting, By Jove*. There was plenty for the money in those days. Brooke was billed as 'The Hibernian Roscius, fourteen years of age'.

The Times, the *Sun* and the *Observer*, the leading papers, ignored the Hibernian Roscius, but the *Morning Advertiser* was there and after a bit of criticism as regards the choice of part said:

"The performance of young Brooke was astonishingly neat and his business and bearing manly and characteristic, far exceeding what could be expected from a boy of his years. Those who are fond of witnessing precocious genius will experience a great treat by seeing the Hibernian Roscius . . . the young gentleman met with a very flattering reception from a very crowded house."

He played for some time and then fell ill. When he reappeared the *Morning Chronicle* damned him with faint praise, and quoted Doctor Johnson's dictum about the performing dog. It was not too brilliant a London début—but London was always unlucky for Brooke.

By 1836 he was so sure of himself that he shed the title of Hibernian Roscius and was content to be billed as Mr. Brooke. He toured and he triumphed and returned to Dublin. He had begun to study the part of Othello which he designed for the astonishment of the

Dublin audience who had first acclaimed him. But to Dublin he was
no longer a prodigy and different levels of criticism were directed at
him. So in 1837 the Dublin Press would have none of Mr. Brooke and
compared him most unfavourably with Macready. But the public
came in crowds and liked his Hamlet and his Norval. He came back
to England, playing Shylock, Jaffier (in *Venice Preserv'd*), Romeo and
Iago. In the latter part he was accused of not knowing his lines. This
was not true. His conception of the character was of an easygoing,
off-hand villain, loving villainy for its own sake—using a bluff
exterior to hide his vileness. Laurence Irving, a magnificent Iago,
played it the same way. Brooke's fame and success grew and his
charming manner, his grace of movement, endeared him to audiences
who were getting tired of the strutting, bombastic style of acting.

In Sheffield, in 1838, Brooke played Claude Melnotte in *The
Lady of Lyons*. This was quite a new play, only Macready had played
it and he was to be a stumbling block to Brooke, too. But the young
man made a terrific success and it became one of his most famous
parts. He was now playing all the big leading roles.

London had not seen him since he matured. It was his fate that
the Metropolis should never see him at the full flight of his powers,
but only when he began to deteriorate. This great actor truly
belonged to the Provinces. But Macready, who was then at Drury
Lane, heard about him. Maybe he remembered the boy who had
come to see him in Dublin. But at any rate the rising fame of this
young man was not pleasing to the eminent tragedian. He did not
want another Richmond in the field. He sent his scouts to investigate.
They found Brooke at Dundee in 1840. Their report was enthusiastic,
perhaps a bit too enthusiastic. Macready thought he had better have
this youngster under contract to him and under his own eye. So
he offered Brooke an engagement at Drury Lane and Brooke
accepted. Gustavus had now broken with home ties. His mother no
longer toured with him, although the greatest love existed between
them. The young man was feeling his feet, and like most young men,
was kicking up his heels and sowing wild oats. His physical attraction, his charm and grace were drawing the attention of the ladies—
his *bonhomie* and celebrity were bringing all the 'good fellows' of
the towns around him. Brooke was drinking deep of the cup of Life
and leaving no heel taps.

But he came to Theatre Royal, Drury Lane, in December 1841.
He was determined to stand no nonsense from Macready—he was
not afraid of him. The great actor was busy with a production of
The Merchant of Venice. Brooke, under contract, went down to the
theatre and studied the cast list, which was displayed in the Green

Room, as usual, to see what he was to play. He found that a very
minor character had been allotted to him. Now he considered himself a star—and he regarded this as an insult. He tore down the cast
list and announced to all and sundry—and one may be sure the
whole company gathered round—that he, Gustavus Vaughan
Brooke, was not accustomed to play second fiddle to anybody. He
strode out of the theatre, vowing vengeance. Macready issued a
writ against him and said he had intended that Brooke should play
Othello to follow this small opening part. Brooke maintained that
he had been engaged for 'leading business' only and threatened to
disclose the whole of the terms of his engagement. Macready withdrew the writ. Brooke went back to the Provinces. His second venture
on London had been no less fortunate even than his first.

His evil star arose. He formed an attachment to a lady called
Marie Dufret, a fascinating woman and a very fair actress, who lived
with him for eight years. But for her—how different his career might
have been. He turned down all London offers, rather than be parted
from her. She probably persuaded him to do so. They lived at the
top of their bent—wine, song and Marie Dufret was the motto. But
if he did not come to London, Brooke was the hero of Manchester.
Put him in any of the theatres there and let Macready or any London
star be at the others—Manchester went to see Brooke. His Hamlet,
his Richard III, and above all his Othello, defied competition. He
was still only twenty-five and his method of life had not yet told
upon him.

But there is no stability in the Theatre. His Manchester management closed down, so Brooke went on tour again. He went to
Berwick-on-Tweed, which was quite an important theatrical town
until the railway came. He took his Dufret with him, her maid and
all her pet dogs. They caused a sensation and when he opened as
Sir Giles Overreach he nearly burnt the town down with excitement. They liked Dufret, too, when she played in *Jack Shepperd*.
Brooke brought theatrical glory back to Berwick and he basked in
its rays. He sat at the window of his lodgings, in a wonderful red
dressing-gown with his stage costumes spread all around him. Then
he and Dufret rehearsed love scenes; the crowds which thronged to
see 'the theatricals' were agog with curiosity. There was always a
big crowd outside the house—it was excellent publicity. The gentry
of the district lionized him—he was invited to their houses and fêted,
but Dufret was not asked. This upset her, and to bring herself into
public notice she took poison in the street, immediately repented
and yelled for a doctor. Her life was saved, of course, but it caused
a scandal and Brooke thought it best to move on. He left heavily in

debt, despite his success, for Dufret had helped to make the money fly. He played in small towns, but congenial company in the inns often prevented him from appearing. Then London made him another offer. It came from Edward Stirling, who was running the Olympic. Brooke sent a polite refusal, saying that after his treatment by Macready only the most advantageous terms could tempt him. But he also sent a list of his 'dates' to Stirling, in case that manager might raise the terms. But nothing came of it—yet the Olympic was to be the scene of his real London début.

He was an actor-manager now, but when he had a good week the publicans and Dufret got the money. But in 1834 he did very well in Glasgow although he failed in Liverpool. Then, with Dufret, he went back to Manchester, his spiritual home, again. The theatre was the Queen's.

There was a blow awaiting him on his arrival. He discovered that the management had already engaged Macready for a visit and Brooke would have to play second fiddle to the man he regarded as his enemy. He wanted the money badly, he had no choice—he had to submit. He played as indifferently as he possibly could. The 'eminent tragedian' rebuked him, which must have been gall to his soul. As soon as Macready had gone—he was himself again.

His power was now remarkable and his voice even more so. They liked big-voiced actors then—there were no microphones. And few, if any, in those days could equal Brooke's vocal power. So when another actor came to co-star with him, expectation rose to fever heat. For this was an American called Forrest. It was said of him that he could drown the voice of any living actor. Brooke was not afraid of this transatlantic son of Boanerges. For a couple of nights he let the American roar. Then he played Iago to Forrest's Othello. Forrest let his mighty voice have full scope. Brooke accepted the challenge. He too used his full vocal power. There has never been such a theatrical shouting match before or since. Brooke shouted the American right off the stage, to the mortification of Forrest and the astonishment of all auditors. Only a mutual hatred of Macready kept the peace between the two men.

Brooke remained Manchester's idol. But his way of life was beginning to tell on him. His late nights, with the ever-flowing brandy bottle in convivial company, were roughening that mighty voice, coarsening those handsome features, slowing up that grace of movement. And still London had only seen him as a child.

In the capital there was a dearth of talent. The year was 1848. Macready was on the verge of retirement, most of the others were second-rate. The Town was ready for a new actor—and then it was that Brooke stepped in. He accepted an offer to play at the Olympic, that strange old theatre made out of the timbers of French men-o'-war, now swept away. He would show London what real acting was, he said. They had seen Macready—well, now they should see Gustavus Vaughan Brooke.

He elected to open as Othello. The night before his London début he spent drinking with new-found friends and casual acquaintances, informing them all that Macready must look to his laurels on the morrow. And the morrow came. On Monday, 3rd January, 1848, the Olympic was packed to see the new actor. He strode on to the stage, looking magnificent. He got a grand reception and the audience settled down to listen. Somehow, he did not capture them. They became restless, an undertone buzz of talk was heard—he was not 'getting over'—that dread sound of boredom—persistent coughing—was heard. He began to lose his grip on himself. The stage manager came on to demand fair play. The audience responded and gave him a cheer. But Brooke was beginning to despair.

Then one of those strange things which only occur in a theatre happened to him. It was indeed an odd freak of Fate. It so fell out that the newspapers had been full of a story concerning Adb'l Kader, Emperor of Algeria, who had, in battle, saved a number of women and children from being burnt alive by cutting his way to them, single-handed, with his scimitar, through the ranks of his foes. The action of the play reached the Quarrel scene and suddenly Brooke rushed on the stage, burst through the fighters, sweeping his gleaming scimitar through the air, crashing it into the clashing swords like a flash of lightning and shouting, "Hold, for your lives." A man in the gallery, carried away by the force and grandeur of Brooke at this moment, cried, "Abd'l Kader, by God!" The house was electrified, and rose to its feet cheering. Brooke was saved.

It acted on him like a tonic. He had them now, in the hollow of his hand. He knew what to do with them—and he did it. To an audience hushed and listening intently, save when it burst into spontaneous applause, he swept to triumph. At the end of some of his speeches the cheers of the audience startled passers-by in the street. In the interval, there was excited discussion and terrific praise. Crowds gathered outside, and were told by lucky seat holders that a new actor had indeed arrived. It was like Edmund Kean over again.

Brooke held them prisoners to his every utterance. At the end, pandemonium broke loose. There had been nothing like it since that bleak winter night thirty-four years before, when that blazing comet, Kean, arose. Next day the Press was unanimous—with the single exception of John Forster of *The Examiner*, who was a great Macreadyite. Otherwise it was complete triumph. *The Times* was ecstatic, the *Morning Post* said, "With the single exception of Edmund Kean, we have seen no such Othello."

Brooke had, it seemed, conquered London. The management, following the Kean precedent, raised his salary from £10 to £60. He played Othello twenty-five consecutive times at the Olympic, but he never reached the heights of that first performance again. Then, like Kean, he triumphed as Sir Giles Overreach in *A New Way to Pay Old Debts*. And the Kean resemblance was working in other ways, too. For on the night he played Overreach he was very late indeed—he was almost not there at all. The curtain went up three-quarters of an hour late, with a cross and impatient audience in the house. But still his acting held them, although it was not the complete triumph of Othello.

The announcement of his Richard III packed the theatre, but he played the old Colley Cibber version and the critics cooled off. His Hamlet failed, his Shylock was seen only once, but he finished up the season with Virginius. Here was a direct challenge to Macready and the eminent one got a nasty jolt. Brooke may not have been so classic but he was terrific in the part.

He had failed to live up to his initial triumph. The fault was his own. Success, as usual, had gone to his head, in the form of too much liquor. On nights when he was not playing at the Olympic he dashed off to Brighton with his Dufret and appeared there. There were nightly carousals—which continued all day. Yet Benjamin Webster made him a handsome offer to appear at the Haymarket, which he refused. It was for £15 per night for 100 nights. Instead, he and Dufret went off to Hull.

But he came back to the Olympic and did new plays. They were bad plays, but his acting got high praise. Again he was off to the country to star with Dufret. He spent the money as he got it and was soon penniless. He and his enchantress crept back to London. He was given a Benefit at the Olympic. A scratch company was collected and he played Richard III. There was an excellent house and all seemed ready for a great 'come-back'.

But the woman who held such power over him ruined it all. She stood in the wings, holding a black cloak to throw over him when he came off. But she was also holding a large bumper of brandy. As he went on she cried, "Hurrah, Gustavus is on his own boards again!"—but every time he came off she gave him great gulps of brandy. By the time the last act was reached he was not sober. His wig got askew. He could not get it straight. The audience burst into laughter. He tore off the wig in anger and finished the last fight holding it in his hand. The audience split their sides. It was more tragic than the tragedy he played.

He took to the 'road' again, insisting that Dufret should be starred also and billing her as 'Mrs. G. V. Brooke'. It was observed that his magnificent voice was failing and the only treatment he gave it was more and more brandy. He sank low—he borrowed from every possible source.

He returned to Manchester, where he had always been successful. Despite his now apparent defects, he succeeded again. And then a great blow struck him. His beloved Marie Dufret left him and bolted to America. She decided he had run his course, there was no more to be got, so she hitched her wagon to another star and crossed the Atlantic. So far as he was concerned, there had been great love. But Brooke took it philosophically. He discovered she had saved the money which he had showered on her and had amassed quite a large sum, about which she had said nothing when bad times came upon them. She took it all away with her, as well as the magnificent stage wardrobe he had bought for her. His epitaph on his dead love was that perhaps it was the best thing which could happen to him. It is a pity that realization came so late.

He steadied himself under this shock and he returned to the Olympic, hoping for and confident of success. And it seemed assured. Then another of those blows which London always dealt him caught him right between the eyes as it were. The Olympic was then under the control of a man called Walter Watts. He was a clerk in the employ of the Globe Assurance Office. Nobody seemed to think it odd that a man in so humble a position could live so well, drive a handsome carriage and pair—and run a theatre. Eventually somebody woke up to the anomaly and it was discovered that Watts had robbed his insurance company of £70,000. The Olympic closed at once—Watts was sentenced to ten years' 'hard' but hung himself in his cell.

Brooke was perhaps the worst sufferer. This job had been his only hope. When he came to London to fulfil it, he had been arrested for debt by a firm of theatrical costumiers. Watts undertook to pay the bill. Now Watts was a criminal—and dead. Brooke managed to get some sort of an engagement at the Marylebone Theatre, filed his petition and so dodged the threatened arrest.

His voice was now playing him tricks, but with the temptress Dufret out of the way, he worked hard and paid off his debts somehow, or at any rate the most pressing of them. He had hoped for engagements at the Haymarket or the Princess's, but in vain. An

Scenes from *Oklahoma*, which holds the Drury Lane record both for
takings and length of run

A portion of a typical gallery queue waiting for an evening performance of *Oklahoma*. They waited patiently all through the matinee performances

offer came from America which he accepted. But there remained an interval before he sailed. The Olympic reopened and he played there a few times. His old enemy Macready came to see him act. He watched the man who might have been his rival very closely and at the end he showed himself a big man as well as a great actor. He went round to see Brooke—who always disparaged him publicly—and told him that, if he took proper care of himself, he was the only actor capable of sustaining the grand line of tragedy. It was a good deal for Macready to say, but say it he did.

Brooke went on tour to bridge the gap between then and his departure for America. And in Birmingham he got married to a Miss Marianne Elizabeth Woolcot Bray, of good connections and respectability. He seemed to have taken Macready's advice to heart, for he was acting superbly.

He sailed for America on 22nd November, 1851. He took the States by storm. There seemed no hard feelings on account of his defeat of Forrest. But he went into management for himself and disaster resulted. At St. Louis he nearly died of rheumatic fever, only his wife's patient nursing pulled him through. When he reappeared he was a public hero. In Boston they presented him with a public address. He bade farewell to the States at Philadelphia, and in spite of some heavy losses he came back home with £8,000 in his pocket. And he went straight on tour again. But London wanted him.

An extraordinary showman, named E. T. Smith, was in charge of Drury Lane. He had not done that place much good—he had reduced it to the level of a booth. He was a publican and an ex-policeman, yet he had a hand in running most of the important theatres. He turned up at Drury Lane, at the Lyceum, at Her Majesty's (the old house in the Haymarket), and at the West London. His whole idea was blatancy and advertising, mixed with sensation. When he was running opera at Her Majesty's—or rather, when he got Colonel Mapleson to run it for him there—he horrified that opera lover by playing, as an afterpiece to *Don Giovanni* by Mozart, Dibdin's little opera *The Waterman* with Braham singing in it—and singing a new song dedicated by Smith to the Metropolitan Board of Works, which Smith said, with some reason, was a most influential body. He got hold of Her Majesty's almost by a trick at a time when he had little money and he ran it in his own way. He left the musical side to Mapleson's hands but he saw to the publicity. When running Her Majesty's he invited the stars and the composers attached to that theatre to go to see The Oaks at Epsom. Some of them went—including Arditi, Titiens, Giuglini—all famous names. Smith drove them down in a really smart and glittering conveyance. They

M

noticed as they drove along that they created a good deal of attention —maybe they took it as a gesture to their own celebrity until, at one of the stops, Giuglini happened to get down and at the back of the coach saw a large board on which was painted, in glaring letters: 'E. T. Smith's Operatic Company'.

Smith wanted to stage the two famous pugilists, Sayers and Heenan, directly after their famous fight, all bruised and battered —on the almost sacred stage of Her Majesty's, as an adjunct to the opera, and Mapleson had great difficulty in preventing it. But Smith did actually stage them—at the Alhambra, which he was running as well. He always had ideas for getting more money into the house, for outdoing his rivals. One was that the stage at Her Majesty's should be divided into two floors, an upper and lower, and that double performances of *Il Trovatore* should be given simultaneously by different casts and at no extra cost to the public. He had his eggs in many baskets but most of them got broken. He was at one and the same time running Drury Lane, the Alhambra, Her Majesty's and a travelling circus. He was landlord of the Radnor Tavern, at the top of Chancery Lane, wine merchant, picture dealer, land agent, bill discounter and moneylender, and a newspaper proprietor. His full name was Edward Tyrrel Smith. In his youth he had determined to be wealthy and as a policeman on the beat he weaved his plans. He knew one great cardinal fact, that to appear to own money gets credit. At one time in his career he hired a £1,000 note, at the rate of £1 per day, just to be able to show it casually to people with whom he was doing business. It was lent to him by a moneylender named Sam Genese. By means of it he made large purchases and avoided giving any deposit, such was the confidence that note inspired. He would attend sales, make what purchases he required, tender his £1,000 note for the deposit, well knowing that nobody could change it, get the goods, resell them at once and pay for them out of the proceeds, pocketing the difference as profit. He wrote his name on the back of the note and from time to time his moneylending friend would replace the one so endorsed by a brand-new one—and Mr. Smith would be seen to endorse that. So everyone believed that £1,000 notes to him were as half-crowns to ordinary people. He bid for St. Dunstan's Villa in Regent's Park and it was knocked down to him for £10,000. The deposit was exactly £1,000—the value of Mr. Smith's note—which was not his to pay with. But he was a quick thinker. He announced then and there that he was going to turn the villa into a sort of Cremorne Gardens, which could not fail to draw tens of thousands and make him lots of money. The outraged auctioneer informed him that nothing of the sort could take place—

and cancelled the sale, to Smith's considerable relief. He missed a
train from Brighton and had two hours to wait. He could not bear
to spend them unprofitably. He strolled along the promenade and
saw a handsome corner house up for sale. He went to the agents,
found out the price and bought it out of hand. He gave orders for the
windows on the ground floor to be knocked out and replaced by
large ones of plate glass. That night he went to Paris and bought a
big consignment of bonnets at a most moderate price. He was going
to turn his Brighton house into a Parisian Milliners. He persuaded
two smart young saleswomen, of attractive appearance, to come
back with him and run the shop. He opened it under the name of
'Clementine'—and did such wonderful business with the latest
bonnets from Paris, sold by real French girls, that in a few weeks
he sold out at seven hundred pounds profit. On another occasion,
national mourning caused all the London theatres to close. E. T.
Smith was not going to lose money by a little thing like that. He
gave a Masked Ball at Her Majesty's. Tickets were a guinea each,
which included supper. Two days before the event, huge fires were
lighted in the property rooms, the paint room and the wardrobe and
there were cooked some hundreds of chickens which had been purchased, after ordinary market hours, at a very low price. Wine was
an 'extra'. He made large purchases of what purported to be
Heidsieck, Pommery Greno, Perrier Jouet and other popular brands
of champagne—only instead of buying it in Epernay or Rheims, he
bought it in Whitechapel, at a very much cheaper price. He invited
Mapleson, his manager, to taste some of it and a bottle was opened
which, according to the label, was of a famous name and vintage.
Mapleson said the bottle and label were all right but the wine was
terrible. It did not worry Smith and his stock of wine was completely
sold out to his masked customers when the ball took place. Much
later, after retiring from the theatrical business, he wrote to Mapleson
asking for a couple of tickets for his wife, whom he described as his
'old woman', and himself and announced that he was now in the
metal business and adding as a postscript: "Do you ever want any
tin?"

Yet E. T. Smith has a claim to be a Pillar of Drury Lane for he
ran that theatre for seven years, at a rental of £3,500. He opened it
on Boxing Night, 1852, with *Uncle Tom's Cabin*, then in the zenith of
its fame. He did all sorts of things. He ran Italian Opera at cheap
prices—4s. stalls, 2s. 6d. dress circle, pit and second circle 1s. and
both the galleries at 6d. A box was a guinea—it is a pity he did not
think of the slogan later used by the famous pills. He had Rachel
the tragedienne, Miss Glynn, Charles Mathews, Chinese magicians,

a circus and a man who crawled across the ceiling like a fly. And he also brought to Drury Lane Gustavus Vaughan Brooke.

Brooke reached that Valhalla of all actors under an engagement for twenty-four nights. He was always news because of his ups and downs and was just the sort of sensation that Smith wanted. He opened there, of course, as Othello. He was terribly nervous but he soon settled down. He was received with unbounded applause, cries of "Bravo, Brooke", and a very good Press. And indeed his Othello was the finest until Salvini played it. He kept sober and he worked hard. He was specially praised for his Iago, but his Virginius was his greatest success. He was entertained at a luncheon by friends and admirers and E. T. Smith took that opportunity of announcing his re-engagement. Brooke was now doing magnificent work. Maybe Drury Lane inspired him, as it has done so many. He had made people forget that Smith had pulled down its prestige and he was filling it again with glory. His first engagement over, he went to Belfast where he spent Christmas, and he distributed 125 blankets to the deserving poor. But he returned to Drury Lane on 31st January, 1854. Unluckily, Smith's showmanship had run away with him again, as it was always prone to do. He over-boosted Brooke to a remarkable degree. Brooke played Brutus in Howard Payne's old tragedy of that name, a great favourite with Edmund Kean. He got a very lukewarm reception. He played Richard III using the old Cibber version. Now Charles Kean had recently done a beautiful production of that play with the correct text at the Princess's. Smith used old tawdry scenery and costumes and the now despised version. Once more, London turned its back on Brooke. He tried again, with *The Corsican Brothers*, which he had played in America. They now called it *The Vendetta* and Smith gave it a most elaborate production. But everything went wrong and its five acts and nine tableaux were loudly booed by a bored audience. The season was a failure—but Brooke had managed to pay off his old debts and even settled with creditors who had not filed claims against him when he went into bankruptcy. It is almost redundant to recall all of Brooke's remaining career. He went back to touring and after his London rebuff he went back to brandy. But he was engaged to go to Australia. Before sailing he played a few more performances at Drury Lane. Although the Crimean War had broken out he did well this time. He made a wonderful farewell at a special performance in the best Vincent Crummles manner—and then reappeared the next night in aid of the Licensed Victuallers' School and Asylum. They should have given him a Benefit, not he them.

Then, 400 influential people signed an appeal for yet another performance, at the City of London Theatre, in Norton Folgate. Despite his two farewells, he played there for a limited number of performances and every night hundreds were turned away. He went to Dublin and bade his mother farewell. He promised to drink her health at 5 p.m. every day. He had no difficulty in keeping that promise.

He was an enormous success in Australia. He made large sums. He made the same mistake as in America. He went into management, and into speculations. He left Australia at last owing £1,500.

He got home in 1861. A change had come over theatrical affairs. Charles Kean had set a new fashion for acting and production. Brooke's methods were out of date—blood and thunder was at a discount. Yet he went to Drury Lane again. Smith was still there and gave him an indifferent cast—yet Brooke's power made them stand and cheer—he 'pulled them out of the plush'. He played his last at Drury Lane on 30th November, 1861. And now the Provinces looked on him askance. London was the arbiter of taste and Brooke was said to be old-fashioned. At Belfast he took only £44 in four nights. He refused to appear again and men carrying banners paraded the streets to tell the public. But he had one faithful friend, Avonia Bunn, who had been his leading lady at Drury Lane. She stood by him. He wanted to go back to Australia—he had not the means. He was arrested in Birmingham at the instances of E. T. Smith, for debt (it will be remembered that Smith did a bit of usury). He was put into Warwick gaol. Avonia Bunn pawned her jewels and got him out. He went bankrupt for £2,267. He tried Manchester again but drink and disaster made him inaudible—he who had driven stentorlike Forrest from the stage. Fechter went to see him and was heartbroken.

He crept back to London and was engaged at the City of London Theatre, but was often too drunk to appear. His mother died and it sent him to the depth of woe. His wife had died some time before and plucky Avonia Bunn married this fallen star—she wanted to help him. He sank lower and lower—he was hooted off the stage at Cork, too drunk to play Hamlet. In a tumbledown little theatre in Northampton all the few patrons saw was a stout, drunken man reeling about the stage and feeling for his words until the curtain was rung down on the play unfinished. He even played in an empty railway arch in Kilmarnock. And all the while, sick in heart and in body, he yearned for the sunshine of Australia, where he believed success would come again. He played for the last time in his own country, at the old Theatre Royal, in Belfast, on 23rd December, 1865. He was to appear as Edgar in *The Bride of Lammermoor* and

Captain Murphy Maguire in *The Serious Family*—for Brooke was an accomplished comedian as well as tragedian—when sober. As he stood in the wings his eye caught the bill of the play for that evening. It said 'Last Night of Mr. G. V. Brooke'. He gazed at it awestruck. "Last Night," he murmured. "It seems like sounding a fellow's death knell." Little did he know how right he was. Photographs of that bill were kept as mementoes by his friends and admirers. He played his parts, he made a farewell speech—he made his last exit from the stage where Siddons, Cooke, Kean and the great ones had played. The version of *The Bride of Lammermoor* had been written by old Calcraft, who had given Brooke his first engagement in Dublin. The wheel had come full circle.

His wife had scraped together the fares to Australia. His sister Fanny was to go with him. They had registered in the name of Vaughan, for Brook was still on the run from his creditors. The ship on which they were to sail left the Port of London, very much over-loaded. Brooke and his sister were to board her at Plymouth. There he took a last farewell of his wife, and there he had a narrow escape from being arrested at the last moment, and the ship was detained by bad weather. At length they put to sea just after midnight on Friday, 5th January, 1866, just missing the unlucky sailing day of Friday. There were 163 passengers on board and a crew of eighty-nine. A gale was raging, a terrible sea was running, but the ship steamed on.

By the Tuesday she was so battered that everything was battened down. The captain decided to return to Plymouth. But a heavy sea struck her, the cargo shifted, sea got into the engine-room and extinguished the fires. The sails which the ship carried were blown to tatters. Water flooded all cabins. A minister on board held Divine Service, for all feared they were lost. Brooke's sister, who had a weak heart, died in his arms.

All through this stress, Brooke behaved like a man. Bareheaded, barefooted, in a red shirt and a handkerchief round his head, he toiled at the pumps, he worked where the danger was worst, he did his best to keep up the courage of the passengers. He was a host in himself. The captain decided to abandon ship. As they cast off the boats, one was lost, another got away with sixteen passengers aboard. The captain stood by his ship. As the last boat left, the man in charge saw Brooke. He had helped get the women and children into the boats, taking all risks and showing great calmness. Now, in his red shirt and handkerchief, he stood waiting for this last call. "Will you not come with us, Mr. Brooke?" shouted the sailor. "No, no," replied Brooke. "You have enough. Should you survive, give my last farewell to the people of Melbourne. Good-bye." Those were his last words. The ship lurched and sank and down into the wastes of the Atlantic went the Tragic Tragedian, playing his last part better than any he had played before. Upright and brave to the end, everybody's friend and his own enemy, a man of great talents and wasted opportunities, he had risen to the heights and fallen again. But in his career he had been a Pillar of Drury Lane and had brought prestige and success to it when that theatre needed them. London had always been unlucky to him and it proved so to the end. For the name of the ship which was his grave was . . . S.S. *London.*

CHAPTER TWELVE

The Pantomimes and Drama of Druriolanus

D RURY LANE is the actual home of Pantomime. That form of
entertainment—which is really the only completely British
contribution to the world of Drama—was born there in the
year 1702, when a merry mixture of topsy-turvydom, extravaganza,
music, singing, fun and dancing, entitled *The Tavern Bilkers*, was
produced. It was concocted by John Weaver, a dancing-master of
Shrewsbury, and it was the germ from which Pantomime evolved.
It was not actually labelled as such, but it was announced that it was
'an attempt in imitation of the ancient pantomimes and the first of
the kind that has appeared since the time of the Roman Emperors'.
That was mainly true. The Roman Pantomimes were entirely
different, and *The Tavern Bilkers* was a considerable elaboration on
them. It was a success and was followed by another similarly topsy-
turvy show called *The Libertine Display'd*, produced the following
year. In 1717 John Rich, at Lincoln's Inn Fields, produced a piece
which he actually labelled as 'Pantomime'. But the honour of birth
must be accorded to Drury Lane. And there Pantomime held
revel at Christmas time, almost without break, until 1921—219
years. Today, it is different, as may appear later. But Pantomime
was a Pillar of Drury Lane.

Colley Cibber produced them, so did Garrick—and good ones,
too. Incidentally, he made his first appearance in the professional
theatre as Harlequin, deputizing at a moment's notice for his
friend Yates, at the long-vanished theatre in Goodman's Fields,
Whitechapel. Sheridan is believed to have actually written a version
of *Robinson Crusoe*. Edmund Kean played in Pantomime. It was a
definite form of art, not to be despised. And down the centuries,
crowds flocked to Drury Lane for the annual mid-winter treat.

F. B. Chatterton, that good manager, was actually bankrupted
by it—proving the exception to the rule, for Pantomime spelt
Money. He was in his time a King of Pantomime and old Doctor
Doran, that historian of the Theatre, has left a delightful glimpse of
what it was like in his day. He went down to Drury Lane on the
afternoon of Boxing Day, 1865, "passing through some of the worst of
'the slums' which find vent therein. . . . There was a going to and
fro of groups of people, and there was nothing picturesque in them;
assemblings of children, but alas, nothing lovable in them. It was a

184

universal holiday." Then he goes through the stage door of Drury Lane Theatre to see the last rehearsal of the show to be produced that evening. . . .

"The change from the external pandemonium to the hive of humming industry in which I then stood, was striking and singular. Outside were blasphemy and drunkenness. Inside, boundless activity, order, hard work and cheerful hearts. There was very much to do, but every man had his special work assigned him, every girl her allotted task. An unaccustomed person might have pronounced as mere confusion, that shifting of scenes, that forming, unforming and re-forming of groups, that unintelligible dumb show, that collecting, scattering and gathering together of 'young ladies' in sober-coloured dresses and business-like faces who were to be so resplendent in the evening as fairies, all gold, glitter, lustrous eyes and virtuous intentions. There was Mr. Beverley—perhaps the greatest magician there—not only to see that nothing should mar the beauty he had created, but to take care that the colours of the costumes should not be in antagonism with the scenes before which they were to be worn. There was that Michael Angelo of pantomimic mask inventors, Mr. Keene, anxiously looking to the expressions of the masks, of which he is the prince of designers. Then, if you think those graceful and varied figures of the ballet are easy to invent, or to trace, as they seem, and are at last easily performed, you should witness the trouble taken to invent, and the patience taken to bring to perfection—the figures and the figurantes—on the part of the artistic ballet master, Mr. Cormack. But, responsible for the good result of all, there stands Mr. Roxby, stern as Rhadamanthus, just as Aristides, inflexible as determination can make him, and good natured as a happy child; he is one of the most efficient of stage managers, for he is both loved and feared. No defect escapes his eye and no well directed zeal goes without his word of approval. Messrs. Falconer and Chatterton are meanwhile busy with a thousand details, but they wisely leave the management of the stage to their lieutenant-general, who has the honour of Old Drury at heart. . . ."

It is a warm and well-drawn picture of a pantomime rehearsal in 1865, ninety years ago. Mr. Beverley was, of course, the most famous of scenic artists; his name was starred on the bills. His work was done on the paint frames back-stage at Drury Lane and they are still there.

Dr. Doran gives some interesting figures. He states that the average expenses of Drury Lane Theatre at Christmastide, when there are extra performances, amount to nearly £1,500 a week. The rent was £4,500 for 200 nights, every additional performance above that being at the rate of £5 per night. There must be £160 in the house before any profit could be reckoned upon. The figures today would make him swoon with amazement. Yet Old Drury carries on. There were over 200 children in those panto-mimes, and the proportion of girls was higher than boys. The management preferred quiet and dull children, to those who were 'smart and lively'. These latter, says the good Doctor, were more given to 'larking about' and thinking of their own cleverness. The quiet and dull children were

> "more teachable and can be made to seem lively without flinging off discipline. These little creatures are thus kept from the streets; many of them are sons and daughters of those employed in the house, and their shilling a night and a good washing tells pleasantly in many a humble household to which, on Saturday nights, they contribute their wages and clean faces."

The salaries of children appearing at Drury Lane today, in *The King and I*, are more than those of second principals in Chatterton's pantomimes—but the truth about the cleanliness and discipline still stands. The children are all the better for their stage experience and certain local councils, who object to their employment, would be usefully employed if they made a personal inspection of the children's fitness, character and happiness and the conditions under which they work.

The Doctor continues:

> "Then there are the indispensable but not so easily procured 'ladies of the ballet'. They number about five dozen; two dozen principals, the rest in training to become so. Their salary is not so low as is generally supposed—twenty-five and occasionally thirty shillings a week. They are 'respectable'. I have seen three or four dozen of them together in their green room, where they conducted themselves as 'properly' as any number of well-trained young ladies could at the most fashionable of finishing establishments."

Maybe the Doctor did not see all of the girls who made up those vast pantomime crowds. Later on, all sorts of people got in—and many of the chorus and show girls were, at other seasons, 'ladies of the town', who could, by virtue of their seasonal engagement at Drury Lane, claim to be described in the charge sheets when arrested as 'Actresses'. The writer himself, when managing the Drury Lane pantomime of 1921–22, had his office invaded by an irate nymph who claimed she had suffered physical damage during the progress of the show. On being asked to describe her injury, she did so, in most picturesque terms, and not content with that insisted on displaying the portion of her anatomy, a portion not by any means usually displayed to public gaze, even in these revealing days.

The young ladies of the ballet would not look at thirty shillings a week today. They would be receiving anything from £10–£12 a week and more in pantomimes.

The Doctor goes on:

"To return to more general statistics, it may be stated that, in busy times, four dozen persons are engaged in perfecting the wardrobes of the ladies and gentlemen. Only to attire these and the children, forty-five dressers are required; and the various coiffures you behold have busily employed half a dozen hairdressers. If it should occur to you that you are sitting over or near a gasometer, you may find confidence in knowing that it is being watched by seventeen gasmen; and that even the young ladies who glitter and look so happy as they float in the air in transformation scenes, could not be roasted alive, provided they are released in time from the iron rods to which they are bound. These ineffably exquisite nymphs, however, suffer more or less from the trials they have to undergo for our amusement. Seldom a night passes without one or two of them fainting; and I remember, when once assisting several of them to alight, as they neared the ground, and they were screened from the public gaze, that their hands were cold and clammy like clay. The blood had left the surface and rushed to the heart, and the spangled nymphs who seemed to rule destiny and the elements, were under a nervous tremor; but almost as soon as they had touched the ground, they shook their spangles, laughed their light laugh and tripped away in the direction of the stately housekeeper of Drury, Mrs. Lush, with dignity enough not to care to claim kinship with her namesake, the Judge; for she was once of the household of Queen Adelaide, and now has the keeping of 'the national theatre, with nine servants to obey her behests'."

The 'flying conditions' today, when indulged in, never cause
faints but Dr. Doran draws a delightful picture of life at Drury Lane
ninety years ago. It has altered in very many ways now, but it had not
altered to any extent when Augustus Harris, one of the very greatest
of all the pillars, took control of 'the National Theatre' in 1879, a
mere fourteen years later. How he did this, in such exciting circumstances and with only £3 15s. od. in his pocket to start with, has been
told elsewhere. He had always had the ambition to control 'The
Lane' when he was managing the Royalty Theatre, in Dean Street,
for Edgar Bruce. That is a very small theatre, much too small for the
soaring soul of Harris. The first person to whom he confided his
desire was George R. Sims, the famous journalist and dramatist.
They were having supper at Kettners. Sims was astonished to hear
that Harris was even after Drury Lane. He knew, like everyone else,
of its closing—which indeed had been hailed as a national calamity.
He considered, experienced man of the Theatre as he was, that the
running of that theatre was a most difficult affair, and although he
knew the volatile and energetic Harris well, he had never regarded
him in that capacity. But Gus, as everyone called him, told Sims that
he had not only made his offer but had his plans. If he got the
theatre he would run drama and pantomime—'on a scale of mag-
nificence hitherto unprecedented'. He would open with Shakespeare,
despite the fact that Chatterton had said it spelt ruin, then pantomime and then drama. Indeed, he had his drama, written by Paul
Merritt, Henry Pettitt and himself—he had his finger in every pie.
It had the very modest title of *The World*. And only the whole world
was big enough for Harris. Today, of course, he would have cast his
eye on Space itself and somehow compassed it. He got Drury Lane
and he reckoned that a capital of £3,000 would see him through.
That alone shows the difference in theatre finance then and now.
He never got that £3,000, he started with £250 short of it. He took a
gamble and he won. Sims warned him that 'The Lane' might ruin
him. Harris laughed. "It can't," he said. "I've nothing to lose."

That was the spirit which made for success. If Gus had not got
the money he had the ideas, and in the Theatre ideas count. He
started with Shakespeare on 1st November, 1879, with a tremendous
revival of *Henry V*. He did this in a most spectacular manner. That
fine actor, George Rignold, played Henry V, and the cast included John Ryder, Stanislaus Calhaem (playing Fluellen), Charles
Harcourt, Mr. Odell—later that familiar figure at the Savage Club
—as Pistol, Dora Vivian as Katherine and Miss Brabrook Henderson
as Chorus. Harris made the military and battle scenes a speciality.
He had lots of horses on the stage and filled it with banners, marching

and counter-marching, the clash of swords and shimmer of steel. It was a big success. *The Era* said: "The entire production augured well for Mr. Harris's enterprise and seemed to be the dawn of a new day in the history of Drury Lane." That critic was dead right. Almost at once Harris leapt into the front rank of the managers of his day and into the front rank of the great ones of Old Drury. He had to follow Shakespeare with pantomime—which was one of the pillars of his plan. He had left it a bit late, naturally, to get the people he wanted, and had, perforce, to fall back on the Vokes Family, who had ruined Chatterton. But he had them under control —they had had a bad fright and were not so aggressive and grasping. The pantomime was *Bluebeard*, which Harris announced as 'By the Brothers Grimm' and E. L. Blanchard. Music by Frederick Wallenstein. It was produced on 26th December, 1879, and he did it on the most lavish scale possible. The Vokes Family figured largely— Fred Vokes as Bluebeard, Jessie Vokes as Lelion, Fawdon Vokes as Luacabac, Victoria Vokes as Fatima and Mrs. Fred Vokes as Sister Anne. There was a double harlequinade—two of everything which mattered. The Clowns were Fred Evans and Will Simpson, the Pantaloons were Gellini and Carl Waller, the Harlequins were Deane and Romaine and the Columbines Mesdames Hedlington and Conway. There were extra characters, too. Miss Wilson played Arlequen Parisienne; Miss Harvey, Pierrot; Miss Murray, Panette; and Miss Leaver, Polichenelle. Harris produced the whole thing himself, his invariable rule. At the end he appeared on the stage in his evening dress and Inverness cape and facing the audience, he demanded, "Well, are you satisfied?" A burst of cheers told him they were. This became his changeless custom. Sometimes he did not even wait until the end of the show before taking a bow. The pantomime ran for eighty-one performances. Again *The Era* praised: "Mr. Augustus Harris has begun well; he has not only deserved success—he has attained it."

Harris used a theatre as a theatre should be used. No sooner was the pantomime over than on went *La Fille de Madame Angot*. This popular opera by Lecocq was no novelty but Harris gave it a production such as no light opera had ever known before. *The Times* said:

"Clairette has never before declared herself the daughter of Madame Angot amidst such surroundings. Mr. Augustus Harris, in fact—like his father before him an expert in such matters—has done his best and it must be confessed has succeeded in his endeavours to excite the attention and gratify the taste of those upon whom the words 'Old Drury' exercise a certain spell."

Nor was the *Daily Telegraph* behindhand with praise.

> "The entire representation was characterized by a completeness in every department rarely attained and its merits were recognized by the crowded and delighted auditory with a heartiness of appreciation seldom more strongly manifested and never more thoroughly deserved."

To use the resources of that magnificent stage was child's play to a man who had managed to put Grand Opera, on its grandest scale, on a stage about three times too small for it—as he had done on tour and at the St. James's Theatre. A Grand Ballet was a feature of *La Fille de Madame Angot* with Mlle Palladino as the *première danseuse*. It ran for ten weeks and was not the only attraction of the evening, being preceded by a revival of that famous drama *Lady Audley's Secret*, with Louise Moodie in the title role.

Harris then staged Shakespeare again. He put on *As You Like It.* He did it well. He had Marie Litton, then the leading actress of the day, as Rosalind, Herman Vezin as Jacques—one of the finest exponents the Stage has ever had—Kyrle Bellew as Orlando, Lionel Brough as Touchstone and old William Farren, the last of the great classic actors, as Old Adam. He got much kudos and acclaim from the Press and public, who both agreed it was an artistic treat of the highest order, reflected the greatest credit on all concerned—and Mr. Harris—and that no more truthful embodiment of the author's conception had ever been seen on the Stage! It ran from May 1880 until July of the same year.

Then Harris launched his first great drama—the one of which he had told Sims—*The World.* He produced it on 31st July, 1880, a time when few other theatres were open. That did not worry him— he would have less opposition. He was not content with being manager of the theatre, holder of the Royal Patent, producer and part author of the play—he performed in it himself. That fine actor William Rignold played Sir Clement Huntingford (known as Charles Hartley), and Gus Harris played Harry Huntingford, Sir Clement's younger brother. The cast is worthy of recording because this was the beginning of a new dramatic era at Old Drury. Besides the two names already mentioned, there were W. T. Ford, Charles Harcourt, Harry Jackson, J. R. Gibson, R. S. Boleyn, Augustus Glover, Arthur Matthison, A. C. Lilly, Philip Beck, A. Weldon, James Francis, Mr. Ridley, Mr. Storey, Mr. Jones, Mr. Turner, Miss Helen Barry, Miss Fanny Josephs, Miss Fanny Brough (to become a pillar of Drury Lane herself), Miss Annie Lambert and Miss Macnamara.

The World had everything in it that the fertile imagination of Harris could devise. A critic said: "An ingenious sensational drama of the day, in which a series of the most exciting episodes were strung together and illustrated with a degree of realism in the scenery and accessories that within our knowledge has scarcely ever been surpassed." Amongst those scenes was the embarkation of a liner at Cape Town, the explosion of what was described as 'an infernal machine' on board, which wrecked the ship and led up to the very sensational and much applauded scene of a raft at the mercy of the waves, on which crouched four survivors of the disaster. This was so well done and so exciting that it drew thunders of applause. In *The World* Harris began his idea of staging a scene which was familiar to most people, especially Londoners, and here it was the inside of the Aquarium at Westminster, with its crowds, and music and entertainments—and it was much brighter and jollier than its original had ever been. People marvelled at it. Just for makeweight, too—in the five acts and nine tableaux, Harris threw in a scene in a lunatic asylum and at a Fancy Dress Ball. There was no doubt about the success of *The World*. He appeared at the end with his question, "Well, are you satisfied?" And they were! *The World* was a big success in New York, where Osmond Tearle played in it and, indeed, *The World* was played all over the world. Gus Harris was now the biggest thing in the biggest theatre and Old Drury was itself again.

Gus then staged his pantomime *Mother Goose*. Here he had a cast indeed—Mother Goose was Little Addie Blanche, John Ridley was The Goose, Agnes Hewitt was Mother Shipton, Mark Kinghorne, King Folderol the First, Kate Santley was Prince Florizel—Principal Boy; Frank Wyatt was Punch and Mr. Ross was Judy, a small boy named Master Bertie Coote was Tobie—he afterwards became a big star and will be remembered for his sketch *A Lamb on Wall Street*, and his show *The Windmill Man*; Fred Storey outdid the Vokes Family in leg agility and played Rifum Tifum; Ada Blanche was Princess Bella and the comedy was in the most expert of hands— the great Arthur Roberts as Dr. Syntax and James Fawn as Yokel. What a couple of laughtermakers to work together! Roberts, the king of gagsters, was himself a pillar of the Theatre and of Drury Lane. There was again a double harlequinade. It got a wonderful Press—and deserved it. Harris pressed on. Hot on the pantomime came a revival of *Virginius*, starring the great American tragedian John M'Cullough, supported by John Ryder, J. H. Barnes, Lydia Cowell, Mrs. Arthur Stirling, Miss Macnamara—and Mr. Augustus

Harris as Icilius. A critic mortally offended Harris by referring to his performance as 'a penny Ice-ilius'. M'Cullough also played Othello, supported by Herman Vezin, John Ryder, J. H. Barnes, Gus Harris (as Roderigo), Bella Pateman (as Desdemona) and Mrs. Arthur Stirling as Emilia. Gus spread his net for the world and brought to Drury Lane the famous Meiningen Court Company from Germany with a varied repertory—from Shakespeare in German to Schiller and Molière. This added laurels to Harris and Old Drury. That was in April 1881.

In the August of that year Harris launched his second drama— *Youth*. It was in five acts and eight tableaux—written by Paul Merritt and, of course, Augustus Harris—and Harris played in it, too. It was a Military Drama, and a tremendous success. Harris gave it a fine cast—John Ryder, A. Matthison, W. H. Vernon, H. Kelcey, Caroline Hill, Harry Nicholls, John Ridley, Louise Willes, Mrs. Billington, Marie Litton, Miss Macnamara, Maude de Vere, Miss Miska, Helen Cresswell, Amy Coleridge and himself. The story does not matter much, though it was good and well contrived. It was the production which really mattered. Here was a country church, the Upper Thames, which changed into the Boating Cottage— with sub-title, *The Moth and the Flame*; Frank's Rooms; Mrs. Walsingham's Soirée; the Convict Prison; Departure of a Troop-ship (many will remember that this was done again in *Cavalcade*); the Defence of Hawke's Point; and Beechley by Night—this was the old home to which the hero returned, whiter than the driven snow. Everything was remarkable, but the highlight was the battle scene. This was truly thrilling and stirred the audience to yells of enthusiasm and a fever heat of patriotism. It was one of the best battle scenes ever staged. No less a person than General Sir Frederick Roberts, V.C., G.C.B., afterwards Field Marshal Lord Roberts, the beloved 'Bobs', personally congratulated Harris. He came to see it and remarked that "although he had heard how wonderfully realistic was the scene of the Defence of Hawke's Point, he had no conception that it was so faithfully represented". Lord Wolseley— 'All Sir Garnet'—the Commander-in-Chief—wrote saying: "You are at liberty to announce my entire approval of the Military Scenes in *Youth* which were represented with a vividness and reality quite startling." What could one wish for more—from the two most famous soldiers of the day? Harris gave some special performances for the troops who had recently been fighting in Egypt under Wolseley—and *Youth* proved just the stuff to give the troops. George Augustus Sala said: "The drama is from first to last intensely interesting and it achieved a distinct, unequivocal, triumphant and

Above : Walter Donahue and Mary Marlo in *Oklahoma* (Everything's Up to Date in Kansas City) *Left :* Isabel Bigley and Harold (now Howard) Keel in *Oklahoma*

Scenes from *Carousel* at Drury Lane

well-deserved success." "No stage battle, even with the liveliest recollection of those fought under Ducrow in the old Astleyan days of yore, can be compared with that, bearing so terrible an aspect of reality when the Drury Lane troops are engaged in the defence of Hawke's Point."—this the *Daily Telegraph*. The *Daily Chronicle* noted that "something like delirious excitement was manifested" and *The Echo* said *Youth* was "the most elaborate and most finished production that has ever been placed on the English stage". *Youth* ran for 114 performances and then had to make way for the pantomime—to be revived for a run of 69 nights afterwards. It went all over the world.

Then came *Robinson Crusoe*, on Boxing Night, 1881. This was written by E. L. Blanchard with music by Oscar Barrett. Again there was a wonderful cast—the comedy was led again by Arthur Roberts as Mrs. Crusoe and James Fawn as Mr. Timothy Lovage. Robinson Crusoe was Fannie Leslie; Will Atkins, Harry Nicholls; Friday was Charles Lauri, Jnr.; Polly Lovage, the Principal Girl, was Miss Amalia. Naturally there were animals in this—stage animals—Messrs. John Ridley and Abrahams were The Pug Dog; the Great Little Rowella and Weldon were The Cat; and Mr. Charles Ross was The Goat. The Sisters Watson and the Robina Quartette were the Days of the Week, John D'Auban was Ketchi-windo and Luna and Stella were the Principal Dancers. Harris gave them staggering effects. A ship left London Bridge and sailed down the Thames. By means of a double panorama, both sides of the river were shown. There was a wreck and the audience saw the ship descend to the bed of the ocean and become the scene of a glittering undersea ballet; there was a procession of Indians—probably black cannibals are meant—passing through a ravine, with crowds watching them—and there was a Street in London with a Procession of Trades. This was the beginning of Harris's obsession for processions. It was such a success that every pantomime had a procession from then on. There were one hundred in the chorus alone, apart from supers and children. Harry Payne was now the Clown in the Harlequinade and a mirror ballet which had succeeded the previous year was repeated. *Robinson Crusoe* ran for 122 performances. And the papers began to remark—and continued to do so for years—"Augustus Harris has surpassed himself." And at the curtain fall on every first night, he was there with his question, "Well, are you satisfied?" The answer was always in the affirmative.

The pantomime was followed by a season of German Opera with Richter conducting. Then Madame Ristori visited Drury Lane and played Lady Macbeth and Elizabeth, Queen of England—

N

Giacometti's historical play. In *Macbeth* William Rignold played Macbeth and J. H. Barnes, Macduff. On Saturday 5th August, 1882, Gus Harris presented his third drama. This was again a single word title—maybe he borrowed the idea from Tom Robertson, and it was a good one. The drama was called *Pluck*. It had a first-rate cast— J. H. Barnes, Arthur Dacre, Harry Jackson, Harry Nicholls, John Ridley, Caroline Hill, Agnes Thomas and Lydia Foote—and also Augustus Harris. *Pluck* did not get the paean of praise ladled out to its predecessors, but it succeeded. He went in for scenic display, of course, and lots of it. The big effect was a train smash—often repro- duced on 'The Lane' stage afterwards, but then a novelty. There was also a house on fire. And a very realistic foggy night. But it ran 103 nights. Henry Pettitt and Augustus Harris were the authors. For good measure, it had a little farce as a curtain-raiser—*The Opera Cloak*— written by L. D. Powles—and Augustus Harris. The energy of the man was amazing.

Then came the pantomime and it was *Sindbad*, again by E. L. Blanchard with music by Oscar Barrett.

The cast was brilliant, Arthur Roberts and James Fawn, Harry Parker, Fred Storey, Chas. Lauri, Jnr. (a poodle), Harry Nicholls, John D'Auban, Charles Ross. Sindbad was Nellie Power, Fatinitza was Constance Loseby—a very fine performer. And, as Captain Tra-la-la, there was Vesta Tilley.

And a new comedian joined Drury Lane, a very big fat man destined to be a pillar indeed. His name was Herbert Campbell and he played Kabob.

Of course Harris had a procession. It was a complete record of the Kings and Queens of England, from William the Conqueror right down to Queen Victoria. Everything was to be perfectly accurate, down to the smallest detail of costume. The children of England would be able to see the complete cavalcade of English history—and presumably learn it—in the space of about six minutes. Alas, at the first performance it all got mixed up and immense confusion ensued, much enjoyed by the audience but not by Gus Harris, who, like Queen Victoria on another occasion, was not amused at all. But they told him they were satisfied, all the same, and he soon got it right. *Sindbad* was a big success, at 102 performances. At the end of the season, Harris gave special performances for the thousands of poor children, a custom he kept up all his life thereafter. The date was Xmas, 1882. The Carl Rosa Opera Company played a season beginning on 26th March, 1882. Carl Rosa himself was in charge and produced two new operas, *Esmerelda* by A. Goring Thomas and *Columba* by A. C. Mackenzie, afterwards knighted and the Principal of the Royal Academy of Music. Both were successful at the time—and perhaps *Columba* was the best of the two.

On Saturday, 4th August, 1882 (Saturday was Harris's favourite opening night), came the drama *Freedom*—still the single word title—written by George F. Rowe and Augustus Harris—and the amazing man also played a Royal Naval Commander. *Freedom* had an Egyptian setting and had a topical appeal as it took place on the banks of the Nile and dealt with the Egyptian Slave Traffic, then in the news. It had James Fernandez, Henry George, Harry Jackson, Harry Nicholls, John Ridley, George F. Rowe—both authors played parts—Sophie Eyre, Miss Bromley and Lydia Foote in the cast. The scenery was magnificent, opening with a scene in the bazaar of an Egyptian city. There were scenes in the desert, murders, fights, escapes over roof tops and all the mixture which Harris knew so well how to blend. *Freedom* ran for fifty-five nights and was taken off to make room for another drama, by Robert Buchanan and Augustus Harris, called *A Sailor and His Lass*. This had an immense cast—it included, of course, Augustus Harris who played the hero. And that was a mistake. So long as he stuck to villains, or semi-villains, he got by, but Gus was neither the shape nor make of which heroes are fashioned. It was lurid melodrama, this show, and he did not help it. With him were James Fernandez, a magnificent actor, Harriet Jay, Sophie Eyre, Harry Jackson, Harry Nicholls, a real pillar of 'The Lane', John Ridley, who could play anything and did, Clara Jecks, Arthur Chudleigh, afterwards to become a well-known manager, and scores more. There were apple orchards and real cows, and a real four-wheeled cab, a midnight orgie in Ratcliffe Highway, an explosion, a ship at sea, a storm with real rain, a fight in the rigging, a wreck, preparations for a hanging and a last-minute reprieve—enough for anyone, even Drury Lane. It ran for forty-eight nights and made a lot of money on tour.

Then Harris staged the most popular of all pantomimes, *Cinderella*, the work of Blanchard and Barrett again. Harry Parker was the Baron; Fred Storey, General Sharpwitz; Minnie Mario, the Prince—here called Prince Pastorelle; Miss M. A. Victor was the Baroness; Harry Nicholls and Herbert Campbell the Ugly Sisters; Cinderella was Kate Vaughan; George Lupino was Ignoramus; Emma Palladino was the Principal Dancer. There was also The Rosa Troupe, and children trained by Katti Lanner, and the Clown was Harry Payne. An important thing about this pantomime, produced on Boxing Night, 1883, was that Harris started the idea of two performances daily—and it proved a big success all through January. He gave ten performances weekly and the 100th was reached on

February 29th, it being Leap Year. Up to that date it had cost him £30,000 to run. His father had done *Robinson Crusoe* years before at Covent Garden and it had been hailed as the most expensive ever. That had cost £16,000. Things were going up, even then. But it was an immense success.

Harris had now done five years at Drury Lane. He had changed failure into triumph, the prestige of 'The Lane' had never stood higher. He had a policy and he pursued it. The public responded. Going to 'The Lane' became a habit and every time it was said "Augustus Harris has surpassed himself".

He had his upsets and his setbacks but he never wavered. It always came right in the end. His activities were amazing, he could not keep still. He controlled tours, provincial theatres, Covent Garden and Drury Lane—making a bigger success of it than had Bunn. He was a newspaper proprietor, too. His audacity was equalled by his pluck—he was the biggest thing in the world of the Theatre. It is not possible here to give details of all his plays and all his pantomimes, though the latter may be listed as being very important. They were as follows:

1884–85: *Dick Whittington.* Fanny Leslie (Dick), Kate Munro, Harry Nicholls, Herbert Campbell, Dot Mario, Minnie Mario and Charles Lauri, a perfectly marvellous cat.

1885–86: *Aladdin.* Grace Huntley (Aladdin), Nellie Leamar, Kate Leamar, Harry Nicholls (Widow Twankey), Herbert Campbell (Abanazar), Victor Stevens and Charles Lauri.

1886–87: *The Forty Thieves.* Edith Bruce (Ganem), Connie Gilchrist, Minnie Mario, Dot Mario, Miss M. A. Victor, Herbert Campbell (Cogia), Harry Nicholls (Ali Baba), Victor Stevens (Ally Sloper), Robert Pateman and, as a donkey, Charles Lauri.

There was a bit of trouble about that pantomime. Gus considered so small a number as forty for the thieves too inconsiderable for Drury Lane. There was an impasse when he refused to produce it. They told him there must be only forty thieves, as the children knew the story and would resent alteration. He found a way out. "All right," he said, "have forty thieves—but every thief shall have ten servants." And they did. . . .

1887–88: *Puss in Boots.* Miss Wadman (Jocelyn); Letty Lind as Princess; Herbert Campbell and Harry Nicholls as King and Queen; Charles Danby and Lionel Rignold as the Wicked Brothers and Charles Lauri as The Cat.

In case anybody thinks that 'fan mail' is something new, a letter exists which was sent to Miss Wadman, the principal boy of that pantomime, by two small children who saw it, a brother and a sister. The brother was the prime mover, for he proposed marriage to Miss Wadman, admitting his tender years—they were about nine—and being quite sure she would wait for him. He said he thought she was the nicest girl he had ever seen. The children put the ladies of the show in the order in which they esteemed them, with her on top and Letty Lind second, and said she had better not tell the others in case they got jealous. Did Miss Wadman reply to that declaration? She did not. She refused to take delivery of the letter because it was unstamped. The children had not a stamp, nor money available to buy it and did not dare tell their parents. So the letter was returned and they got into trouble. What a pity Miss Wadman, who was a lovely creature, never knew of her youthful admirer.

1888–89: *Babes in the Wood.* Harriet Vernon as Robin Hood; Florence Dysart; Maggie Duggan; Harry Nicholls and Herbert Campbell as the Babes; Victor Stevens as the Wicked Uncle—and, as the Wicked Aunt, Dan Leno— his first appearance at Drury Lane. Charles Lauri played a poodle.

Thus into the tapestry of Drury Lane came one of its most famous figures, that of Dan Leno. He did not partner Campbell in that pantomime, but he did so in the next, and that peerless combination lasted for years. Harris went to the Music Halls for his pantomime people and that was excellent judgment. Actually, it was Arthur Conquest at the old Surrey Theatre who got him to go over there and see Dan Leno. Conquest knew Harris would want Leno and unselfishly he let him have him. Thus that prayer which Dan Leno had offered up on the steps outside Drury Lane came true.

1889–90: *Jack and the Beanstalk.* Harriet Vernon as Jack; Agnes Hewitt; Maggie Duggan; Harry Nicholls; Herbert Campbell; Charles Lauri (as Puck) and Dan Leno as Mrs. Simpson.
1890–91: *Beauty and the Beast.* Lady Dunlo as Beauty; Vesta Tilley; Herbert Campbell; Harry Nicholls, and Dan Leno as Mr. Lombard Street.
1891–92: *Humpty Dumpty.* Little Tich as Humpty Dumpty; Fanny Leslie; Marie Lloyd as Princess Allfair; Herbert Campbell and Dan Leno as King and Queen of Hearts; Mabel Love as Dancer.

Mabel Love was one of the most beautiful and most photographed women of her day, a Queen of the Picture Postcard Craze. She graduated into straight comedy and had quite a distinguished stage career, dying only recently and beautiful to the last.

1892–93 : *Little Bo-Beep*. Ada Blanche as Boy Blue; Marie Lloyd as Little Red Riding Hood; Marie Loftus; Dan Leno and Herbert Campbell; Little Tich; Arthur Williams; Mabel Love.

1893–94 : *Dick Whittington*. Ada Blanche as Dick; Marie Montrose; Dan Leno and Herbert Campbell; Fawdon Vokes; Joe Cave.

1894–95 : *Cinderella*. Ada Blanche as The Prince; Isa Bowman as Cinderella; Alexandra Dagmar; Dan Leno and Herbert Campbell; Lionel Rignold; Sophie Larkin and Emily Miller.

That pantomime of 1894–95 was the last Harris ever did, for he died on 22nd June, 1896, aged only forty-four. He had then controlled Drury Lane for seventeen years, raising it from an empty theatre showing a To Let board to the height of prosperity and fame. He had never spared himself and overwork killed him. He had been knighted, not for his services to the Theatre in general but because he had been a Sheriff of the City of London when the first Emperor of Germany paid a visit and he had arranged all the entertainments in connection with the event. But if he received no title from the Theatre, the public paid him a tribute. Public subscription paid for the erection of a drinking fountain to his memory, surmounted by his bust, and fixed to the front of the theatre he loved and served so well—Drury Lane. There it stands today as a memorial to him. How many theatre magnates of today would get such a tribute?

Despite his own many interests, Gus Harris was a real Man of the Theatre—he was never really happy outside it. He reduced everything to terms of Theatre. As has been shown, he wrote his own dramas, at any rate as part author—and of those seventeen pantomimes of his, he was part author of six and producer of them all. A great personality, a man of tremendous power—he loved being before the public. To him, that was Heaven. He was never at a loss, he would make a come-back after every rebuff—and any unfortunate incidents on first nights he usually turned to his advantage. As regards his acting ability, it was only second-rate—Arthur Collins always said that he played in the shows so as to qualify for membership of the Drury Lane Pension Fund. But to him Old Drury was almost sacred, a Temple of which he was High Priest, and indeed he served it well. Small himself, he liked everything about him as big as possible. He believed in realism as a means of illusion—and he knew quite well that the Theatre's job is illusion. But he knew that the public were always amazed at seeing real things on the stage, which led him to use real bulls when he staged *Carmen*. He had many irritating methods and often they seemed mad, but there was always method in them.

He believed implicitly in Pantomime and in the magic thereof. He always made magic and beauty a part of his Christmas shows. He gloried in the Harlequinade and its tricks. He kept bright and shining the romance of Harlequin and Columbine. And his Transformation Scenes were something at which to wonder. Scene after scene unfolded before the wondering eye, each with its own special company, dancers and costumes—the beauties of the English countryside gave place to the Mountains of the Moon, the middle of the rainbow, the bed of the ocean—in which great oyster shells sailed on to the stage, and, opening, revealed lovely girls as pearls therein. Cloudland was compassed and led to a valley gleaming with jewels, and from there to the planet Venus, suitably inhabited, was a mere step. Change after change, as the music swelled and thrilled, and the figures on the stage swirled and sang—until at last the entire depth of the massive stage was revealed, and on a glowing mountain peak stood the Fairy Queen herself, whilst about 600 turned to acclaim her as she extended her wand in blessing on all—the Triumph of Virtue over Vice . . . a spectacle indeed of colour, and stage management . . . and then, a crash on the band, a blare on the brass, a zing of the cymbals and a bang of drums and with red fire and blue fire blazing in the wings, on rushed the four great Figures of Pantomime—Clown, Pantaloon, Harlequin and Columbine. The children cheered as they joined hands in a wild ring-a-roses and then shouted their slogan—the Proclamation of Pantomime itself— 'Here We Are Again'. . . .

No wonder, when Gus Harris asked his usual question, "Well, are you satisfied?" a delighted house, almost exhausted with laughter, wonders, magic and mystery, sated with music—carried away to the realms of Illusion by the genius of that small bearded Inverness-cloaked figure, yelled back: "Yes."

CHAPTER THIRTEEN

Dramas and Pantomimes—Harris and Collins

ONE cannot dismiss the work of a pillar like Gus Harris without further reference to some of his later dramas. They were all big and stupendous and as the years went on their stories and their thrills improved. Gus grew into Drury Lane and took on its quality and polish. Expert stage technician as he was, there were first-night hitches on some occasions—the only wonder is that there were not more. Mention has been made of that cavalcade of English history, timed to last twenty minutes. It lasted much longer for all the characters got inextricably mixed up; and the audience beheld, with astonishment, a complete jumble of partners and periods: George II walking with Henry VIII; Mary, Queen of Scots, with the Duke of Wellington as escort, and similar odd things. But he soon got it right.

He had been a pioneer of the cinema, one of the very first to show animated pictures, as they were then called, at an exhibition in Olympia. He used the cinema in a very excellent drama which he produced at Drury Lane, called *The Great Millionaire*. Charles Fulton played the millionaire and J. Farren Soutar, that well-graced actor, played a ruined, impoverished peer. There was a scene in which a motor-car was seen speeding along a road and finally dashing over a cliff to destruction. This was done by a film thrown from the circle. Soutar on the stage had to rush to the brink and gaze after it. On the first night, he nearly went over too. Gus decided he could do better than the film. He did the scene in actuality on the stage. The car came hurtling down a long winding road and dashed over the cliff edge, to the amazement and thrill of the audience.

The first time a horserace was staged at Drury Lane was in *The Prodigal Daughter*, a Harris drama of 1892. There had been real horses on the stage before, but they had never raced. Gus made them do so. Not only a horserace but—the Grand National, jumps and all. And as the winner of the stage race, he used an actual winner of the National—Voluptuary. The Grand National in the National Theatre was indeed a thrill. There were all sorts of other scenes, country mansions, stately homes on the lawns of which the hounds 'met' with huntsmen in pink, and the Grand Hotel, Paris, to name just one or two. But the Grand National was the thrill. It was terrific, with no detail omitted; there were the horses, the jockeys, the owners, the trainers, the touts, the bookies, the great mobs of yelling, excited people—and the excitement in front of the house was as great as that on the stage. It was written by Henry Pettitt and Augustus Harris. There was a fine cast headed by Henry Neville, that superb actor, James Fernandez, Leonard Boyne, Julius Knight, Harry Nicholls, J. L. Shine, Arthur Williams, Miss Millward, Miss B. Horlock, Fanny Brough and Mrs. B. de Solla.

In 1893, Gus played a topical card again. Weapons known as Maxim guns, considered the deadliest implements of war the world could produce, had been making history. Gus decided that Maxim guns should have a place at Drury Lane. Or it may be that they were Gatlings and Nordenfeldts. The point is that they were machine-guns. So machine-guns starred in Old Drury's autumn drama. It was called *A Life of Pleasure*. One of the pleasures of life which Harris showed his public was a small detachment of British troops cut off by dacoits in Burma. The situation is desperate, they are surrounded by masses of men determined on their destruction. Are the British dismayed? Not a bit of it. They prepare to meet the crisis. Someone must try and get through to the main body and tell them of the plight. A young officer volunteers. He has, of course, been wounded, but he will do—and dare. He rides away for his life and the lives of his comrades. The dacoits try to cut him off—he puts his steed at a dreadful jump, a yawning chasm, he clears it—and is off on his mission of rescue. He dashes through the enemy and disappears carrying the hopes of his comrades. The Burmese attack as the British strive to retire from a perilous position. The battle-field is dark and grim, a deep ravine and a roaring cataract. Rifles crack through the darkness with spurts of flame, and cries are heard when one reaches its mark. The British captain's calm, confident voice gives the commands, but he and his men are outnumbered. They have to get a bridge across that ravine to escape. They do it, too, and then the battle is really joined as the redcoats—our soldiers fought in red coats then, despite the jungle—get to the other side and form for the real attack. Then pandemonium breaks loose, the Gatlings and the Nordenfeldts rattle and crack, their flashes illuminating the scene like darts of lighting. A deadly hail of lead sweeps into the charging dacoits, who are mown down by the hundreds and seen falling and dying in the light which comes from those new and deadly machine-guns. And then a bush fire lights up the whole scene. It drove the audience into paroxysms of excitement and such enthusiasm has seldom been seen. It was by no means the end of the show; but Gus rushed in front of the curtain to receive his reward—

and he got it. He always cashed in on news and topicality. He imported an American sporting drama called *Gentleman Jack* and he adapted it for the needs of Old Drury. That was in April 1894. Here, he had a special attraction, for 'Gentleman Jack' was none other than Gentleman Jim Corbett, the heavy-weight champion of the world who had recently beaten Charlie Mitchell and John L. Sullivan, and was a popular hero on both sides of the Atlantic. He was a pretty good actor, too; he was seen in training, punching the bag, and then in an actual fight, of course knocking out his antagonist. As a play it may not have been first class, but as a piece of showmanship it was in the champion class. Corbett took a hearty call on the first night and made a charming speech of thanks—so did Gus. It was a success.

He had another setback on the first night of *The Derby Winner*, his own home-made drama in the same year as *Gentleman Jack*, 1894. Again there was a magnificent cast, Mrs. John Wood, Beatrice Lamb, Louise Moodie, Pattie Browne, Hettie Dene, Amy Abbott, Arthur Bourchier, Evelyn Hughes, Charles Cartwright, Rudge Harding, Ernest Lawford, George Giddens, Lionel Rignold and Harry Eversfield. No need to dwell on the plot, it was the settings and the effects which mattered, and they included a grand military ball, ablaze with uniforms and gorgeous dresses, a scene at Tattersall's and, of course, the race for the Derby itself. That came unstuck. The favourite did NOT win. But Gus was equal to the occasion. He dived in front of the curtain and confronted an audience roaring with laughter over the mishap. "Ladies and gentlemen," he said, "I know what you are laughing at—but—as a matter of fact the real winning-post is half a mile further down the course. What you have seen is a portion of the race, and although the villain's horse was ahead when you last saw it, I can assure you that Clipstone, at the winning-post, beat it by a neck." At once came cheers—just as they did when Arthur Collins, Harris's successor, by a quick turn of wit, turned disaster into success on the first night of *The Whip*, years later, as has been related elsewhere.

Before saying good-bye to the great Gus Harris, it is worthy of note that in that last pantomime of his, *Cinderella*, she went to the ball, for the first time in Stage history, in a motor-car. Gus must always be up to date.

And also to pay tribute to two more of his dramas, one was *The Royal Oak*, in 1889. This was a thing of considerable beauty and rather a better story than usual. The woodland glades were done magnificently and Charles II was played by Henry Neville. Winifred Emery, that lovely actress, was leading lady. And another of outstanding merit in every way was *The Armada*, produced in 1888 to mark the tercentenary of the defeat of that so-called Invincible Fleet. It was written by Henry Hamilton and Gus Harris. It had a big cast which included Winifred Emery, Ada Neilson, Leonard Boyne (hero), Luigi Lablache, Harry Nicholls, Victor Stevens, and many more. Here was a story of love and adventure finely told and wonderfully staged. A wicked Spaniard carries off the fair English girl (played by Winifred Emery), and the hero, Vyvyan Foster (Leonard Boyne), goes in pursuit. There was the villain's palace in Madrid where he threatens to hand the girl over to the Inquisition if she will not surrender to him. The hero, being a hero, got access to her and said he would come to the rescue. His ship was attacked and there was a most spirited fight. Vyvyan captured his attacker, no less a person than the Alcalde, and from him wrung the secret of when the Armada is to sail. What is he to do—return at once and warn his country, or stay and rescue his girl? Love or duty? Duty wins and he sails for home, but tells the Spaniards he holds the Alcalde as hostage for his sweetheart's safety. He sees Queen Elizabeth, and the great commanders, Effingham, Walsingham, Raleigh, Drake, Hawkins and Frobisher. He calls for volunteers, in a very beautiful scene representing the village of Charing, in Kent. Naturally, he gets them.

The famous Bowls scene on Plymouth Hoe was reproduced—after the picture by Seymour Lucas—and there was a perfectly marvellous reproduction of the English Fleet fighting the Armada, which drew volleys of applause. The little matter of defeating the Armada being over, the hero went to Spain to get his girl. She was in the hands of the Inquisition and was condemned to death. There she stood, in the next scene, tied to the stake, with the howling populace all about her and the deadly torches about to be applied to the pyre, whilst the priests chant the *miserere*. And then, through the throng, burst the hero and his gallant crew. In a fight they cut down the Spaniards and cut loose the girl. And so back to England, with a knighthood for the hero from the sword of Queen Bess and a pageant of her triumphant progress to St. Paul's—a happy wedding —red fire—the final curtain and a delighted and enthusiastic audience. No better piece of stagecraft was ever seen than that battle with the Armada. To advertise this play Harris issued tens of thousands of little metal coins, of brass, and about the size of sovereigns. On one side it said '1588 The Armada 1888'—surrounded by the words 'Drury Lane Theatre Every Evening'. On the other there was a representation of a sea fight, surrounded by the words 'Augustus Harris, Lessee and Manager 1888'. Thousands of those little 'coins' still exist and people write to Drury Lane concerning them and ask if they have any value. Except as curios, they have none. These words may reach the eyes of those who may come across one—and are thus answered.

Augustus Druriolanus Harris was succeeded by Arthur Collins, a man as great and in some ways greater. He carried on the traditions and he had more taste and often better judgment. He ruled 'The Lane' wisely and well and his story has been set forth elsewhere, for at Drury Lane he will never be forgotten. It was whilst Collins was in command that the great partnership of comedy between Dan Leno and Herbert Campbell was broken—irrevocably broken by death. Those two wonderful men, the firmest of friends, departed this life within a few months of each other. Campbell, the man of thunderous voice and gigantic stature, went first. He died of a stroke in July 1904. He and his friend and partner in laughter had played together in the pantomime of 1903–4. Campbell had seen the shadows engulfing Dan and had grieved, but there they were together again and they sang on the Boxing Night:

> "In the panto of Old Drury Lane
> We have both come together again,
> And we hope to appear
> For many a year
> In the panto at Old Drury Lane."

And the audience thundered an 'Amen' of joy at the sight of them. But it was not to be. Campbell, so big, so forceful, so truly British, died. . . . And in October 1904, men, women and children of Britain heard with a shocked sense of grief that a man whom few of them knew personally, but whom they all regarded as a very old friend, had passed away. There is a tribute which the British pay to those whom they love and they always paid it to him; they call such people simply by their Christian names. There is no need to say any more, everyone knows who it is. In this case, they called him Dan. For he was Dan Leno, the greatest comedian the land, which has produced so many great comedians, ever knew. He was a household word. A whole generation had known him from its childhood and many more loved him for the gift of laughter he had given them.

Dan Leno, whose name was George Wild Galvin, was born at Eve Court, King's Cross, London, in 1860. The site of that house is now covered by St. Pancras Station and it was Dan's delight to say that they really meant to call it St. Dancras, in memory of him, but owing to an unfortunate misprint it got called St. Pancras instead!

His father and mother were good, hardworking professionals, so he took to the Stage as a duck takes to water. He started very young, dancing on the tables in working-men's clubs and being rewarded by coppers. Long before he ever considered himself a comedian, he earned his living by his feet—and earned it the hard way. But those feet of his danced him to the top. He became Champion Clog Dancer of the World. There was an attempt to trick him out of his title, but Dan won. He was always working. He played in pantomime with his father and mother at the famous Argyle Music Hall, Birkenhead, and in the report book is a record of his excellent performances and behaviour. He was still only a boy. And when he got to London, he worked three halls a night. It was at the Middlesex Music Hall that he became a comedian. The manager suggested that he should sing a comic song. Dan doubted if he was good enough, but he tried. He sang a song called 'Milk for the Twins'. There was no more need for dancing, here was a comedian of the first quality, but he never quite put his clogs away—he was an amazing dancer to the end.

Strange that his first fame should have come to him in that old street called Drury Lane. For Dan had the greatest veneration and respect for the historic Theatre Royal, which takes its name from that thoroughfare. Once, when passing it with a relation, he crossed the road, went up its steps, and knelt down in prayer. When asked what he was doing, he said, "I was praying that one day I might play there." That prayer from the heart was heard and answered.

As a comedian, he went right to the top. His songs were as individual as himself. He made a big success with a parody of a then popular song—'Queen of my Heart'—parodies were to the popular taste then; and then came those character songs which he made his own. There were 'The Railway Guard', 'Mrs. Kelly (You *must* know Mrs. Kelly)', 'Nevermore', 'The Shopwalker', 'The Tower of London', to mention only a handful of gems. Always he was exactly the character about whom he sang. He could fill the stage with imaginary people and by his art you saw and heard them. He made everything so real. You saw the customers when he was the shopwalker, you heard the trains when he was the guard—and when he was a huntsman there was the whole meet before you, although he always protested he never got any. But when he mentioned that he preceded his horse over the fence, you both heard and felt the impact. 'The Tower of London' was a masterpiece. There he was a guide, showing the people around, but never losing sight of the refreshment-room, to which he constantly drew attention. You grew thirstier and thirstier with him in his anxiety to get that drink. He would take as his subject an ordinary egg and discover things about it of which nobody had dreamed before but saw quite clearly when he pointed them out. He was always struggling with adversity; his clothes gave him perpetual trouble—shirts and collars were always at war with him, trousers were too big, and coats too long. But he always won. What he did with a harp beggars description. Also, he would suddenly appear to be at a loss for a word. It would evade him. He would gesture, he would think and concentrate, he would have his audience on tenterhooks—they wanted to shout and tell him—and then out would come that wonderful smile of his, and a word entirely different from the one they had expected would knock them out of their seats with laughter.

When he played a woman he was marvellous; they were pieces of superb caricature in the best sense of the word and always recognizable as real people—to be met with anywhere. In him the characters of Charles Dickens came to life, for in many ways Dan Leno was the Charles Dickens of the Music Halls and pantomime. He was real Music Hall. He was one of the very greatest of the great Individualists who made Music Hall what it was. In pantomime he was a veritable king.

He played pantomime at the Old Surrey Theatre for Conquest, who controlled that fine playhouse. He had no part given to him. "Just come on when you like, Dan," they said. They knew he would play fair—and he did.

Conquest, knowing Dan's greatness, invited Gus Harris to come over from 'The Lane' and see him. Harris came, and Dan Leno went to Drury Lane. That prayer was answered. He went there in 1887–88—he stayed there every Christmas until his end. He and Herbert Campbell were something quite unique, it is almost impossible to explain what those two men were like. They were a complete contrast, Dan so small, so quiet, so wistful, Campbell so big, so noisy, so forceful. They loved each other like brothers—they were completely unique together—and they died within a few months of each other. Dan belonged to everyone. Dukes and dustmen, bishops and barmaids, clerks and coalheavers, aristocrats and plebeians, all fell beneath his spell. He had something for them all. They all loved him. With the children in the audience he was quite wonderful. He never played over their heads, he never played 'down' to them. They recognized him as one of themselves—there was a perfect understanding. He was never 'blue'—he was never vulgar. He had no need to be. He was the true Clown; he had the gift of tears as well as laughter. Only a knife's edge separated them. He could be wildly comic and then, in a flash, he was a poor, weak, downtrodden creature, his big eyes yearning with sorrow, his face a mask of tragedy, bringing tears to the eyes of his audience—and then, in a breath, he had them laughing again. But no matter how absurd the things he did, there was always the basis of reality—that was his great strength. These creations lived. It was not so much his songs, but the patter with them that mattered. Such genius as Dan's comes very seldom. He was the greatest comedian of his time, maybe of all time. There have been many others but none quite like him. The nearest is Charlie Chaplin, but he worked in another medium, and to get his full force he had to be the same. Dan was always different. He had his Royal Commands. They called him 'The King's Jester' and of that he was justifiably proud.

He always gave of his best and he always gave all he had. Indeed, he gave too much. They waited for him outside the stage doors of Drury Lane, the London Pavilion, the Tivoli, the Oxford, all over the land. "Good old Dan," they shouted, and he threw them all he had in his pockets. Every Sunday morning he read and answered all the letters which poured in asking for his help. None was refused. He gave more than that. He gave delight to millions by his consummate art—art which it is impossible to describe in mere words. Perhaps of his Drury Lane pantomime triumphs *Mother Goose* was supreme.

Let us forget the tragic end of this great little man. Let us remember that on that dull November day in 1904 his funeral passed through a vast crowd of mourners, drawn from every rank in life, standing bareheaded in the murk and gloom to say farewell to him who had always brought them sunshine. Traffic was stopped, the shops were closed and shuttered, the people stood hushed and tearful as that small flower-covered coffin passed by. A nation mourned him as their Monarch of Mirth and Laughter. He was only forty-four when the shadows engulfed him and the last curtain fell. He is indeed a Pillar of Drury Lane, worthy to rank with the greatest—with Betterton, Garrick, Siddons, Kean—a genius who gave joy—and memories to linger on. . . .

To try to do Arthur Collins justice in so small a space is not possible. Much has been written before of his consummate mastery of stagecraft and of the Theatre—much will be written again, when once again the annals of Old Drury are penned—and the writer hopes to accomplish it. But mention must be made of some of those who added lustre to 'The Lane' at Arthur Collins's command; some gone a good while, others passed on whilst this chronicle was being written. Some drama, some pantomime—and of the latter, the memory of the woman whom Arthur Collins, who was a judge indeed, always said was the best Principal Boy he had ever seen. Her name was Nellie Stewart. She only played there twice, but she left an indelible impression. And no wonder, for she was a woman of amazing talent and power. She was an Australian, born Woolloomooloo—in Woolloomooloo Street, Sydney, New South Wales. The number was 41. It was afterwards Cathedral Street. She had theatrical blood in her veins, for her mother was descended from Mrs. Yates, a fine actress of Garrick's day—indeed, it was her husband for whom Garrick deputized when he made his first appearance as Harlequin. Her mother, herself, had worked at Drury Lane. Her name was Theodosia Yates and she had taught the choruses how to sing. She went to Australia and there she married, first James Guerin, and when he died, she married again, Richard Stewart, of mixed English and Welsh blood. Unlike so many theatrical children, Nellie Stewart had a happy childhood. Her half-sisters, by the first marriage, both went on the Stage. She lived in a theatrical environment. She was taught singing, dancing, fencing, everything an actress should know—and of course, she went on the Stage herself. She started right at the bottom, playing pages and the like, and in due course she rose right to the top. Naturally her career started in Australia and she proved to be one of the most gifted and talented of all the wonderful people which that land of sunshine has given to the Theatre. She could, and she did, do it all. She was complete Theatre. She saw and learnt from all the great ones who visited there, such as Nellie Farren and Sylvia Grey. She was as good in drama and comedy as she was in light opera—and even grand opera. There was just nothing she could not do. There is no time to trace that remarkable career in detail. It included Gilbert and Sullivan, *Dorothy*, all the famous roles in light opera. She sang Marguerite in *Faust* as easily as Fredigonde in *Chilperic*. In London in 1892, she was in *Blue-Eyed Susan*, a burlesque by Geo. R. Sims, with Arthur Roberts; there was nothing she could not do. She was now famous in London, New Zealand, Australia and America. And then in 1899, Arthur Collins persuaded her to go to Drury Lane as Principal Boy in *The Forty Thieves*. He paid her £50 a week—two shows daily. She has left it on record how well they did things at Drury Lane and of the wonderful costumes that wizard Charlie Alias made for her—she had a jewelled snake round her tights which intrigued her immensely. She loved the Theatre, too, and was responsive to its atmosphere—the ghosts of the great ones whispered in her ears and she felt inspired by them. She was a big success, but the English climate did not suit her. It affected her throat. Engaged for the succeeding pantomime she rehearsed but throat trouble

Dame Sybil Thorndike unveiling the memorial to Ivor Novello in Theatre Royal, Drury Lane

Above: Bill Nagy, Ray Walston and Mary Martin in *South Pacific*
Left: Wilbur Evans, Mary Martin and Michael Mellinger in *South Pacific*

prevented her from opening on the Boxing Night. But she was back as soon as possible, to play Jack in *Jack and the Beanstalk*. Personal memory sets down that she was the finest Jack of all time. She could sing, she could act, she could dance and she could not help looking beautiful. She made the Principal Boy something more than a figure of pantomime, she made 'him' the real hero of a Fairy Story, a creature out of the land of Romance and Magic—neither man, boy, woman nor girl—but Jack as the children imagined him. Yet she was a quite ravishingly beautiful woman, and old eyes can see her now, in the Finale, dressed in black armour, fitting her magnificent figure like a glove, her mass of pure golden hair surmounted by a black helmet—a great light blue sash across the front and a sky-blue cloak behind—something at which to marvel and to wonder—and remember indeed. She only played 'The Lane' twice, but she should always be remembered. Afterwards she did all sorts of things—*Il Trovatore, Lohengrin* she took in her stride. And overseas in Australia she played *Sweet Nell of Old Drury*—and she looked it. She played that delicate comedy of *Mice and Men*—the part which Gertrude Elliott played here—and Shakespeare too; indeed, she played Romeo to her daughter's Juliet superbly. And needless to say she looked lovely. This most remarkable woman, one of, if not the best of, Old Drury's Principal Boys, challenged only by Fay Compton in more recent years, died in 1931 at the age of seventy-two, beautiful to the last. Recently there was an occasion organized in her memory and the promoters wrote to Drury Lane asking if some memento of her remained there. The writer of this book sent one of his precious programmes, bearing her name—he has only one more left—and had a charming acknowledgment. Drury Lane had not forgotten her. Australia is justly proud of her memory.

Collins engaged for his dramas the finest casts he could get. Some of those people contributed to the atmosphere and tradition of Drury Lane, and not the least of them were Lyn Harding, Basil Gill and Constance Collier. All three are dead now, Gill and Constance Collier dying whilst these pages were being written, within a few days of each other. And the careers of those three people were always crossing and recrossing. And all three of them gained what was perhaps their greatest glory with Sir Herbert Tree at Her Majesty's Theatre. Yet they belonged to Drury Lane too and their names are chronicled here, for otherwise they may languish into obscurity, and that should not be.

David Llewellyn Harding was born at Newport, Monmouth, in 1867. He went on the Stage against his family's wish—stern, Non-Conforming Welsh people did not approve of such things. That he

took that step and braved his family's anger is something for which
the British Theatre must be grateful, for he was in the very front rank.
He toured in drama, he played in stock, in fact he toured the world
and learnt his business the hard way. His first London appearance
was at the Shakespeare, Clapham, in 1897, in *The Silence of the Night*.
His first London success was scored at the Grand, Fulham, in 1902,
in *The Prophecy*, quickly followed by *A Snug Little Kingdom* at the
Royalty. The eye of Tree was upon him and he went to Her Majesty's
—then His Majesty's—in 1903. There he met Basil Gill and
Constance Collier; there he played a round of great parts superbly.
Nobody who saw them will forget his performances as Inu in *The
Darling of the Gods*, Bill Sikes in *Oliver Twist* (that was great indeed),
his Cassius in *Julius Caesar*, his Fred Bayham in *Colonel Newcome*,
Bolingbroke in *Richard II*, Burrus in *Nero*, and his Enobarbus in
Antony and Cleopatra. He went to Drury Lane first in 1907, playing
Sheanagua in a Red Indian play, *The Last of His Race*. He played
opposite Basil Gill. Alas, it was a deadly flop and Old Drury's
shortest run. No blame attached to the actors. He was Noel Ferrers,
the villain in *The Sins of Society*, and in that 'autumn drama' at 'The
Lane' he proved the finest villain the great theatre had ever had. He
was there again, still a villain, as Jem Callender in 1908 in *Marriages
of Mayfair*. Poor Lyn Harding was doomed to be a stage villain and
could be so much more, as he proved time and time again. He was an
actor of presence, power and strength. A big man with a fine voice
and wonderful diction, he could—and did—play anything. He was
Crichton in a revival of *The Admirable Crichton* and that is not a
villain's part. His Dr. Grimesby Rylott in *The Speckled Band* was one
of the most powerful pieces of acting our Stage has ever known. His
Drake at His Majesty's was outstanding. His career was long and
distinguished and he came to Drury Lane again in Ivor Novello's
Glamorous Night in 1935. Once again he was the villain, Lydyeff, and
his acting put a polish on the whole production of that musical
drama. Lyn Harding loved his Profession and reached a good old
age. Shortly before he died—on Boxing Day, 1952—he sent the
writer, an old friend, his obituary notice, written by himself.
"Popie," he wrote, "I am not well and I don't like it. I am sending
you this. You will know what to do with it when the time comes.
Bless you." And the writer did know what to do and did it. He got his
old friend a fine farewell—and he even got into the printed obituary
notices what Lyn had written at the end. "Dame Irene Vanbrugh
said of him 'He was not only a great actor, but a great gentleman'."
That went in too—because it was true.

Basil Gill played more often at Drury Lane than did Lyn

Harding. The two men were friends and associated at Her Majesty's for years. They were direct contrasts in everything save ability—there they were the same.

Gill was born in Birkenhead in 1877. He was destined to be an artist but he preferred grease-paint to oils and in that medium he painted many splendid portraits. Had he suddenly come upon the scene today as a young man Hollywood would have bankrupted itself to get him. He was an actor with the Grand Manner, which is now extinct. He was noble to look at, noble in voice and noble in his art. He was one of the handsomest men who ever trod the stage. It was his misfortune, perhaps, to be a contemporary of Lewis Waller's, and later of Henry Ainley's. Gill had not Waller's dynamic force and dash—but he got his effects just the same. Ainley's superb manly beauty and resonance of voice, his wonderfully romantic appearance, rather overshadowed the quieter Basil Gill. Yet he was a splendid actor. Drama claimed him and he began his career in *The Sign of the Cross*. He came to London when Wilson Barrett did a season at the Lyric—and Constance Collier was in the company, too. He toured as Marcus Superbus in *The Sign of the Cross* and he lived up to that name. Adoring women went every night of the week to see him. This handsome, well-built man with the perfect voice and diction and the faraway, dreamy eyes, swept them off their feet.

He always seemed something apart—and that attracted them. When making love, he had a way of yearning over the girl in his arms which was quite irresistible, and when he spoke the word 'beloved' he hung on to the second syllable, making it seem like a long-drawn-out, passionate caress. He went to Drury Lane in 1902, playing Messala in *Ben Hur*. He was acclaimed. His splendid physique, the classical beauty of his face, made his appearance in Roman attire noteworthy. He was not much given to movement, but when he did move it was with the sudden, lithe grace of a panther. He could just stand there and look a noble Roman and be the centre of attention. His voice was bell-like and he knew how to use it. He spoke lines like the playing of a symphony orchestra, too, so full of tones was he. He joined Sir Herbert Tree at His Majesty's in 1903 and it was his natural home—there he was a thing of grandeur amidst grandeur. Few today can realize the brilliance of the company of which he made one. He played all sorts of parts. He never argued about it. He just took what was given him and he played it for all it was worth and always made it seem worth more. All he wanted to do was to act—he never showed temperament. If the part did not appear 'fat' that did not worry him, he put the fat in by his talent. Nor was he ever afraid to follow another actor in a part—he knew he could hold his own. In Tree's magnificent production of *King Henry VIII* he followed Ainley as Buckingham and his delivery of that speech on the way to execution, "All good people, pray for me," was better than Ainley's had been. It was more human, more sensitive, less declamatory—he made you feel he was gazing into the eyes of death. He played an extraordinary round of parts at His Majesty's—for although he would leave for a while he always went back. Many will remember his Kara in *The Darling of the Gods*—a thing of romantic beauty. His Brutus was second only to that of Lewis Waller, which is saying something; and just to show his versatility he was a remarkable Cassius, too. Parts as widely differentiated as Lysander, Edwin Drood, Steerforth, Henry IV, Octavius Caesar, Harry Maylie, he just took in his stride. He was the best Joseph Surface of his generation and his was a generation of giants. A vivid memory of him is recalled in a scene in Tree's *Nero*—between Gill and Constance Collier—Gill as Otho, to whom she had been faithless, she as Poppæa. His fierce denunciation of that beautiful woman as she lay enticingly on a couch, his voice, his anger, his noble anger—and his final rushing exit crying "To Lusitania, to Lusitania"—will never be effaced. His Duke Orsino too was notable; his voice had that dying fall of the music mentioned.

He was a dear, nice, gentle fellow, with whom it was impossible to have a row. Maybe he stood in his own light, but it was his way. He shared a dressing-room with Lyn Harding for years—and Lyn could be difficult—and there was never a wry word. His Drury Lane background was Messala in *Ben Hur*, the original production; Niatawa, in the ill-fated *Last of His Race*; Nigel Villiers, the hero in *Marriages of Mayfair*—and what a hero, too—filling 'The Lane' with his voice and personality, that voice which on occasion could contain floods of tears; and as The Rev. Verner Haslam in the celebrated drama *The Whip* in 1909. He played a clergyman who was inclined to drunkenness and was betrayed into crime by the adventuress. He portrayed the mental struggles and the eventual victory over his failings as a great actor should. He was also at Drury Lane for Forbes Robertson's farewell season, when he played Bassanio, and again in 1920 as Count Anteoni—opposite Godfrey Tearle—in *The Garden of Allah*, a most sensitive performance. Shakespeare, drama, comedy—it all came alike to him because he was a real actor. In his later years many will remember his Lieutenant Osborne in *Journey's End*, one of the best things he ever did. He was as welcome in America as in Britain. He stood for distinction, grandeur and the honour of his Profession, and he never let it down. He died in 1955 at the age of seventy-eight, handsome and charming to the end.

And that great lady of the Theatre, whose career was mingled with those of Lyn Harding and Basil Gill, and whose name was Constance Collier, was complete Theatre through and through. She knew more about it than anyone the writer, whose dear friend she was, ever met, except Sir Herbert Tree who had taught her so much. And well she might. She was born of it, in theatrical diggings in Windsor. Her mother used to carry the new-born baby down to the theatre every night in a blanket and put her under the dressing-table whilst she played her part. Constance breathed grease-paint from her earliest days and it was always her favourite perfume. She was on the Stage herself almost as soon as she could walk, playing Pease Blossom in *A Midsummer Night's Dream*. She had a hard and unhappy childhood, although she adored her mother. She never had a real home. She was one of the bravest women in the world. All her life she fought adversity, ill-health and bad luck—and she always won. She went to look for work at the age of fourteen, when she had fourpence in her pocket. She walked into the Gaiety stage door and demanded to see the great George Edwardes. The stage-door keeper, Jupp, nearly died! But Edwardes happened to be passing and was struck by her dark beauty. He gave her a job all right. She was in the chorus of the Gaiety, she went on tour, and then Edwardes, who also controlled the Empire in Leicester Square (not a cinema then), put her into some *tableaux vivants*—together with Hetty Hamer and Marie Studholme. They were contrasted types and the three most beautiful girls in London. All London went to see. In a ballet he cast her for Cleopatra, thus showing the shape of things to come. She did not want musical plays. She got into *The Sign of the Cross*, and met Basil Gill. She was a success. She was with George Alexander. She made her first big success later at the Comedy Theatre in 1899, in a play called *One Summer's Day*, in which she played Chiara, the beautiful gypsy. She wanted desperately to get to His Majesty's with Tree and at last she succeeded. She played Pallas Athene in *Ulysses*, and she looked so lovely that it was breath-taking. She was the 'clear-eyed goddess' to the life. She played in *The Eternal City*, *The Merry Wives of Windsor*, *The Man Who Was*, *Twelfth Night* and Nancy in *Oliver Twist*—and that was one of her greatest roles. She went to Drury Lane to play in *Ben Hur* as Iris; Gill played Messala. She was superb. She returned to His Majesty's to create Poppæa in *Nero*, as has been mentioned. She played Trilby and in *Colonel Newcome*, and then she played Cleopatra in *Antony and Cleopatra*. That was something to see indeed. She was the only actress who ever lived who could both play Cleopatra and look it. Both acting and beauty made one understand Antony's cry:

"Let Rome in Tiber melt, and the wide arch
Of the rang'd empire fall! Here is my space."

She and Gill were amongst the company which Tree took to Berlin and which astonished the Berliners, who thought they had the best. She was at Drury Lane again in *The Last of His Race* with Gill and Harding, and in *The Sins of Society* in 1907. There she shone, an ideal actress for that great theatre.

There was nothing she could not do. Her performances as the sordid Nancy and the glowing Cleopatra showed that. She wrote *The Rat* with Ivor Novello and started his successful career. Much that he knew of the Theatre he learnt from her—and proudly admitted it. Her career was too long and too distinguished to have justice done to it here. Famous on both sides of the Atlantic, she spent most of her later life in America, coaching the stars and teaching them how to speak the Queen's English. She nearly died at one period of what was looked upon as an incurable disease. The gates of death were opening for her and she gazed upon them bravely. Then a miracle occurred. A new drug was tried upon her. It saved her life. She came back from the jaws of death to new triumphs. She was the first person in Europe, one of the first in the world, to have this drug administered. It was insulin. Late in her life, shortly before she died, her sight failed. She bore it bravely. She was told that there was a possible operation but at her age nothing could be guaranteed, even life itself. She took the risk, like the brave woman she was—and her sight returned, to her joy and that of all who loved her. She was a superb actress and a very lovely woman and the annals of Drury Lane are the richer by her name.

None of those three people would ever have used, in respect of themselves, that much abused word of nowadays, 'Star'. There were no stars then. They were leading actors and actresses. They learnt their jobs and did not become leading people until they had qualified. There was none of that nonsense about 'stardom in a night' for young people barely out of school. Nor did they rely on publicity. They relied on the effect of their acting on their audiences; and thus their fame was made and endured, and endures yet in the memories of those who saw them. Nor did any of them belong to what is now called 'Show Business'. They were members of the Theatrical Profession—and proud of it. That was their calling and they strove to please. They always did their best. They respected tradition and quality; they acquired quality and having got it, never sank below their standard. Lyn Harding, Basil Gill and Constance Collier, three great ones of the Theatre, three masters of their most difficult art—the art of acting—also added to the story and the lustre of Theatre Royal, Drury Lane. And they had pride in doing so.

CHAPTER FOURTEEN

Ensa

WHETHER or not Ensa can claim to be a pillar of Drury Lane is a very moot point, but there is no doubt that Drury Lane can claim to have been a pillar of Ensa. Without that famous theatre as its headquarters, it might have had far more troubles than it did—and it had enough, in all conscience.

Ensa—Entertainments National Service Association—was born in the Munich Crisis, when Basil Dean, who had done excellent work in troop entertainment in the First World War, foresaw that some form of entertainment would be very necessary in the clash which seemed inevitable. He knew how much unorganized amateur work there had been in 1914–18. He knew that despite the keenness and the enthusiasm of the kindly people who gave it, something organized and of a professional nature was necessary. Those who served in the First World War will not need to be reminded of some of the things which the troops, incapacitated by wounds and consequently unable to escape, had had to endure—the endless round of children from dancing academies, the bands of amateurs, full of kindness but empty of talent, who invaded the wards, sang, played and tried to be funny. The troops had to suffer and smile. At one hospital when the entertainers arrived, they found the ward empty. The men had taken to flight and were hiding in the grounds. They were brought back by a sergeant-major who rounded them up, fell them in, and addressed them. "Men," he said, "I sympathize with you, but play the game. They like doing it, don't let's spoil their enjoyment." The men responded. . . .

Basil Dean wanted to stop all that and to have a properly organized service. Many leading people in the Profession rallied to his call. Leslie Henson christened the organization. It was known that initials were of great importance in the Services, and Ensa sounded easy to remember. So Ensa it became. The writer of this book was appointed Honorary Publicity Man. He sent out the story to the Press, which got headings like 'Actors Want To Do Their Bit', and that did not please Mr. Dean, who is of a rather serious disposition. But it did reflect the public idea. However, after many meetings, at which matters of great import were discussed, the organization began to take shape. Everyone had their own ideas, of course, and being actors, expressed them at length. Certain words became of great pith and moment. At one of the meetings somebody used the word 'envisage'. It caught on at once. Everybody 'envisaged' all sorts of things. And meanwhile war marched nearer with relentless tread. Basil Dean showed the greatest energy. The War Office accepted the idea—but could not see how it was to be used. Organized entertainment laid on to the Services in war was something new—and in this country, as Ensa was to discover, something new is always suspect. But Dean's work in the First World War had been attached to the Navy and Army Canteens Board—the old NACB. Here, at any rate, was a precedent. So Mr. Dean and his incipient Ensa were handed over to the successor to the NACB, which was the Navy, Army and Air Force Institutes—Naafi—or as pronounced by the troops, Naffy. Now this was the first blow which Ensa had to suffer. Naafi was, and is, a remarkable organization working with efficiency and enterprise, but by the very nature of its monopoly and ubiquity, most unpopular with the troops. To them, Naafi was a joke. And here was Ensa as part of it. That was one of the major tragedies of Ensa. This magnificent idea, which might have achieved so much, became and ended as a comedian's gag—a certain laugh.

Yet, despite small encouragement from anyone, when war finally arrived on 3rd September, 1939, Ensa was ready. That is, the hard core was ready. A small band of experienced Theatre people had their jobs and were standing by. Sir Seymour Hicks had been persuaded to accept the title of Controller of Ensa, and said he never knew what he had to control. He was, of course, the Leader of the Stage; Basil Dean was Director of Ensa (for Naafi); Sir Kenneth Barnes, then Principal of the Royal Academy of Dramatic Art, was General Secretary; Jack Hylton was Chief of the Music Section; Thorpe Bates and Greatrex Newman were to look after Concert Parties; Leslie Henson was chief of Musical Comedy; Jack Buchanan, Chief of Revue; E. P. Clift, a well-known theatre manager, in charge of Theatres and Production; Alec L. Rea, in charge of finance; Stanley Bell, once stage director for Sir Herbert Tree, was chief of Equipment and in charge of R.A.F. contacts— he had a distinguished flying record in the First World War; William Abingdon, Old Drury's expert stage director then, was Chief of Staff and W. Macqueen-Pope, Chief of Publicity. Eric Tissington of Naafi and Bob Locardo, for Variety, were other members and there was Mr. Purdom, of Equity, in charge of something known as Central Registry.

War had broken out and Ensa found itself at once with a private war of its own on its hands. Many of the great ones of the Theatre stood aloof. In some cases they disliked Ensa, being of the opinion that they could do the job more efficiently themselves. There was also a considerable difficulty over the position of Agents, for Ensa could pay only token salaries. On 3rd September, Ensa's office was a small room in Naafi's headquarters and it was obvious that something more important was wanted. To get matters smoothed out and into the open, a meeting of all concerned in the Theatre was called for Friday, 8th September, 1939, at the offices of the Society of West End Managers. It was largely attended. There were scenes of strife and dispute from the very opening and Sir Seymour Hicks, in the chair, had a terrible job on his hands. Nobody agreed with anything or anybody—many distinguished Theatre people walked out, shaking the dust of Ensa from their shoes. Outside, the Press was waiting, licking its lips for a good scandal story. Inside a riot raged and at times it looked like personal violence. Something had to be done and done quickly. The time had come to play a trump card. Basil Dean and the Publicity Chief left the meeting and sped by car to the War Office. Dean went inside and was back in less than ten minutes. He told the Publicity Officer it was all right. Ensa could announce that it would take over Drury Lane Theatre as its headquarters. He did not return to that meeting but the Publicity Man did so, finding the storm still in progress. He spoke to Sir Seymour, who was a close friend of his, and got permission to make an announcement. He rose to his feet and got order for a moment, for he had not spoken before. "Gentlemen," he said, "it is my privilege to announce to you that Ensa has acquired Theatre Royal, Drury Lane, as its headquarters and from there it will operate. I am just about to issue the official announcement." By a miracle the storm died down. 'The Lane' as headquarters!—this was something important—this mattered. The immense prestige of that building had its effect. A new feeling came over the scene and more friendly discussions ensued. Drury Lane had won the first battle for Ensa. And that afternoon the story went out to the world.

On Monday, 11th September, that small staff moved into the great playhouse. What had been dressing-rooms became offices, that of Mrs. Siddons was H.Q. Publicity. And, in those historic walls, Ensa got to work.

Whatever may have been said since about Ensa—and much has been said—it lost no time. It went into action at once. On 25th September, 1939—only a fortnight after actual work had begun—the first ration of entertainment went out to the troops. Twelve first-class concert parties, whose seaside seasons had been cut short by hostilities, were ready to go. Each had its own portable stage, made at Drury Lane, first class and fully equipped with their own lighting

installation. They all assembled on the stage at Drury Lane and Sir
Seymour Hicks addressed them and wished them luck. Reporters
thronged, cameras flashed. Ensa was off on its career.

It had all been done at lightning speed, in face of immense
difficulty. Nobody really knew where the troop concentrations were
and the War Office was most chary of information. There had been
a little liaison between the distinguished playwright, also a soldier,
who was in charge of War Office publicity and the publicity man of
Ensa. The W.O. wanted all issues of news to be submitted to them
first. The Ensa man knew better than that. He wrote a carefully
worded communiqué, which he was going to issue to the Press, and
sent that in. He also sent it out to the Press. Some three weeks later
he was told his communiqué was passed and that it should be the
model for all future Press releases. It had been printed weeks before
—but everyone was happy.

The names of those concert parties which went forth from Drury
Lane into the unaccustomed black-out and mystery of wartime
conditions—to do a job which nobody had done before—are worthy
of placing on record. They were as follows:

> George Ellis's 'The Troupers'.
> Will Seymour's 'Bubbles'.
> Murray Ashford's 'Hullo, Happiness'.
> Murray Ashford's 'The Piccadilly Revels'.
> John Berryman's 'Crazy People'.
> Bertram Montague's 'Sunny Smiles'.
> George Thomas's 'The Evening Stars'.
> Willby Lunn's 'The Spotlights'.
> Dennis Redhead's 'Fools in Fantasy'.
> Cecil Johnson's 'Margate Entertainers'.
> 'The Eight of Us.'
> 'Let's Be Gay.'

Murray Ashford, since dead, was the King of Concert Parties
and contributed two splendid troupes.

They went out into places hitherto unknown to most people—
places like Ludgenhall, Porton, Bovington, Fittes, Waddington,
Manby, Duxford, Stradishall, Debden, Watton, Burscough, Penrhos,
South Corney, Upper Heyford, Ollerton, Catfos, Wytton, Winter-
bourne Gunner—names to become familiar to tens of thousands later
on but then right off the map. These people were plucky pioneers.
There was the question of lodgings and the like, and it was not

possible to arrange accommodation beforehand. Somehow they got through.

They deserve remembrance for their work and their courage. Jack Buchanan, right from the start, took out star-decked shows, including himself and artists like Elsie Randolph, Fred Emney, Raymond Newell, and others. One such was given at a big barracks near London. The Public Relations Officer on the spot did nothing about it. He never came to the show. He stayed in the Mess. He said he knew it would be a failure. The Ensa Publicity Man took along the Press and cameramen and by virtue of a kindly regimental sergeant-major, got them all in. The result was a resounding success and lots of valuable publicity. That publicity was not needed by the artists in particular but was a splendid boost for morale, especially as directed to those who had sons, husbands and male folk serving. The sight of them having a good time brought cheer. Harold Holt, too, since dead but then the leading Music Impresario, got into action right away and did some fine concerts.

But it soon became apparent that the Forces were composed almost entirely of dramatic critics. They sneered at the shows, for which, a few weeks earlier, they had paid good money to see by the sea. Nothing suited them. The Press assailed and baited Ensa, certain papers being most violent in this. The Publicity Man resisted and fought all attacks. One scribe, who stated in his paper that the Ensa portable stages took forty-eight hours to erect, was challenged to come to Drury Lane, select a stage himself, select the men to erect it and time the result. He did not want to accept but he had to do so. He came down, he picked his stage, he picked his team from the men assembled. The stage went up, ready for use and also lit, in twenty-five minutes. That was that. Later, when Ensa began to send out ballet, another scribe delivered a slashing attack. He said this was cruelty to the troops. He had, he stated, a younger brother serving and he wanted to protect him from this outrage, but that brother was lost in the mists and security curtain of war. He did not know where he was. The Ensa Publicity Man told him. That brother was an Entertainments Officer at a certain camp and was one of those who had actually asked for ballet as an attraction. Documentary evidence was produced. Those particular attacks stopped.

But everyone was now at war with Ensa. It was a new idea and therefore not to be tolerated. When the first lot of films were sent out, there was a howl of rage because they were not all brand-new pictures which had never been seen by the public. That attack was beaten too. And anyway, it was not possible that everyone in the Forces had seen all those pictures.

And whilst on the question of films, that was one of Ensa's bad and radical mistakes. It had been arranged, before operations started, that the entertainment provided would be 75 per cent film and 25 per cent living entertainment. That was a most sensible idea. Films were easily portable and required a minimum of transport and equipment. There were plenty of them.

Living entertainment was far more difficult to handle, and quite apart from that, there was the question of personalities. The shows had to be good. As Ensa grew and grew, naturally the living entertainment could not cope with the demand, and the quality—never of the highest in general—sadly deteriorated. One good live show a week would have been a change and something to which to look forward. A surfeit of indifferent and often bad shows had a devastating effect. The film side of Ensa was run with great efficiency and courage by Ben Henry, who won his battles and triumphed in the end.

Contact was established early with the British Broadcasting Corporation. Almost from the beginning, small broadcasts were given. But war broke out between Ensa and the BBC. It was in many ways the bitterest war of the lot. Mistakes were made, there was little give and take or understanding on either side. Yet in the end Ensa won its niche.

But so far Ensa had not got overseas. That was what it wanted to do—for the 'phoney war' was on and boredom was sapping morale. The authorities would not hear of entertainments going to the Front. At home, every sort of show was on the road, including a circus: but not in France. There the ban was heavy—the bar was up. But somebody thought this absurd. That somebody was Gracie Fields. She was determined to sing to the boys overseas. She would not be denied. And she broke down the official resistance. Over she went, supported by Sir Seymour Hicks (who had led the first party of entertainers to go to France in the First World War and now led the way again); Claire Luce, the star of musical comedy (who, being an American, said she was the first instalment of Lease Lend); Tom Webster, the famous cartoonist; Billy Russell, star Music Hall comedian, and some girl dancers. Over they went and they gave their show. At home, the Publicity Man was determined that the show should be broadcast. He had approached the BBC as soon as it was fixed. He had been turned down. But he was a most tenacious Englishman. He assailed the BBC ceaselessly, he rallied the Press to his aid—and they gave it willingly. But it was only on the actual day of that first historic performance that the BBC gave in—and allowed a mere fifteen minutes for the broadcast. The Press actually ran it on contents bills. That first broadcast from France was a most thrilling affair. For the first time, parents, lovers, relations at home heard the voices of their men—or at least they might have been their men—full of cheer and excitement, shouting, laughing and applauding as their beloved Gracie sang to them. It was a first-class morale boost and altogether a most moving occasion, not to be forgotten by those who were present and by the millions who listened. It brought such joy and confidence to them. In a long life composed of many battles, that Publicity Man still considers that fifteen minutes wrung from the BBC his greatest victory and his most valuable one.

And after that, the bar was down. Ensa could go overseas and companies were formed. But attacks on Ensa still went on.

Then Ensa won another victory—and again the Publicity Man had a hand in it. On Friday, 28th November, Their Majesties King George VI and Queen Elizabeth visited Theatre Royal, Drury Lane, to inspect Ensa and to speak to the parties going overseas. It was one of those surprise visits that was known all about by those responsible a long time before, but the secret was well kept from the great majority of those working at Drury Lane. Everything possible was laid on. Their Majesties came prepared for a visit of three-quarters of an hour. They were so interested that they stayed for an hour and three-quarters. They saw a hive of industry. Jack Hylton conducting a full orchestra in the rotunda, clerks and secretaries dashing about with documents and files, a conference in the Board Room full of stars, and Sir Seymour Hicks sticking pins into a map to show where Ensa shows had been given—or might be given at some future time. The Queen asked why some of the flags were red and some blue. The King said they used the red ones when they ran out of the blue. He was perfectly right. They saw Henry Oscar directing a rehearsal of a play in the Green Room—he was head of the Play Section and is a most distinguished actor himself. They met the company which Sir Seymour was to take over the following Sunday—which included Claire Luce, Dorothy Ward, Bertha Willmott, Tom Webster, Lance Fairfax, Billy Russell and some others. The Royal visitors had a handshake for them all. They went on the stage and saw Leslie Henson producing a little musical show which he was taking over—which included Binnie Hale, Violet Loraine, some members of his regular company and a small chorus. They watched this rehearsal for quite a time and they joined in heartily in the chorus of a song called 'Sally' which Arthur Riscoe had written specially for this show. They went on the stage and chatted with everybody, including the chorus. They went under the stage and saw Ralph Reader with his Gang Show, rehearsing in the

Ballet Room. This all-male show was to go right up the line, into the most advanced positions—and did so. They saw a company of variety artists also rehearsing, which included Will Hay and other stars. The King noticed Skeets Martin doing a trick with a match-box. He insisted on learning it before he went on to the next show. He said it would amuse the children at Christmas. And master it he did. Their Majesties met Jack Buchanan, and all the important Ensa folk. They saw a party which was leaving for Home Entertain-ment that very evening, with their full equipment. This was in the charge of Oscar Barrett, for so many years manager of the famous Empire in Leicester Square. The Queen saw some of the sewing women at work on the stage and went over to speak to them specially. Those women went purple with pride as they showed and explained their work to this Great Lady, who obviously knew all about such things herself. One of them, Bessie, a very old servant of Drury Lane, was so overcome with joy and pride that she was nearly speechless for days.

Ensa used to send little cars, carrying two performers (one of whom drove), and a Mini-piano, to the lonely outposts of the Anti-Aircraft defences. One of these was being loaded up when the King and Queen were on their visit. They stopped and watched. Tommy Knox, then the chief 'props' of 'The Lane', was in charge. Maybe it was nervousness at the Royal supervision but the piano was difficult to fit into its small space. "I'll bet you five bob you don't get it in," said the King. "Go on, boys," whispered the Publicity Man who was conducting Their Majesties. The boys went on and the piano went in. The King had not got the five bob—he did not carry money. But the bet was paid all right. . . .

The King and Queen heard the story of the Ghost with great interest and waited quite a time to see if he would appear. The wretched spectre, who is now world famous, did not oblige. What made it worse was that he was in full view, twice, during the follow-ing day. The Queen asked if there was a canteen and on being told there was not, said she thought there ought to be. One was promptly opened and was of great benefit. At least you could find people when you wanted them—they were in the canteen—otherwise they were lost in the vast dim spaces of Old Drury. When the King and Queen left they were loudly cheered by a big crowd that had gathered. A photographer had been allowed in and got a splendid picture of Their Majesties fraternizing with Leslie Henson's little company, chorus and all. This visit got much publicity and stopped the attacks on Ensa for a time.

On the Sunday evening, 30th November, those parties to go

overseas left Victoria station, steaming out of the London black-out into the mists which shrouded the battlefields of France. And doing yeoman service.

When the actual fighting broke out, in the spring of 1940, Ensa had over two hundred artists overseas. Plans had been made at Drury Lane for the eventuality. It was called the Z Plan. The Publicity Man got the news in the small hours of the morning—he took all the overnight calls from France on his bedside telephone. He rang Basil Dean, who left for France that afternoon. And every one of those artists got home safely, properly fed and cared for, and not even a handbag lost. Ensa was not always in a muddle.

And the stage of Drury Lane showed a curious sight early one morning at the time of Dunkirk. It was filled with sleeping men, in battledress. They were the Naafi men who were attached to Ensa and also Ensa guides and field managers. They had got through. Some of their portable cinemas had been giving shows in the very teeth of the German advance. But all got back safely and they were addressed by Mr. Dean on that stage, as curious a picture as it had ever held—and as dramatic as any—weary, dishevelled men with the mud still on them, who had escaped under the shadow of death, at Dunkirk.

Old Drury had its own A.R.P. department and it had its own detachment of Home Guard. Thus history repeated itself, for a company had drilled at Drury Lane, composed of the actors, during the '45 Rebellion—were they not His Majesty's Servants?—and many had joined the many Volunteer detachments which grew up when Napoleon threatened. Drury Lane even then had its own company of Fencibles.

H.R.H. The Duke of Kent, and the Duchess, attended a special matinée at 'The Lane', when Maurice Chevalier flew specially from France to join Gracie Fields in an entertainment for the special benefit of the Anti-Aircraft Brigade—this was just before the Blitz gave those then weary, bored men so much to do. General Pile himself was there to thank Their Royal Highnesses. It was a memorable occasion at Drury Lane. Chevalier used the Publicity Man's office as his dressing-room. They were old friends. That very great artist, one of the world's greatest, gave a wonderful show.

The battles between Ensa and the world in general went on without ceasing. That with the BBC never stopped for a moment. Ensa got a weekly half-hour on their air—and every broadcast was a pitched battle. The programmes, which included Geraldo and his orchestra, had they not been sponsored by Ensa, would have been praised. Geraldo gave splendid service all through. But there was

His Majesty King George VI, and the present Queen Mother leaving Drury Lane Theatre after seeing *South Pacific*. In the background can be seen the present Queen and the Duke of Edinburgh. This was King George's only public appearance during the interval between his illness and his death. He died exactly a week after the visit

Above : A typical first night scene in the Rotunda at Drury Lane *Below :* The chiefs of staff at Drury Lane. *Left to right :* Ronald E. Gray (Secretary), Bertie Stoll (Catering Manager), W. Macqueen-Pope (Historian and Publicity), S. F. Webb (Manager) and Ernest Kingdon (Assistant Manager)

another programme, which went out from Drury Lane, of which the general public knew nothing. This was called 'London Carries On' and it went out on the Overseas Service. It ran for two solid years, with never a row or a bicker. It had a host of listeners amongst the troops, who would write to the participants and when on leave come and see them. So far as that programme was concerned the utmost friendliness prevailed between the BBC and Ensa—possibly because the Higher Command took not the slightest interest in so small an affair as this. Yet it always announced itself as coming from Theatre Royal, Drury Lane, and every programme was written and devised by the Publicity Man, who always did the opening announcement, saying, "From the world's most famous playhouse, Theatre Royal, Drury Lane, we who work there send you half an hour of London." Every programme had a London slant—music and songs illustrative of the city. It was immensely popular and it was always a joy. Sometimes, indeed quite often, Cecil Madden, now one of the Chiefs of the Television Service and also one of Television's pioneers and a most cheery man, would come along and take part himself. It was a friendly, informal party—as Ensa itself should have been. The cast was small and hardly changed. Now and again there would be a guest artist. But the stock company, as it were, consisted of Stephen Williams, who had been chief of Luxembourg Radio and who produced; Jack Leon and his Orchestra, who did wonderful service and who played every show; Joan Young, who became a star of stage and radio; Harry Hudson, a famous Music Hall star when he had partnered Kirby, as the Hudson of Kirby and Hudson, and was a tower of strength; golden-voiced Gloria Kane, and pretty, clever Maidie Andrews. That was the main team, though for a good time there were also Henry Oscar and Bernard Clifton. Margaret Harper Nelson was script girl and of the greatest value. She now holds a high executive position in the film world.

That little show was a very happy part of Ensa and gave great joy. One fan from India invited all the members over, as soon as they could come, he said, to a tiger shoot. R.A.F. pilots told how they listened to it in mid-air when on bombing raids; men from the Merchant Service and the Royal Navy wrote letters of thanks. Soldiers wrote from all parts of the world, asking for songs and repeats. 'London Carries On' did two pantomimes; one of them, *Cinderella*, was actually given the honour of being broadcast in the Home Service. In the other a very small child played the part of the Fairy Queen. It was one of her very first radio efforts. Her name was—and is—Petula Clarke. The pantomime was *The Babes in the Wood*. There was never any trouble over 'London Carries On'

P

because, although always announced as an Ensa show, it did not attempt to do propaganda for the undertaking. Its main object was amusement. Ensa carried on, too, at Drury Lane despite increasing opposition and difficulties. There came a day when two things happened. The German battleship *Bismarck* was sunk—and so was Ensa. *Bismarck* disappeared beneath the waves but Ensa, like London, carried on—only it was no longer officially Ensa. It had become the Department of National Service Entertainment. Basil Dean was now Director of National Service Entertainment. Old Drury was, for the time being, a Government Department. It did not think much of that position, nor did its old inhabitants. In their opinion a Theatre Royal was better than a Government Department. Nor did the troops take the slightest notice of the change. They still looked upon Ensa as part of Naafi—and treated them both as a joke. According to the Navy, Ensa meant 'Even Naafi Stands Aghast'. The comment of the Army on Ensa was 'Every Night Something 'Appens'. Comedians everywhere had only to say Ensa to get a roar of laughter. None of that was really fair. Ensa made mistakes, very many of them. It never seemed able to find out the proper formula for a Troop Entertainment and there certainly was one. It always insisted on giving the troops what it thought they should have and not what they felt they wanted. The Forces were, of course, composed entirely of men and women of the general public—torn up by the roots from their natural way of life, and although doing their duty, harbouring a certain resentment against the war in general and all concerned with it. Ensa was part of the War Machine and easy to assail. So they assailed it. Quite extraordinary things happened. A show which had been derided in one camp was applauded in another. It was found out, by probing, that locality and conditions had much to do with the public taste. Certain camps were happy places, others were not. In the case of strict, unpopular concentrations, Ensa got the bird—and when it took the same material to more pleasant conditions, it got applause instead. That is just one of the many obstacles which Ensa had to face.

Many Ensa shows were, under the restricted conditions imposed upon them, very good indeed. Archie de Bear, that splendid producer of revues and the man who made 'The Co-Optimists', did excellent service, and his miniature revues, often written by Reginald Arkell, another man of experience and talent, were most popular. Perhaps Archie de Bear himself was not too popular at Drury Lane with the brass-hats of Ensa. He is a man of wit—and that wit can be trenchant. He is afraid of nobody and says what he thinks. He has a

great sense of humour. He would, in company with the other heads
of departments, attend the meeting of Ensa chiefs, when Basil Dean
would take the chair and the proceedings assumed the importance
and solemnity of a cabinet meeting at times of crisis—and all times
held crises for Ensa. It is to be feared that neither Archie de Bear
nor the Publicity Man—called the Public Relations Officer (he was
also promoted to be Director of Broadcast Programmes but had
little power in his office)—were impressed. They played a little
game together, passing each other notes across the table and going
into fits of suppressed laughter. They used to take the view that
Ensa, now a Government Department, should really form a Government itself and they would appoint Cabinet Ministers for all
occasions. There were certain phrases which, for a short time, would
be in everyone's mouth in Ensa. For a while the 'words of power'
were '*Ad Hoc*'. The two malcontents promptly created a Minister for
Ad Hoc. On another occasion, one of the chiefs used the phrase *coute
qui coute*. Instantly a Minister was appointed. Both men were
publicly reproved by Mr. Dean for 'undue and ill-timed levity'.
They could not have cared less. In their opinion, Ensa wanted a lot
more levity. It is the considered opinion of many of those who
worked at Drury Lane for Ensa that had that organization kept its
identity as being simply a professional source of entertainment—and
behaved itself as such—its path would have been easier. But it ran
itself like a portion of the Civil Service—it worked on Government
lines—on Service lines. Now the Services, both fighting and civil,
knew more about that sort of thing than did Ensa. Thus the positions
were reversed—the Services became the professionals and Ensa the
amateurs.

But nothing stopped Ensa, it went grimly on. And perhaps that
word is not ill-chosen. It fought every inch of its way. Basil Dean,
who created it and who carried it through to a tremendous achievement, does not deserve the blame which was so often piled upon
him. He made his mistakes, but they were mistakes of personality.
Basil Dean is more of a fighter than a strategist; he was all for frontal
attack when strategy would have proved more successful. He would
rush ahead building a line over unsurveyed country and then reach
what seemed an impassable river or an unclimbable range of
mountains. Somehow he got over both. Often inside organization
was considered more important than composition of entertainment.
He did what he did—and he did much—almost single-handed. He
never received the support of the great ones of the world of the
Theatre. It is to be feared that a good deal of personal feeling and
jealousy went into that. Had there been proper support, Ensa could

have been the finest contribution to national effort the Theatre ever made. But he never got it. The reason may have been partly his own fault. He is not an easy man to know or to work with. But there is a sterling quality and a tremendous power of drive and determination beneath the reserved surface. This is a naturally shy man who covers up by an armour of forcefulness. The forcefulness is part of him, but he never kept it in control. He, too, would have words of power, which those two rebels, de Bear and the Publicity Man, seized upon. He used, for a time, the word 'tendentious'. Every minute those two malcontents wrote to him—and they saw to it that they wrote many—contained that word several times over. They used it on all occasions. Mr. Dean never realized his leg was being pulled. At one time he informed all and sundry that everything must be 'stark'. Those two men went about being stark in their own way. A keener sense of humour in the Higher Command might have helped a lot.

But Basil Dean did it—did what he intended to do. He made Ensa the greatest organization of entertainment that history had ever seen. Ensa circled the world—and everywhere on earth where British troops were stationed, there, too, was Ensa. It was achieved with the greatest difficulty and in face of determined opposition; much of the opposition coming from quarters from which support should have been afforded. Basil Dean went ahead like a tank and overrode things which might have daunted a lesser man. When munitions became of paramount importance he sent Ensa into the factories and munition works. The first of such concerts was given at Woolwich Arsenal and the Rt. Hon. Ernest Bevin came along himself to launch it. The star of the party was Will Fyffe, who did grand work for Ensa. The workers sat around in their canteen eating their food and surveyed the preparations rather grimly and with hostile stares. But Ernie Bevin was equal to it. He got on that platform and smiled at them. "Well, mates," he said, and they cheered. Ernest Bevin took a great interest in Ensa. He agreed to a scheme for a central bureau where players liable for service could be registered and set to do entertainment work rather than scrubbing floors and peeling potatoes. He took the liveliest interest in that Bureau—which he always called 'The Burroo'. He was a great man, and a great Englishman, too. During an Ensa broadcast to America, an ordinary munition worker, a Mrs. Brown of London, spoke a message from the workers of England to President Roosevelt. The President received it and was most gratified. It did national relations good service, and a good understanding between the two countries was most necessary. And a great opportunity was missed, in connection with these Munition Concerts. The Publicity Man had an idea. He wanted to bring over, one at a time, the greatest film stars in America and take them round the tour of factories in which Ensa gave entertainment. As a booster of morale this would have been wonderful—and the workers deserved it. It would have helped international relations, too, for all the stars would have come. They could not have stayed out, the publicity value was too great. On returning home they would have told wonderful stories of their adventures and of Britain under war conditions. They would naturally have 'hit the whole thing up'. They would have had columns and columns in the Press, eagerly read by people who would pay no attention to what politicians, government officials and ordinary journalists said. A film star commands—and gets— attention. Imagine the impact of Deanna Durbin, then at her zenith, on a crowd of grimy, red-eyed workers in a munition factory, striving to keep up supplies and fight the Blitz at the same time. Imagine what the effect would have been on American readers of that young lady's story of her adventures on what she would rightly regard as a battlefield. Had this scheme come off, Ensa might have stood on top of the world. But it never materialized. The originator of the idea never quite discovered why. He believes that inter-departmental jealousy had a good deal to do with it being scotched. One of the objections was that the transport difficulty was too great. All that was wanted was a couple of seats on a plane once a month; that could not be obtained. Yet many small fry, doing quite unim-portant work, had no such trouble. It is possible that had a depart-ment other than Ensa conceived that idea, it would have taken place. The Publicity Man also believes that had he been allowed to take it himself to high quarters, he would have got it through. He had done things quite as difficult in the First World War. But Ensa was a Government Department, he was not even chief of a Division. So a grand idea was wasted.

Ensa did a remarkable pageant on the steps of St. Paul's Cathedral. It was a most imaginative affair, written by Clemence Dane and performed by Dame Edith Evans, Henry Ainley, Leslie Howard, Roger Livesey, Mary Clare and other stars. The orchestra and choirs were conducted by Sir Henry Wood. Dense crowds packed Ludgate Hill, right down to the Circus. It was a great success. But Ensa got into trouble for upsetting the traffic of London. It was always like that.

Drury Lane was now a completely changed building. It had been bombed and patched up; it never stopped working for a day. Its workshops were as busy as any munition factory. Every available inch of space was partitioned off into offices, which invaded two-thirds of the stage itself. And Ensa overflowed it—into scores of other buildings. But Drury Lane remained the hard core and the prestige of that great name was of immense value. Many of the best people left Ensa, through disagreements mostly brought about by official restrictions and government red tape. Had Sir Seymour Hicks remained in charge, the story might have been different. With Seymour to charm the High Ups and Dean to do the work, much might have been different. Amongst those who left, after three years' service, was the Publicity Man. He was—and is—an Old Druriolanian, bound to that theatre by family ties over two centuries in span. But he could not stand what was going on. He did not agree with the turn things were taking. He informed the authorities that he was not a Civil Servant—he had never been a servant, he said—and was rarely civil anyway, so was entirely out of place. And he shook off the dust of Ensa and departed.

He returned shortly before Ensa's demise, at the request of Basil Dean, to help wind matters up. He assisted in giving Ensa a decent burial. At a Press Conference he summoned, the journalists, after listening to a statement, decided that Basil Dean, the much assailed, really deserved a vote of thanks. And said so.

And so Ensa died, and its flag which flew on the roof of Drury Lane was hauled down by Harry Leggatt, the fireman, now dead. It had done its job and it had gained much by its background of the famous theatre. Basil Dean received a C.B.E. They could not have given him much less. Some of the blame was his, but he never received the praise to which he was justly entitled. He has had a distinguished career in the world of the Theatre which he still adorns. He has had many successes. But the writer believes that his happiest hours were those which he spent in the general manager's office at Drury Lane, as Director of Ensa, riding the storm, continually dictating letters and reports, continually attending meetings, continually fighting fresh foes and surprise attacks. For Basil Dean loves Theatre Royal, Drury Lane, and he found it a pillar in his support during his darkest—but to him no doubt—most glorious hours. . . .

Ensa was gone. Drury Lane shook itself clear of government bonds—and prepared to be once again, Theatre Royal. . . .

CHAPTER FIFTEEN

Drury Lane—1947–1953

THE period when Sir Alfred Butt controlled Drury Lane has already been recorded elsewhere. It was one of reconstruction, enterprise and success, for Sir Alfred Butt knew, and knows now, though retired, all about running a theatre. He stands amidst its pillars, by no means the least. The outstanding feature of his regime was the beginning of the series of big musical productions from America, starting with *Rose Marie*. One often hears complaints about the fact that American shows so often fill Old Drury. There is something to be said about that which few people know.

In the early part of the 18th century an actor named Macklin slew another actor, as a result of a quarrel, in the Green Room before a fireplace which can still be seen. He was charged with manslaughter, and although the penalty was being burnt in the hand, branded by a hot iron with the letter 'M', Macklin's hand was never so marked. His story has been told. But the name of the actor killed was Hallam. He had a younger brother working in the theatre—which has always been a family house. That younger brother was nervous. He had his eye on the violent, quarrelsome Macklin and he reasoned it out. "If Macklin killed my brother, he may kill me" was the result. So Hallam left Drury Lane. He recruited a small company of English actors and actresses and they sailed from Bristol to Boston, Mass. There in a barn in Boston they gave the first performance ever given on American soil by professional actors and actresses, thereby founding the American Theatre—as a result of a killing in the Drury Lane Green Room. That theatre, therefore, is the parent of the American Stage, and when American plays come there they are only coming home.

The great ones of the Butt period were Edith Day, Derek Oldham, Harry Welchman, Sir Cedric Hardwicke, Marie Burke, Paul Robeson, Clarice Hardwicke, Billy Merson, Evelyn Laye, Gene Gerrard, Raymond Newell and afterwards Richard Tauber (although Sir Alfred had gone then). Noel Coward had produced *Cavalcade* in association with Sir Charles B. Cochran. Julian Wylie had revived pantomime with glory. Basil Dean had given a memorable production of *A Midsummer Night's Dream*, bringing Shakespeare back to Drury Lane, from which theatre it had been absent for many years. After Sir Alfred Butt left, H. M. Tennent took over the general management, which had been held for a short time—during which Tauber appeared—by George Grossmith. 'The Lane' was in difficulties and Ivor Novello put it back on the peak of prestige. Ivor Novello, Mary Ellis, Dorothy Dickson and Olive Gilbert are all in the tapestry of Drury Lane. Prince Littler did a splendid panto-mime, with Binnie Hale as Principal Boy, and Tom Arnold had staged *Babes in the Wood*, with Fay Compton as Robin Hood. Nor must the name of G. S. Melvin, in pantomime, be omitted from Drury Lane annals.

And for a great part of this period, Drury Lane, run as it is by a limited company, had a most distinguished chairman in Lord Lurgan. He loved Drury Lane and gave it ceaseless service. Tall, handsome, fresh-complexioned and with silver hair, he was a fitting figurehead for the grand old theatre. He could conduct a meeting with grace, charm and persuasive tongue—when needed. He took the liveliest interest in everything which went on. He attended rehearsals and he knew what he was talking about. When, in its bad time, Drury Lane wanted attractions, nobody worked harder than Lord Lurgan to get them. He smoothed over many difficulties, he brought people together and made negotiations easier. He was the epitome of Victorianism, and in himself showed its sterling quality, its courtesy and its demand for a high standard. He had served his country in the Army in the Grenadier Guards. He served it well at the 'National Theatre'. He stands amongst its pillars, too. His son, the present Lord Lurgan, is a worthy son of his father, with all the charm and warm-hearted grace, lives in South Africa, but takes the keenest interest, not only in Drury Lane but in the Theatre in general, is an accomplished lover of music and a Vice-President of the Royal General Theatrical Fund. Lord Lurgan was succeeded as chairman by Walter Payne.

The outbreak of war in 1939 closed Drury Lane, as it closed every place of amusement throughout the country, and Ensa took over. Drury Lane's contribution to the history of the Drama in war-time was war work. During those years the Higher Command had changed. A new Board had taken over, which reigns today, consist-ing of Prince Littler (Chairman and Managing Director), Charles Gulliver, Emile Littler, Stewart Cruikshank, T. Flaming Birch and S. R. Newsome. Drury Lane itself, wounded and scarred, the war over, awaited demobilization and a return to its real position as the premier theatre.

When Ensa was disbanded, repairs were put in hand. All the Ensa debris was swept away and the war scars hidden by such reconditioning as post-war restrictions allowed. What was done was accomplished in a remarkably short space of time. 'The Lane' began to look like itself and to stand once more in majesty.

The opening play had to be decided upon. There were those who would have liked to see the curtain rise again, just as it had fallen, upon a revival of Ivor Novello's *The Dancing Years*, but that was not to be. Prince Littler commissioned that other giant of the Theatre, Noel Coward, who had scored such an outstanding success with *Cavalcade*, to supply the opening attraction. Mr. Coward wrote and composed a musical play called *Pacific 1860*. His view was, at that time, that the public, sated with the alarums and excursions of war, would like something gentle, soothing, charming and nostalgic. So he wrote a love story of the 1860s and placed it, as an antidote to battlefields, in the so-called Pacific Ocean, on an island. The play was beautifully mounted and dressed under the direction of Mrs. Gladys Calthrop. It had an excellent cast, but it was not really a Drury Lane show. At Her Majesty's it would probably have scored an emphatic success. Mr. Coward, of course, wrote sparkling dialogue, and some very charming music. But it lacked movement and dancing. As a sop to the old-timers at Drury Lane he put in a ship which sailed from the quayside. But those old-timers pointed out that at Drury Lane a ship had to do rather more than that—it had to catch fire, blow up and sink, at the very least.

Noel Coward brought over a star from America to play the lead—Mary Martin. She was known here only through her films, in which she was most popular. But in *Pacific 1860* she had very different material with which to deal. She played a prima donna who fell in love with a young man, resident on the island, who belonged to a very serious family indeed, who naturally, in their Victorian way, would have nothing to do with a woman who was on the Stage. Mary Martin, clever as paint, cute and most fascinating—and at that time red-haired—arrived at Drury Lane and was fêted. Expectations ran high. The cast also included Maidie Andrews, that talented and pretty actress who knew 'The Lane' well, Carl Jaffe, Sylvia Cecil, whose lovely voice found full scope in the music Mr. Coward gave her to sing, Cyril Butcher, Tudor Evans—to whom fell the honour of speaking the first words of the play on the reopening, Helen Horsey, Daphne Anderson and Graham Payn, who was the leading man and did well. There were many more. *Pacific 1860* reopened Drury Lane Theatre on 19th December, 1946. The theatre was thronged with celebrities. It was a night of excitement and memories and although the reception was good, much of the applause was for the theatre itself. Mary Martin played and sang delightfully. But something was missing. The Press was not enthusiastic. Mary Martin was cramped by being cast out of her real style. But all the same, *Pacific 1860* had bad luck. It struck the worst winter this country had known for years. Bitter, freezing cold clamped down, snow fell deep and laid where it fell, there were constant fuel and lighting cuts—the theatres could not be properly warmed, and the box-office had to sell tickets by candlelight. But *Pacific 1860* managed to run for 129 performances—and what mattered was that Drury Lane was open again. Mary Martin made herself very popular with the Druriolanians—and the public. She, her little daughter and her handsome husband, Richard Halliday, endeared themselves to the theatre staff.

Mr. Littler arranged for an American musical play, presented with immense success in New York—and all over the States—by the Theatre Guild of New York. It was called *Oklahoma*. Its fame had been bruited abroad by people who had visited America, by servicemen who had been there and seen it and who had brought home records. To the general public it meant little. But it had been written by Oscar Hammerstein II—who knew all about Drury Lane—and composed by that magician of music, Richard Rodgers. It was based on a story called *Green Grow the Lilacs*, a simple study of American life in Oklahoma at the beginning of the 20th century. It was produced in New York by Rouben Mamoulian. It was a small, intimate show and there were no names which anybody knew in the cast. But it was to come to Drury Lane. It had played—and was still playing at that time—at the St. James's Theatre, New York, which is about the same size as its celebrated namesake in London. People wondered if this show would suit the vastness of Old Drury. And Old Drury wanted a success.

The interests of the Theatre Guild were handled here by the firm of H. M. Tennent Limited, the premier producing organization of this country, whose founder, then recently dead, had been general manager of Drury Lane. Hugh Beaumont was in charge. The time came when *Oklahoma* should move into London. Disaster began to happen. The ship in which the company was to travel with its belongings was burnt right down to the water's edge. It was extremely difficult, in those immediate post-war days, to get transport. So the costumes were transferred to the *Queen Elizabeth*, and sailed in that great ship, as did also Lawrence Langner, one of the two real controllers of the Theatre Guild, and Jerome Whyte, who was to produce *Oklahoma* at Drury Lane. The *Queen Elizabeth* made history by running on a sandbank and occasioning further delay. The company had to be sent over as best they could. Some came by air and they arrived, totally unknown by name in this country, at London Airport on 11th April, 1947. It was perhaps an omen that for the first time after that long and desperate winter, spring looked through the clouds on that day and it was one of gentle, golden sunshine.

Oklahoma was to make history by being the first Drury Lane production ever to open out of Town. It was to be produced at the Opera House, Manchester. There was further trouble at the airport over one of the dresses—which had been brought over in an un-finished state and led to arguments with the Customs. A train call had been arranged for the company; but that had to be cancelled as they did not all arrive on the same plane. But eventually they were assembled and left for Manchester, pretty tired and weary, at about six in the evening. But still they were not all there. Eight of the principals had come by sea on a freighter. They were still at sea, delayed by adverse weather and fog. Nobody could say when they would arrive. The decision to open in Manchester was a wise one. The management of Drury Lane wanted to have a look at the show and to judge the effect of the variety of American accents on the public.

The path of *Oklahoma* continued to be stony. In Manchester further snags cropped up. It was not possible to open on the advertised day—the company was not at full strength. The theatre was sold out, and Mr. F. Appleby, the manager of the Opera House, had to cope with disappointed customers over a postponement. He managed it. The company were still unregistered aliens. That had to be dealt with. The costumes were still actually in bond to the Customs. The company had to be provided with ration books, etc. The difficulties were immense. But they were met with grim deter-mination by Ernest Kingdon, who was managing the company for H. M. Tennent Limited and the Theatre Guild, and who is now assistant manager of Drury Lane. He worked wonders. The police were most helpful, so were the Customs, so were the Food Office officials. They all actually came down to the theatre and dealt with the matters on the spot, so as not to interfere with rehearsals—other-wise it would not have been possible to open that week. It shows that officialdom has its human side—and the police always have had. Also the company's salaries were stated on contracts in dollars, and rates of exchange had to be worked out daily. Equity raised a difficulty. The 'Oklahomans' were not members of British Equity. There was talk of stopping the show until this was achieved. But Hugh Beaumont had foreseen that and dealt with Equity head-quarters in London, so that when the local Equity leaders came

along and raised vexatious points he defied them and referred
them back to their chiefs. The Drury Lane Publicity Man, who had
gone down to Manchester where he is well known, helped him in this.
He and Hugh Beaumont had a council of war early in the morning
whilst Mr. Beaumont—popularly known as 'Binkie'—was in his
bath. And the Equity difficulties were smoothed away—if they had
ever really existed save locally. But one great snag remained. Those
eight principals were still at sea in their freighter. It was possible to
open, for everyone in the cast knew every word of the show and
could play anything. Still, Drury Lane was taking no chances.
It was not possible to postpone again. But there was the great snag
of the Press—who would see what was, instead of a first night,
merely a dress rehearsal with eight understudies! The Publicity
Man took a hand. He knew the Manchester Pressmen—no finer in
the country—and they knew him. He called a conference with the
help of Mr. Appleby, who did wonderful service, and he got them to
surrender their tickets for what was to be the opening night and
come the night after, when there was a chance of a full company
and a proper show. They agreed. And he would like to register here
his deep appreciation of this most sporting gesture in the interests of
fair play.

Jerome Whyte had conducted rehearsals. He was cool, calm and
imperturbable. He just walked over difficulties and he won the
hearts of the Manchester stage staff by telling them that he had
never seen a better. It was true enough. For Jerome Whyte difficulties just did not exist. One of the cast—a girl—came to him and
said: "Oh, Mr. Whyte, I've got an awful attack of laryngitis. I
cannot speak properly, let alone sing." "Pay no attention to it,
honey," replied Whyte, "just sing right through it." And she did.

But still those missing principals were at sea and time sped on.
There could be no more postponements. At length they were
located. They were off Dungeness. Elsie Beyer, then general manager
for H. M. Tennent, performed a seeming miracle. She chartered a
tug, she got those people off the ship and to shore, she hired a fleet of
fast cars—and the missing Oklahomans, on the very day of opening,
sped northwards therein. At Manchester things were agog with
excitement. Would they win the race to beat the curtain? At the
stage door was the Publicity Man, and the Press and photographers
of Manchester, waiting on what was a wonderful story! The box-
office was besieged. Thousands were disappointed. The vast Opera
House could have been sold out over and over again. But would the
missing performers do it? That was the anxiety of the management.
And, three-quarters of an hour before the rise of the curtain, those

missing Oklahomans arrived at the stage door. They were photographed, they were interviewed at high speed; they were cramped
and hungry from their long dash. Some of them said they had not
got their land legs, they still felt the motion of the ship. They were
rushed to their dressing-rooms and into their costumes. . . . In front
of the curtain, and to face a huge and expectant audience, stepped
Frank C. Marshall, general manager of Theatre Royal. That
audience hushed. What was this? Bad news? But Mr. Marshall was
smiling. He had good news indeed. He told the audience of the
arrival of the balance of the company and the difficulties which
had been overcome—he was cheered. The lights dimmed, the
orchestra played—and *Oklahoma* had started. It swept to success
in Manchester.

But there was still London—still Drury Lane. To that place
came *Oklahoma* on the night of 30th April, 1947. Drury Lane was
packed to capacity. The patrons of the pit and gallery had waited
for days—literally days—to be there. Here was an unknown cast—a
play unknown—music unknown save by those who had American
records; for the performance of the music had been banned in this
country until after the opening night. It was an evening of
tremendous excitement in the Theatre, such as seldom comes.

At the back of the grand circle stood a man who had watched so
many Drury Lane first nights from that same position. He was
quietly confident on this occasion, for he had been to Manchester—
still, in the Theatre one never knows! His memory took him back
over forty-nine years when on 12th April, 1898, he had been taken
as a boy of ten years old as a birthday treat (a day late), to see a first
night at the Shaftesbury Theatre. It had been an American musical
play, too. It, also like *Oklahoma*, had a cast utterly unknown to
London which had come over under tremendous difficulties—and on
money borrowed for fares. He had seen that play triumph and every
member of its cast become a popular favourite the next day, for the
play had been *The Belle of New York*. He had never expected to see
the like again. Yet here history might repeat itself and he took it as a
good omen that he had met the *Oklahoma* company at the airport on
11th April—only that had been his fifty-ninth birthday. Still—it
was a coincidence.

The lights went down—the orchestra under the first-night
direction of Salvatore Dell'Isola—who had conducted in New
York and who in due course handed over the baton to Reginald
Burston, Drury Lane's own distinguished maestro—played the overture. The curtain rose to a gasp of amazement from those seeing the
play for the first time. For here was no traditional Drury Lane

opening. Here was the vast stage seemed shrunk to small dimensions but the scenery was colourful enough—it was a replica of that used in America and painted on the Drury Lane paint-frames by Alick Johnstone. But save for the figure of a middle-aged woman sitting in a rocking-chair, that stage—still very large—was quite empty. Golden sunlight blazed down and the effect was of the warmth and heat of an early summer morning. And then, off-stage a man's voice began to sing and London heard for the first time the opening bars of 'Oh, What a Beautiful Morning.' . . .

The singer walked on, tall, handsome, imposing Harold Keel . . . and *Oklahoma* had started—and had won already. No need now to describe that play and its tremendous and justly deserved appeal. That night was one of thrills. The untraditional opening, the springing of a 'hit' number on the audience within a few seconds of curtain-rise—but then every number was a hit number, so what did it matter? Excitement grew and grew and the fall of the curtain on the first half was like that of a finale. The atmosphere during the 'break' shivered with excitement such as is seldom seen in a theatre. Delighted people gasped remarks to each other. The particular thrill the Publicity Man derived was to see something he had never seen before—or since—the Press Room empty before the end of the interval. The critics, the gossip-writers, the men and women of Fleet Street hurried back to their seats, so as not to miss a minute of this enchantment. If the first act had not been exciting, more was to come. Every number had seemed to 'stop the show', but when the song and the wild, wonderful dance which followed it, 'The Farmer and the Cowman', came to its end—then the show stopped indeed. It is doubtful if there has ever been such applause at a Drury Lane first night. It looked as though it would never stop. Then, suddenly, a shot rang out—and, thus jumped into astonished silence, the audience quietened and stared, and the show went on. It was Mary Marlo playing Aunt Eller who had fired the shot and given the show a chance to continue. This piece of quick thinking got applause and the show just rolled on. Its thrills, its excitements, its desperate fight in the last scene and the concerted singing of *Oklahoma* itself, all were acclaimed. And there was something else—there was the ballet, something new, fierce, original, almost primeval—something so fresh and arresting that it scored its own particular triumph on a night of triumphs, that ballet devised by Agnes de Mille, which set a new fashion and was so much copied. For many, it was the best thing in the show. At the end there were unforgettables scenes—and numbers had to be reprised over and over again. It seemed the public could never have enough. *Oklahoma* had put Drury Lane right on the pinnacle again. That company of young Americans had done it. The youth, the surge of spring, of sunlight, of energy and warmth came to a country tired of war, perils and seemingly endless winter and acted like a tonic. The play had struck the psychological moment. Business was colossal, and *Oklahoma*, one of the smallest shows in numbers, costumes, scenery and properties which Drury Lane had ever staged, took the most money, ran the longest time— 1,543 performances—and broke all records. Every member of that first company deserves a mention but there is not space enough. But Harold Keel—now calling himself Howard Keel—as Curly, got a record fan-mail and deserved every letter of it. He is now a famous film star, then he was unknown. Mary Marlo played Aunt Eller with the poise and experience of a star actress, as indeed she is. Betty Jane Watson, as Laurey, was like a spring day. Walter Donahue as Will Parker was everybody's ideal cowboy and scored heavily with 'Everything's Up to Date in Kansas City'. The Ali Hakim of Marek Windheim must be mentioned and Wm. J. McCarthy, one of the more senior of the company, who was an excellent Andrew Carnes—and his daughter Ado Annie Carnes, played by Dorothea Macfarland, was a revelation in comedy. Her curious accent, her terrific punch and point, made her a big favourite. And when she told them 'I'm Just a Girl Who Can't Say No'—they could not say 'No' to her. The exquisite dancing of Erik Kristen and Gemze de Lappe in the ballet was a revelation and Remington Olmstead was also a sensation; he was a great character, and enjoyed himself. A huge man, light as a feather on his feet, he became very English indeed in dress. After going about Town as a cowboy he suddenly adopted bowler hats, black coats and striped trousers and in that attire he rode a motor-cycle. He then turned to kilts and learned the bagpipes—he even got into the Enclosure at Ascot. A remarkable young man.

Tribute is due to all, but there are still one or two special mentions—the dark beauty and vivacity of Beatrice Lynn, the girl who fell down in 'Every New Day', and the amazing grace and appeal of little Margaret Auld Nelson. She was a blonde with the appeal of a child, as simple and sweet as she looked, and her gracefulness was only equalled by that of Pauline Chase. When Margaret danced she did not seem to touch the stage, and when she fluttered to the end it was like a leaf falling from a tree. She had a personal success. And a great tribute must also be paid to the performance of Henry Clarke as Jud Fry. He acted that difficult character—the homicidal sex-maniac—with supreme skill and no offence, and sang like a man in grand opera.

Everyone will have their own memories of *Oklahoma*—for many it will be the splendid masculinity, rugged handsomeness and fine voice of Howard Keel; for others the fountain-like clarity of Betty Jane Watson, the fun of Donahue and Dorothea Macfarland, or the skilled control of Mary Marlo. For very many it will be the ballet. But for most—it will be the whole of *Oklahoma*, as near perfection as a musical play could be—and returning with skill and modernity to the method of light opera. There were many changes of cast in that long run—from 1947–50—and memorable amongst them was the playing of Laurey by sweet and charming Isabel Bigley.

Oklahoma was a most Royally visited show. All the Royal Family, almost without exception, came to see it. Queen Mary entertained some selected members of the cast in the Royal Room during the interval. It was the Oklahomans first meeting with Royalty. They were nervous but that gracious lady put them at their ease. They behaved very well indeed. One of them perhaps slightly overdid it. He gazed at the Queen a long while and then he said, "You know, Ma'am, you don't look your age." Her Majesty took it as a great compliment and was much amused. It so happened that the August Bank Holiday of 1947 was the birthday of Queen Elizabeth (now the Queen Mother). It was always the custom of King George VI to make all family occasions of importance a reason for a visit to the Theatre. So on that Bank Holiday he brought his wife and his whole family to see *Oklahoma*. Once again the members of the company were received in the Royal Room. They had been warned as to etiquette and special stress had been laid on the fact that they must not ask for autographs—indeed this is a thing which is never done to the Royal Family. They had indeed been told, to stress it specially, that to make such a request was high treason and they might be arrested and taken to the Tower of London. Some of them, if not all, believed it too. They did not ask for autographs, but one got as near as he could. When he found how charming and natural the British Royal Family was, he produced a programme from his pocket. He addressed the King and Queen. "Sir and Ma'am," he said, "I am not going to ask for an autograph. I would not do such a thing. I know what that means." (Their Majesties were a little mystified for they did not.) "But if you, Sir, and you, Ma'am, would be so gracious as just to put a finger on this programme, I would mark the spot and keep it all my life." They did it for him, laughing, and he went away transported—not to the Tower, but in delight. . . . At the end, the entire company and the audience sang 'Happy Birthday To You' and the Queen was delighted.

Scenes from *The King and I* at Drury Lane
Lower picture shows Herbert Lom as the King and Valerie Hobson as
Mrs. Anna

PILLARS OF TODAY

Upper left: Oscar Hammerstein *Upper right:* Jerome Whyte *Left:* Richard Rodgers

Oklahoma was one of the great occasions at Drury Lane.

It was succeeded on 7th June, 1950, by *Carousel*. This was an entirely different sort of play from *Oklahoma*—a musical version of *Liliom* with a tragic theme and a touch of fantasy. It opened in more traditional Drury Lane style—with a scene at a fair and a round-about in full action (a roundabout is, in American, a carousel). There was a big crowd and much colour and the first few minutes, entirely mimed, were amongst the best things in the show, the music being especially delightful. The first act was packed with good numbers, 'If I Loved You', 'When I Marry Mr. Snow', and 'June is Bustin' Out All Over', and a remarkable sailor ballet, too. The second act brought tragedy and the hero—also perhaps a villain in his own right—got to the Gates of Heaven and was sent back to earth to try and right the wrongs he had done. It was a mixture of style and method, of mood and sentiment. It succeeded and ran for 566 performances, but it never had the appeal of *Oklahoma*. The original principals were Stephen Douglas, succeeded by Edmund Hockridge from Canada, Iva Withers, succeeded by Laverne Burden from South Africa, Marion Ross succeeded by Patricia Black, Marjorie Mars, that first-class actress, Eric Mattson, Morgan Davies (of Wales), Jack Melford, William Sherwood and Bambi Linn, who danced like a thistledown in sunlight in the curious but imaginative ballet, also devised by Agnes de Mille.

And then Mary Martin came back. She came back in *South Pacific*. She came back a great star because of that play and her performance as Ensign Nellie Forbush therein in America. The announcement of the production of *South Pacific* caused great excite-ment and Drury Lane was besieged for seats. People clamoured for the first night—expectation was on tip-toe. None of this excitement was engineered on this side of the Atlantic—it had come across of its own accord. It is not Drury Lane's custom to over-boost. This is stressed because when the first night of *South Pacific* took place, it did not get a good Press. There were reasons for it and over-expectation was one of them. It was also very American. It told of the American Navy and Army in the South Pacific and there was very little said about the fact that the British had been in the war, too. Not that it mattered—this was a play, not a political argument, and it should be treated as such. It was a curious play—but it had a good strong story. It was very masculine and there were lots of large, brawny men with very little on but muscular development. But it was a big and overwhelming success, despite the Press and because of the supreme artistry of Oscar Hammerstein, Richard Rodgers—and Mary Martin. The very difficult part of Emile de Becque, the hero, was played by Wilbur Evans, who had the job of being constantly referred to as a 'wonderful guy' and managed to live up to it. His was the duty, too, of singing 'Some Enchanted Evening', and he made it enchanting. The other hero of the play was performed by a young Englishman of not very long experience, Peter Grant, who took his chance. An outstanding hit both in acting and singing was made by Muriel Smith as Bloody Mary, who became at once a Drury Lane favourite. Her performance and her singing, especially of 'Bali Ha'i', were something to remember. And another hit was made by Betta St. John, whose lovely and expressive face and hands, whose grace and beauty as Liat won all hearts. She was succeeded by Chin Yu when she returned to America. Hartley Power, that splendid actor, brought weight and importance to the character of Captain George Brackett, U.S.N., and others deserving remembrance were Ray Walston, who gave a perfect performance as Luther Billis—the American equivalent of a Cockney—Bill Nagy, Wally Peterson (who had been in *Oklahoma*), and John McLaren, who finally succeeded Hartley Power.

South Pacific belonged to Mary Martin. Tens of thousands of people paid to see her 'Wash That Man Right Outa My Hair'— which she did in full view of the audience—and sing 'I'm in Love With a Wonderful Guy', to say nothing of other numbers and dancing. Here was the real Mary Martin, no longer encumbered by a crinoline as she had been in *Pacific 1860*, and with the airs and graces of a prima donna, but as a real American woman, full of verve, pep and vitality. She played her serious scenes like a splendid actress (which she is), and she sang her more rollicking songs just as they might have been sung by the old-time Music Hall stars—can more be said than that? She had cut her hair short and she led a fashion. She had to do this because of the hair-washing scene and the necessity for drying it quickly. But it suited her—and the part, too. She touched the right note of pathos when needed and she hit the octave of comedy with as sure a touch as a great pianist. When she left, after two years, she was succeeded by Julie Wilson, who gave a very good performance indeed. *South Pacific* ran for 792 performances—being first produced on 15th November, 1951. A big, resounding Drury Lane success.

There was an evening of tremendous drama during that run. That great King of this country, George VI, had been ill and undergone an operation. The nation, which loved him, prayed for his recovery and hoped that all would be well. It knew nothing at all save the official bulletins which were issued. No king had ever been nearer to his subjects than he—few if any had been better beloved. He and his people had endured the horrors of war together, the Blitz, the grim hours of mortal danger, and the final triumph and relief of victory. He was not only his People's King but their Friend. So they hoped and they prayed, but the news was scant and nobody, of course, saw him. Then came an announcement that he had gone down to Sandringham for recuperation and convalescence. This was better, this was good, but still people knew so little—and nobody saw him. Then, even the bulletins ceased. No news is good news, the folk said to each other. And then, something occurred in that British Family at Sandringham which, to the King, meant a celebration, a point to be marked, whether hail or farewell. His daughter was going on a world tour with her husband. So the night before they went, the King, following his usual custom, gave a party—a Theatre Party. He brought his family and his wife to Theatre Royal, Drury Lane— and at very short notice indeed. Now, when Royalty goes to the Theatre, it pays—just as does the general public. It does not come in free by virtue of its office. It buys its seats through a certain old-established theatre ticket agency. It is usual, when Royalty attends a play, for it to occupy the Royal Box, although our present Queen is departing from that custom. But that has been the rule for many centuries. When Royalty comes in its private capacity it does not want the slightest fuss made. It wants to give as little trouble to everybody as it possibly can. It does not want, above all things, to disturb an audience and distract attention from the traffic on the stage. So it was always the custom of Royal playgoers, except on State occasions or big charity performances, where they were there in their official capacity or to help, to wait in the Royal Room behind the Royal Box until the auditorium lights were down, the footlights up and the orchestra playing the overture—and every-one's attention directed to the stage. Then they would slip quietly into the box endeavouring not to attract attention. For except on special occasions, no mention must be made of their presence, actual or expected, until they are inside the theatre. No fuss, no bother—there is as a rule more pomp and circumstance over the visit of a local mayor than a visit by a reigning monarch. . . .

The King brought his family to Drury Lane, and those of the staff whose duty it was to receive him saw him for the first time since that illness had begun. What they saw shocked them. This was a very sick man indeed—a man with the marks of suffering on his face and a queer look in his eyes—a man who seemed to be doing what he did by habit and custom, but whose eyes were alive and whose brain was as keen and active as ever. He was doing his job, as he had always done. He and the family went into that Royal Room and there they stood and chatted as usual. The door of the Royal Box was slightly ajar. Outside in that vast auditorium were over 2,000 people, subjects of that King—they came not only from this country but from the Dominions overseas. A rumour went round like lightning, as rumours do, that the King was in the theatre. They wanted to see him—how they wanted to see him! That desire assumed the strength of an electric current, of great magnetic force—the concentrated wish and hope of a great concourse of people, all filled with love towards the person it believed and hoped it would see. It seemed that its force reached the King himself, for instead of waiting in the room as usual, he turned and went into the Royal Box, with the houselights full up and in full view of everyone. The writer wishes that the myriads who were not there could have seen the demonstration which followed—one not only of loyalty but of deep, heartfelt love and affection. In a long life full of incident the writer has seen nothing so spontaneous or genuine before. They stood up, they cheered, and they had tears of pleasure in their eyes. That solitary figure in the Royal Box stood quite still and looked at them. Then, he bowed very low indeed and motioned to the rest of the family to come in. They took their seats whilst the applause went on—the lights went down, the footlights glowed, the orchestra began—and the curtain swept up. In the interval the King received Mary Martin and other leading people of the show. He gave no sign that things were not normal, he made little jokes, he was as kindly and charming as ever.

The second act was on—it was over—the applause came again. 'The King' was played and sung with emotion. And then that demonstration of love began again. Once more the King stood quite still looking at those people, his subjects, a cross-section of the whole Commonwealth of which he was the beloved head. Then he waved to the gallery, he waved to the upper circle, he waved to the Royal circle on a level with his box, he waved down to what had been the pit, he waved to the stalls. He gave each section of those people of his their own special salute. It drove them nearly mad with pride and delight—they stood on the seats, hats, handkerchiefs, programmes flew in the air—and the cheering was something remarkable to hear. That man with the sad, lined face stood there upright and silent and gazed at them. Then—he did it again—that fivefold salute—and if possible the enthusiasm grew even greater. He stood quite still. He looked all round that great building and at that great concourse of his people who stood before him. He took a long lingering look as if to fix that scene in his memory. And he bowed to his subjects, very, very deeply—and turned into the Royal

Room. Mr. Prince Littler, Mr. F. C. Carter and other members of
the staff whose duty it was to receive their King, escorted him to
his car. He shook hands, he got into the car and he drove away
through a mob of his cheering people. But that face and that look
burnt itself into the memory of those who had been near him. It
seemed to them that this man was saying good-bye. . . .

It was Wednesday night. The next day the whole nation saw
just a glimpse of that worn face on television . . . and on the following
Wednesday morning came the news that this King, this great King,
gallant and brave gentleman indeed, had gone from us.

At Drury Lane he was mourned—for there he was well known
and the people of 'The Lane' are His or Her Majesty's servants.
But with that very deep, very real grief that they shared with the
nation was perhaps just a touch of pride that this great and good
monarch had really said farewell to his people in that building which
his ancestor had made Royal and the tradition of which he had so
faithfully maintained. It seemed that a glowing page had been
completed which could never be dimmed in the history of that
Royal Theatre—which had known every monarch since Charles II
had ennobled it—where 'God Save the King' had first been sung,
where 'Rule Britannia' had first been heard by the public and
where George II had received the news of the defeat of the Young
Pretender at Culloden Moor.

Of all the things which have happened in Drury Lane down the
centuries, nothing was more moving, more dramatic, more sad and
yet more inspiring than that last visit of a beloved King. . . .

CHAPTER SIXTEEN

Today—1955

THIS present record of Drury Lane and its Pillars draws towards its end. *The King and I* followed *South Pacific* in October 1953. Once again by Hammerstein and Rodgers, it was produced here, as it had been in New York, by John Van Druten, the eminent dramatist and man of the Theatre, and his artistic, sensitive touch did much for this very lovely play, putting a gloss and patina of beauty on it. He himself, by virtue of his long association with the British and American Theatre and his record of success, takes his place as a pillar of 'The Lane'.

The King and I was to have had Gertrude Lawrence as its leading lady. All the country and Drury Lane looked forward to that, for she had been superlatively good in it in New York. But death intervened and took that great woman of the Theatre away before her time, and before she could come to Drury Lane. Another leading lady had to be found. The choice fell on Valerie Hobson, a star of films but not so well known in the legitimate Theatre. Jerome Whyte took her across to the States to see Hammerstein and Rodgers. She was engaged for the part. There were those who doubted the wisdom of this selection, but that experienced group of men were right, as usual. This play, based on fact, is the story of the adventures of Mrs. Anna Leonowens at the Court of Siam, of her battle with its King who wants to be Western cultured and civilized but who still remains an Oriental at heart—who always yearns for the 'scientific' but whose mind, although born a despot, is always torn by doubt as to what is the right thing to do. To him—it is a 'puzzlement'. The play is a thing of charm and beauty, delicate yet gripping, imaginative yet factual, filled with sentiment yet never sentimental. Miss Hobson had to portray the British woman of education and culture—a Victorian lady faced with sudden Oriental savagery, as governess to the Royal children—more than that, as confidante and adviser to the King himself. It is by no means an easy part but Miss Hobson played it with charm, understanding and grace. She sang the music with clarity of diction and trueness of tone, if with no great vocal power, which was most acceptable. She made a distinct success. The part of the King fell to Mr. Herbert Lom, an actor who had hardly been seen on the stage here but who was a star of films and immensely popular thereon. As the King,

Mr. Lom contributed a veritable *tour de force*. Here was great acting indeed—here was the grip, and complete understanding of the art of acting such as had not been seen at Drury Lane for many a long year—here was the grandeur of the old days come back. It was a masterpiece and a joy to watch. Old-timers on the staff, who had seen so much in Drury Lane and elsewhere, would go in and watch with pleasure. It was something quite memorable, this performance of a complex role, which included singing, and Herbert Lom had never sung in public before. It ranks, in the estimation of the writer, who is old and experienced in the world of the Theatre, as one of the outstanding performances of our time. *The King and I* scored a very big success. It still fills the theatre at the time when these lines are being written, although Valerie Hobson and Herbert Lom are gone and have been replaced by Eve Lister and George Pastell, both of whom perform excellently.

Much of the delight in *The King and I* lies in the performance given by the Royal children of the King. Immense difficulty was experienced in getting these children together—for it was not enough to simply have children—British children—they must, to be convincing, be of Oriental aspect and manner. Many were tried and most found wanting, but at last Miss Terry, the famous trainer of stage children, assembled a little company of children—she found them individually—who were absolutely perfect.

The staging was a series of beautiful pictures, the story one of romance in which tears and comedy are blended. Excellent performances were provided by George Benson, Doreen Duke, Ivor Emmanuel, Ian Mezurus, Ronald Leigh Hunt and Muriel Smith, a firmly established favourite at Drury Lane. Nor must the exquisite and exotic dancing of Sonya Hana be omitted. The ballet—an Oriental version of *Uncle Tom's Cabin*—under the title of *The Small House of Uncle Thomas*, was a show in itself full of quaint beauty. *The King and I* runs on, well into its second year as these lines are written.

It is, of course, the work of those two men, the author and composer of *The King and I*, who have now contributed so much to the history of Drury Lane, Richard Rodgers and Oscar Hammerstein II. They are wizards of the Theatre—they are the perfect combination, the modern equivalent of Gilbert and Sullivan and just as different in personality. The great thing is, however, that they do not fight or squabble. They have founded a great firm which produces their own works and those of others. They stand on the peak of success and they deserve it. They are today the universal providers at Theatre Royal.

Richard Rodgers has achieved his ambition. He always wanted

to be a composer for the Theatre, to spend his life amongst music. He has done so. Born in 1902, he was surrounded by music because his family—who were not of the Stage—loved it and would play the hits from the musical shows of their time over and over again at family concerts. Young Richard drank it in. And very soon, very very soon, he was trying his own little hands on the piano and using his young brain to compose. He adored the Theatre and now he is married to it. No need to delve into his remarkable story, which is like a romance. Of his early attempts, of his partnership with Lorenz Hart which produced so many shows, of his adventures, successes, failures, a book has been written. He first met his present partner, Oscar Hammerstein II, when they were both at college. He regarded Hammerstein with awe, for he was of the Theatre and had actually written and produced a show—at college. But to young Rodgers it did not matter where it was done, the achievement was everything. What is of importance in this place is what Richard Rodgers has done for Drury Lane. And in partnership with Oscar Hammerstein he has done much, very much indeed. He is a quick, energetic man with a very good and clear business brain. That is not so usual in a fine composer. But Richard Rodgers is never usual in anything he does, as his music shows. He does wonders with it. It is always unexpected. It never goes the way one thinks it will—he will change tempo and type and still keep it perfect in form and melody—'Hello, Young Lovers' in *The King and I* is an example of this—the way he changes from waltz to barcarolle and back again is enchanting. He works at top speed and there is he the exact opposite of Oscar Hammerstein. He produced the melody of 'Oh, What a Beautiful Morning' in a matter of minutes. It had taken Hammerstein a long time to write the words. To look at Rodgers you would think he was a smart business man, maybe a successful lawyer—but when you see the eyes, you see the melody.

He and Oscar Hammerstein have now been responsible for Drury Lane's longest run in *Oklahoma*, its third longest run in *South Pacific*, its fourth in *The King and I*, and its fifth in *Carousel*. That is something of a record. They have now composed and written four Drury Lane smash-hits—in the four plays mentioned above—in succession. That has never been done before except by Ivor Novello. He did four in succession—and by himself. And he also played in them. But his shows never ran as long as those of Rodgers and Hammerstein.

Oscar Hammerstein II calls himself so to be different from his close relation—his grandfather, Oscar Hammerstein of Theatre and Opera fame—the man who built the London Opera House, now the

Stoll Theatre. Educated at Columbia University—as was Richard Rodgers—he had the Theatre in his blood. His own father was a theatre manager—how could he escape and become a lawyer? He had taken a B.A. degree. He did not want to be a lawyer although he worked at it. He wanted the Theatre, he wanted to act—and he wanted to write as well. He did all those things. He, like Rodgers, was born in New York. He became a stage manager, he learnt all there was to know about the Theatre. He began to write, libretti and lyrics. He succeeded. He always says his vocabulary is very limited indeed. Be that as it may, if Oscar Hammerstein does not know many words, he has the supreme ability of knowing how to use them. His gift lies in his naturalness and imagination, which he blends together—he is a poet of the every day—and he invests everyday occurrences with romance. He began his connection with Drury Lane quite early. He was part author of *Rose Marie* which, with 851 performances, held the Drury Lane record for years until he and Rodgers knocked it out with *Oklahoma*. But it still holds second place. He was part author, too, of *The Desert Song*, which held second record at 'The Lane' for years, too, until Hammerstein and Rodgers displaced it with *South Pacific*, *Carousel* and *The King and I*. So Hammerstein is now an Old Druriolanian. He was part author of *Show Boat* as well, another big Drury Lane success, and of *Ball at the Savoy* and *The Three Sisters*. He knows, loves and understands Drury Lane. He is a big man, slow but sure of movement, with a rugged, kindly face, a quiet slow voice and a smile which is like a burst of sunshine breaking through grey wintry clouds and heartening everyone He is a kind man with a splendid nature. There is something of Drury Lane itself in him. He is beloved there by everyone. He and Richard Rodgers have done that great theatre magnificent service and they are pillars indeed, of which Old Drury may be justly proud. There is no question of being American or British—they are of Drury Lane, part of its texture.

But they cannot be over in this country all the time—they have vast American interests. So, to and fro between New York and London, comes the man who does the technical, the practical work —Jerome Whyte. Sometimes he stops for months, sometimes a few weeks, it depends what there is to do. But he does it. He knows those two men and they know him. He has produced for them, in this country at Drury Lane—apart from other theatres—*Oklahoma* (for he was operating for the Theatre Guild at that time), *Carousel* and *South Pacific*. John Van Druten produced *The King and I* but Jerome Whyte supervised the production, sorted out the cast and put the show all there. He is a forthright, blunt American with a mind of

his own, born in New York. Physically strong and sturdy, he has a
fresh complexion and chestnut hair—a colour which so often goes
with forceful people. For Jerome Whyte certainly has force. He is a
young man, born in 1908, and he started his theatrical career in
1925 as a chorus boy. He learnt his job the hard way, starting at the
bottom and working to the top. He was in the chorus of *Coconuts*
with the Marx Brothers. He went into variety, and learnt that side.
He had his own act, a double act—Carfield and Whyte—Carfield
was the girl. He went into Stock, and he became proficient in
dancing. He decided to master the technical side of the Stage and he
became assistant to Hassard Short, the famous producer, whose
name Whyte speaks with reverence. He blossomed forth as a full-
fledged stage manager and as such handled many important shows
—and he joined the Shuberts, with whom he remained for five
years. Five years with the Shuberts is an education in itself.

Then he met somebody. He met Richard Rodgers—he worked
on the Rodgers shows—*Boys from Syracuse, Pal Joey, Too Many Girls,*
and others. Then, at the wish of Richard Rodgers, he went to the
Theatre Guild, to work on a play then being written and composed,
and on which Hammerstein was working, too. That play became
Oklahoma—and so the association of Jerome Whyte and the Rodgers-
Hammerstein combination really started—eleven years ago. Today
he is an integral part of the trio which supplies Drury Lane. He is a
tireless worker, he seems to live for auditions. No part is ever
allotted by him unless an audition is given, it does not matter how
eminent is the actor or actress required to play it. Whyte wants to
see for himself—and does. He sits in the stalls at Drury Lane and
watches endless chains of candidates for small parts. When he sees
what he wants, he knows at once. He has a flair for spotting talent.
And very seldom does he make a mistake, though he takes lots of
chances. That practical knowledge lends an X-ray quality to the
eye, a special tone to the ear. His association with Hammerstein and
Rodgers was interrupted by three and a half years war service with
the American Air Force—but he came back safely and started to
work at once. Now he is so familiar a sight at Drury Lane that he is
an accepted part of it. He makes friends easily—but he can turn on
anger which blazes like a volcano. He does not suffer fools gladly.
He has the firmness of an expert—and what is a very rare gift in
the Theatre, he knows what he wants—and what Rodgers and
Hammerstein want, too. He appreciates and understands the
atmosphere of Old Drury and has a right to take his place—by long
and fine service—as a pillar thereof in this present era.

Today, Drury Lane walks in sunshine and success. Much of this is due to Prince Littler as chairman and managing director—a man of vast theatrical experience and a grip of finance, so often missing in the world of the Theatre. He is not at all what one expects a great theatre magnate to be. He is a quiet, dark man, very retiring and rather shy. He does not court publicity—indeed, he rather shuns it—he prefers to show results rather than to discuss plans. And he certainly shows results. He has a friendly manner and a kindly understanding nature and is married to a very charming lady—herself of the Theatre—who was Nora Delany before she became Mrs. Prince Littler. Prince Littler loves the land, and if he were not so occupied in the world of the Theatre—he controls many playhouses and combinations thereof and is the biggest man in theatrical affairs today—he would be a great agriculturist. He has his farm, and when he can get there and become part of it—maybe those are his happiest hours. His smile is an encouragement to those on whom he bestows it. He has guided Drury Lane to success—and may he do so for many years to come. He works ceaselessly and with success for the deserving cause of theatrical charities.

The men who make the wheels go round at Drury Lane are now a mixture of old and rather newer servants. The Second World War took many of the elder brethren—and as the years go on, death takes them, too.

Sidney F. Webb remains the manager—now the senior manager in the West End, with thirty-four years of service to Drury Lane to his credit. Ronald E. Gray, F.C.I.S., is the secretary, an old and valued servant, too. Incidentally, Mr. Webb almost lives on the premises, in a block of flats adjoining the theatre and which the theatre owns. To Sidney Webb, Drury Lane is Life.*

Ernest Kingdon, who did such splendid work at the production of *Oklahoma*, is now assistant manager. Since Prince Littler became chief, the general manager is Frank C. Marshall, who has served Mr. Littler for years and is an experienced practical man of the Theatre, too, in all branches. In succession to William Abingdon as stage director is Jack Miller—with years of experience behind him. The late stage manager Jack Waters, who served for some years and never lost his temper in the most trying times, and his assistant James Smith, both deserve a mention. They have been swallowed

* Old Drury has suffered a loss just as these lines are being written by the retirement of its Manager, Sidney F. Webb, who served it so well, faithfully and loyally. He gave the best of his life to the theatre which he loved, never sparing himself. Ill health is the reason for his going and he will carry with him into his retirement the best wishes of the entire staff and hundreds of friends. He was held in the greatest esteem and affection by all, and was one of the very best Managers that famous theatre ever had. His successor is Sidney Smith, from the Stoll Theatre.

up in Commercial Television. The carpenter is Louis Walton, the property master Edward Boxall—an Old Druriolanian—and the chief electrician is George Wright, also an old servant, who with Ben Anderson, who assists him, did yeoman service during the war in the Drury Lane A.R.P., apart from being experts at their job. May Cole reigns over the wardrobe department. There is Jimmy Pennell still at work on the stage—the famous 'lifts', now so seldom used, are his especial charge—and he has been there for years. In the box-office is T. G. Rees, another old servant, with his assistants, W. J. Mitchell and R. Hurndell. The stage door is guarded by Fred Cavell, another old and valued servant. It needs a smart person to get by him—he was once the gaoler at Bow Street with such illustrious criminals as Crippen under his charge.

Everyone who visits the theatre exclaims about its cleanliness and the way it shines. When parties are taken round on tours—which happens quite often—the first thing the ladies spot and mention is the wonderful polish and cleanliness of it all. That is the work of Mrs. Jordan, its housekeeper, who has served it for years and who graduated there under Sir Alfred Butt from the old Empire in Leicester Square. Outside the theatre, as linkman in chief, is the big manly figure of Bill Girt, an ex-Lifeguardsman who was once part of the escort to King Edward VII. He, too, is an old servant.

In the conductor's chair sits Reginald Burston, who has occupied that difficult position with distinction since Drury Lane reopened. And working hard at Drury Lane is Bertie Stoll, in charge of the catering. And a mention too for Mr. F. C. Carter, who as general manager of Associated Theatre Properties Limited—of which nowadays Theatre Royal, Drury Lane, is part—does much hard work for the famous old theatre. There is another figure on the managerial staff, too—for Rodgers and Hammerstein—who has now been there for some years and looks like remaining, handsome William Stiles . . . whose passion for the Theatre is mixed with a passion for sport.

So Theatre Royal, Drury Lane, goes on, down the centuries. It is a wicked piece of private enterprise and asks to be no more. It has no state subsidy—it earns its own living as it has always done and it prefers it that way. There is another great playhouse in London which has a yearly subsidy, and Drury Lane notices that the figure is usually something about the same amount as Old Drury pays annually by way of Entertainment Tax. It does not grumble for Drury Lane is part of England and therefore likes its freedom, and likes to pay its way. The public are apt to call it the National Theatre and so in fact it is. Another National Theatre is being built now and Drury Lane has no pang of jealousy. Rather the reverse. It wishes that new place all the luck in the world. For Drury Lane has nearly three centuries of tradition and glory inside its walls and that is what makes for greatness. It will take another National Theatre a long time to catch up. Inside 'The Lane' the past lives with the present in perfect amity; it is a modern, up-to-date playhouse whose chief asset is its history and its atmosphere. There it is, standing where it has stood since 1663 and still leading its Profession. It is a patchwork of period, a storehouse of the story of England.

It keeps its continuity. There still remains a small portion of that first theatre which Killigrew built—only a few courses but they are there. There is a great deal of the second theatre—for the main structure rests on the arches which Wren built—and there they are for all to see, as strong and firm as when Sir Christopher Wren put them there in 1674 after the first fire. There is still the fireplace in the Green Room before which Macklin killed Hallam, and in that same Green Room hangs Garrick's mirror. There is a staircase which is an epitome of the building—part of it is 1812, part is 1921 and part is 1674. The Board now meets in the room in which Sheridan wrote *The School for Scandal*. And down in the Green Room, locked in with paper, pens and ink, some anchovy sandwiches and bottles of claret, that same erratic genius wrote at top speed—in direct contrast to his leisurely penning of *The School for Scandal*— another great success which was *The Critic*. The leading members of his company, knowing his dilatory habits, had made him a prisoner —and it showed results.

In the vestibule itself now stands a leaden statue of Shakespeare, a very beautiful thing indeed, the work of John Chere, who was, in the late 18th century, a master of the art of sculpture in lead. For years that statue stood on the portico covered in paint. Everyone thought it was plaster and paid no attention to it. But bomb blast made repairs to the portico imperative. It was then discovered by the men who moved the imagined plaster statue that it weighed a tremendous lot. On examination, it proved to be lead. There was a salvage drive at the time—but this was part of Drury Lane and not going to salvage. It was hidden away deep below street level. And when peace came it was cleaned and many thicknesses of paint removed, showing a thing of beauty which now has a place of honour. It was probably given to the theatre by Samuel Whitbread, for he bought much of Chere's work when that artist died and placed some in the grounds of his Bedfordshire home.

In the vestibule is the record of all those who have held the Patent—and the Cenotaph to those actors who fell in the First

World War. Emblazoned there too is the fine record of Arthur Collins. In the rotunda stand the statues of Garrick, Kean, Balfe and Shakespeare—the Bard is in plaster but the statue has importance. It is a cast of the original statue which Garrick commissioned the great French sculptor Rambouillet to make for him—it is one of the few casts in existence. On the wall is a bronze plaque to the memory of Sir Henry Irving—sent by the united artists of Italy because Irving's last West End production was a dramatized form of their great epic poem, 'Dante's Inferno'. Irving played often at Drury Lane but his real greatness belongs to the Lyceum Theatre—now a dance-hall. So Drury Lane cherishes that plaque. On either side of the rotunda are great doors and over that on the left is 'King's Side' and over that on the right is 'Prince's Side'—a remembrance of the night when old King George III administered a good hiding to his grown-up son, afterwards George IV, when they met at the theatre. That was an historic occasion, for surely never in the history of any nation did a reigning monarch thrash his Heir Apparent in full view of his subjects. Yet it happened at Drury Lane. At the bottom of the great staircase on the right hangs the picture of a very lovely lady indeed, the late Dowager Countess of Dudley. She is there because she was also Gertie Millar, the very embodiment of the spirit of the Gaiety Theatre for many years—perhaps the greatest star musical comedy ever knew. She had nothing to do with Drury Lane but she loved the fine old theatre. She asked Prince Littler, a great friend of hers, if that picture might hang there and he agreed at once, for Gertie Millar was one of the great ones of the Theatrical Profession and deserves her place in that Valhalla. When she died she left the portrait to Mr. Littler, who has given it to the theatre.

At the bottom of the stairs on the left is a fine portrait of William C. Macready, who did such wonderful work at Drury Lane and who lifted its status high. That was given by Brigadier J. Macready, D.S.O., O.B.E., and his son A. J. Macready. It, too, is treasured. There are many other things of interest—and the Ghost still walks. Upstairs on the grand circle level are busts of Sir Johnston Forbes Robertson, who bade farewell to the public at Drury Lane, of Samuel Whitbread and of Ivor Novello. When the time came to place a memorial of Ivor in the place where he did so much, choice fell on a bust of himself which was his own property and which he loved—a very beautiful thing and the work of Clemence Dane, dramatist, novelist, painter and sculptor. It was unveiled by Dame Sybil Thorndike on the same day that Gertie Millar unveiled her portrait and Sir John Gielgud performed the same ceremony on the leaden statue of Shakespeare. Mary Ellis spoke a poem she had written specially for the occasion. It bears just a simple record of the plays which Ivor did at Drury Lane. They speak volumes.

In the picture gallery, on the grand circle level, are many interesting things, including the original of the famous act-drop used on one occasion only when the Emperor of Germany went to a gala performance with King George V. This is by Stanhope Forbes, R.A. There hangs a photostat of the famous Patent of Charles II, the most valuable theatrical document in the world, which shows what that Charter looks like today—almost as good as new—and a portrait of David Garrick, by E. J. Lestarde the Court painter, kindly given by Mr. Clifford Martin.

To enter Drury Lane is to breathe in an atmosphere of greatness and an atmosphere which is the tradition of England. Yet so few are cognisant of it. One sees them hurry through the doors, with hardly a glance right or left, and make straight for the refreshment bars. That is what matters.

But some there are who stop, and look and ponder. And they are not always the natives of this land. On occasions the writer of this humble chronicle conducts parties round Drury Lane and tells an outline of its story. Recently he took a party of Asian gentlemen round—over here to study banking—and they came from many lands in the Far East, but the majority were of the Commonwealth. When the tour was completed, one of them made a little speech. "We love this place," he said, "this to us is part of England and that we like. Here is tradition, here is conquest of difficulties and here is tenacity of purpose in the face of many foes. Here too is quiet grandeur which is not acquired by lavish display but which seems to grow from the very soil. That, to us, is England. And we are proud that we are of the Commonwealth—for we feel that we too have some ownership in this Theatre Royal." Those words were true and the writer appreciated them. The conducted parties go away rather awed by what they have seen and heard, but with eyes aglow.

Drury Lane makes little display of its greatness. Once, along the front of the grand circle where nobody could see them, were a line of tablets each bearing a great name in Drury Lane's story. The tablets are still there but covered by the machinery which works the 'front-of-house' lighting. That is one of the reasons why this little book has been written, to tell the British people, at home and overseas, something of those who helped to make that tradition and atmosphere which is Drury Lane Theatre, a cherished British possession. This book is a companion to *Theatre Royal* written by the same pen some years ago, but it deals more with personalities, although it brings the story up to date. For the history of any theatre and its greatness must be the story of the people who lived and worked in it. It is they who have made Drury Lane, from a mere building, into a jewel-box of excitement and great happenings.

So, when next a visit is paid to Drury Lane Theatre to see a play—or when it is passed by in the daily round—the writer would beg people to remember that this is something more than a theatre. It is part of England, part of our national story—one of the sights of London and by no means its least. There it has stood and there it stands, carrying on through war and peace, bad times and good. It has seen so many changes, it has changed itself but always its heart has remained the same—just as does the heart of Britain. And those who work there, and those who love it as playgoers and Britons, pray that as long as there is this City of London, there may always be that portion of it which is called . . . Theatre Royal, Drury Lane —supported by those pillars—those men and women who wrought for its greatness and splendour.

London. May, 1955.

INDEX

Abbott, Amy, 202
Abingdon, William, 113, 217, 251
Abington, Mrs., 100
Abrahams, 193
Addison, Mrs., 158
Adelaide, Queen, 187
Ainley, Henry, 211, 212, 229
Alexander, Sir George, 21, 22–3
Alias, Charlie, 208
Allen, Bishop, 70–1
Anderson, Ben, 252
Anderson, Daphne, 233
Andrews, Maidie, 225, 233
Anne, Queen, 87, 90, 162
Appleby, F., 235, 236
Arne, Thomas, 90
Arnold, S. J., 119, 121
Arnold, Tom, 232
Ashford, Murray, 219
Austin, 78–9

Baddeley, Robert, 100, 107–14
Balfe, Michael William, 140, 141, 143, 148, 149, 151–2, 254
Barnes, J. H., 191, 192, 194
Barnes, Sir Kenneth, 217
Barrett, Oscar, 193, 194, 195, 223
Barrett, Wilson, 211
Barry, Helen, 190
Barry, Mrs., 86, 100
Barry, Spranger, 154–5, 157
Bates, Thorpe, 217
Beard, John, 159, 160
Beaumont, Hugh, 234, 235, 236
Beck, Philip, 190
Beeston, Thomas, 31
Bell, Stanley, 217
Bell's Weekly Paper, 95
Bellamy, George Anne, 68–9
Bellew, Kyrle, 190
Bennett, Miss, 89
Benson, George, 247
Berry, William, 157
Berryman, John, 219
Betterton, Thomas, 43, 44, 46, 47, 60, 86, 87, 132
Beverley, William Roxby, 185
Bevin, Rt. Hon. Ernest, 228
Beyer, Elsie, 236

Bickerstaffe, Isaac, 88
Bigley, Isabel, 240
Billington, Mrs., 192
Birch, T. Flaming, 232
Black, Patricia, 241
Blakes, 157
Blanchard, E. L., 189, 193, 194, 195
Blanche, Ada, 191, 198
Blanche, Little Addie, 191
Bleak House, 128, 161
Boleyn, R. S., 190
Booth, Barton, 45, 58, 59, 61, 69, 91
Bourchier, Arthur, 202
Bowen, 63–4
Bowman, Isa, 198
Boxall, Edward, 252
Boyne, Leonard, 201, 203
Bracegirdle, Mrs., 100
Braham, John, 135, 177
Bray, Marianne Elizabeth Woolcot, 177, 181
Brooke, Gustavus Vaughan, 89, 167–83
Brough, Fanny, 190–1, 201
Brough, Lionel, 190
Browne, Pattie, 202
Bruce, Edgar, 188
Bruce, Edith, 196
Buchanan, Jack, 217, 220, 223
Buchanan, Robert, 195
Buckhurst, Lord, 51
Buckingham, Duke of (George Villiers), 49, 50
Buckstone, J. B., 22, 164
Bulwer, Edward Lytton, 136–7
Bunn, Alfred, 137, 138–9, 140–53
Bunn, Avonia, 181–2
Burbage, Richard, 41
Burden, Laverne, 241
Burke, Marie, 231
Burston, Reginald, 237, 252
Butcher, Cyril, 233
Butt, Sir Alfred, 231, 252
Byron, Lord, 118

Calcraft, 168–9
Calhaem, Stanislaus, 188
Calthrop, Mrs. Gladys, 233
Campbell, Herbert, 115, 194, 195, 196, 197, 198, 204, 206